D0933571

# ERNEST HEMINGWAY

*A Study of the Short Fiction*

*Also available in Twayne's Studies in Short Fiction Series*

*John Cheever: A Study of the Short Fiction*
  by James O'Hara
*Stephen Crane: A Study of the Short Fiction*
  by Chester Wolford
*Andre Dubus: A Study of the Short Fiction*
  by Thomas E. Kennedy
*Franz Kafka: A Study of the Short Fiction*
  by Allen Thiher
*Bernard Malamud: A Study of the Short Fiction*
  by Robert Solotaroff
*Flannery O'Connor: A Study of the Short Fiction*
  by Suzanne Morrow Paulson
*John Steinbeck: A Study of the Short Fiction*
  by R. S. Hughes
*Peter Taylor: A Study of the Short Fiction*
  by James Curry Robison
*Tennessee Williams: A Study of the Short Fiction*
  by Dennis Vannatta
*William Carlos Williams: A Study of the Short Fiction*
  by Robert Gish
*Virginia Woolf: A Study of the Short Fiction*
  by Dean Baldwin

*Twayne's Studies in Short Fiction*

Gordon Weaver, General Editor
*Oklahoma State University*

Ernest Hemingway.
*Photograph courtesy of the John F. Kennedy Library.*

# ERNEST HEMINGWAY

_A Study of the Short Fiction_

Joseph M. Flora
_University of North Carolina,_
_Chapel Hill_

_TWAYNE PUBLISHERS • BOSTON_
_A Division of G. K. Hall & Co._

Copyright 1989 by G. K. Hall & Co.
All rights reserved.
Published by Twayne Publishers
A Division of G. K. Hall & Co.
70 Lincoln Street, Boston, Massachusetts 02111

Twayne's Studies in Short Fiction Series, no. 11

Copyediting supervised by Barbara Sutton.
Book design and production by Janet Z. Reynolds.
Typeset in 10/12 Caslon by Compset, Inc.

Printed on permanent/durable acid-free paper
and bound in the United States of America.

Library of Congress Cataloging-in-Publication Data

Flora, Joseph M.
    Ernest Hemingway : a study of the short fiction / Joseph M. Flora.
        p.      cm. — (Twayne's studies in short fiction : no. 11)
    Bibliography: p.
    Includes index.
    ISBN 0-8057-8322-9
    1. Hemingway, Ernest. 1899–1961—Criticism and interpretation.
    2. Short story.   I. Title.   II. Series.
    PS3515.E37Z5938   1989
    813'.52—dc20                                                      89-33706
                                                                          CIP

*Once again for Christine and for our sons*

# Contents

*Preface*       xi
*Acknowledgments*       xxi

PART 1. THE SHORT FICTION: A CRITICAL ANALYSIS

Hemingway's Theory of the Short Story       3
Transcending Autobiography       26
The 1930s: New Directions       61
The Stories of the Spanish Civil War       89
The Last Stories       102

PART 2. THE WRITER: HEMINGWAY ON THE SHORT STORY

Excerpts from the Preface to *The First Forty-nine*       127
The Art of the Short Story       129

PART 3. THE CRITICS       145

Tony Tanner • Earl Rovit and Gerry Brenner • Cecelia
Tichi • Michael S. Reynolds • Kenneth G. Johnston

*Chronology*       179
*Bibliography*       182
*Index*       189
*The Author*       202
*The Editor*       203

# *Preface*

Although Ernest Hemingway has been dead for over twenty-five years, he has managed to hold on to our attention—both as a writer and as a public figure. Indeed, the two roles can hardly be separated. The interrelationship may be conveniently illustrated by *The Garden of Eden*, a novel that Hemingway had begun writing in 1946 and worked at for several years, but could never bring to satisfactory conclusion. In 1986 Scribner's published the work, omitting a great deal of the plot but giving a cogent shape to complex material. One of the novel's major subjects is writing: the male protagonist expounds a theory of writing and emphasizes the demands of writing. But the novel has received most attention because of its characters' experimentation with their sexual roles, not an unusual subject for the 1980s but definitely avant-garde for Hemingway's era. The love or sexual triangle of the book is indeed important to the action; the surprise was that a seemingly contemporary theme would come from the great macho of an earlier era. Readers—friends and foes—interpreted the new data differently, but in general they expressed a sense of relief that Hemingway could deal so seriously with sexual role-playing and experimentation. (He had, of course, examined the theme of inversion in several short stories, and the issue of sexual identity was an important part of his novels as well.) In *The Garden of Eden* Hemingway seems to be confronting his own sexual ambiguity more directly. In any case, from the grave, Hemingway appeared to be directing his career remarkably well—remaining controversial, certainly, but also arresting the attention of a large public, both within and outside the academic world.

Almost concurrently with this last of Hemingway's posthumous novels, four new biographies of Hemingway were published. One of them, Kenneth Lynn's *Hemingway* (1987), received great attention because of its thesis that Hemingway's entire life was shaped decisively by the problem of sexual doubleness and ambiguity. The course was set, Lynn argues, by Hemingway's mother, who dressed him as his older sister Marcelline's "twin sister," thereby making his struggle to assert his masculine independence the major battle of his life. In a sense,

Preface

Hemingway's life was like that of Poe's Roderick Usher, who buried his twin alive, but finally had to acknowledge that feminine side of himself. The intensity of the struggle finally brought Usher down; Hemingway also had to struggle mightily with his feminine side.

Lynn brought out new information about Hemingway and provided vigorous readings of several works. It seems fair to say that the shock of Lynn's thesis (though Gregory Hemingway anticipated it in his *Papa: A Personal Memoir*, 1976)[1] made the appearance of his book more dramatic than the publication of the other three biographies. But Jeffrey Meyers's *Hemingway: A Biography* (1985), Peter Griffin's *Along with Youth: Hemingway, the Early Years* (1985), and Michael Reynolds's *The Young Hemingway* (1986) have also provided new information and valuable interpretations. Collectively, the books remind us just how difficult any biographer's task is, how elusive the biographer's prey can be. When the subject of a biography is Ernest Hemingway, who made concealment a major tenet of his art, we need not be surprised that one biographer's subject sometimes seems vastly different from another's.

Griffin's and Reynolds's biographies will be multivolumed, so it seems likely that in the next several years students of Hemingway's life will have ample cause to evaluate this American life and major writer.[2] Meanwhile, the Hemingway Society is prospering—arranging well-attended sessions at the annual meetings of the Modern Language Association, sponsoring the *Hemingway Review*, and holding annual summer meetings at various locations where Hemingway lived and wrote. As the meetings symbolize, the life—like the work—continues to intrigue us.

Finally, all of this activity matters because Hemingway's work matters. By understanding Hemingway better, we also understand the American experience better. Hemingway's sexual themes are not the only themes attracting contemporary interest. Recently, for example, Jackson J. Benson paired Hemingway and John Steinbeck, arguing that they represent contradictory sides of modern existence, "so opposite as to be like the two sides of the same coin." In Benson's scheme, "Hemingway expressed the Judeo-Christian perceptions of nature as subservient to human needs and the frontier attitude that nature is a challenge, an arena in which the male of the species proves his manhood. His [Hemingway's] ongoing efforts to dominate nature became the essence of his public personality." Steinbeck, by contrast, was nonviolent and advocated cooperation rather than competition, seeing himself as "a biological entity, related to other animals and the ecological whole." Steinbeck concluded that although man suffers, he "makes everything around him suffer also."[3]

In the midst of the outpouring of biographies in the 1980s (critical discussion of Hemingway's work has never abated), it seemed especially timely that in 1987 Scribner's published *The Complete Short Stories of Ernest Hemingway: The Finca Vigía Edition*. The two preceding Hemingway books from Scribner's had been *The Dangerous Summer* (1985) and *The Garden of Eden*. Although each book has its intrinsic interest, both exemplify Hemingway's later anxieties and his struggles to complete satisfactorily the work he had envisioned. And both works required major editorial shaping before publication. *The Complete Short Stories*, on the other hand, gives readers the authentic master. In addition to reprinting the stories contained in *The Fifth Column and the First Forty-nine Stories* (1938), it gathered the Hemingway stories that have since been published. It also gives readers seven stories that had never been published. *The Complete Short Stories* provides a great deal of the contours of an extraordinary career, emphasizing how much Hemingway remained committed to the short story. His short stories portray all the major locales of his active life, and they embody all of his major themes.

*The Complete Short Stories* is not, however, truly complete. Even as a high school student at Oak Park High School in Oak Park, Illinois, Hemingway was trying his hand at short stories. The stories that he published in the *Tabula*, his high school's literary magazine, reveal why his classmates thought their Ernie so clever. These stories do not, however, belong in the Finca edition, any more than they would have belonged in *The First Forty-nine*. Hemingway did not write his first serious short stories until after he returned from World War I. Yet those experiments are also excluded from *The Complete Short Stories*, though Peter Griffin does include five of them in *Along with Youth*.[4] Although in their foreword to the Finca Vigía edition Hemingway's sons do not discuss their reasons for the exclusion of these stories (unpublished before Griffin's book appeared), the omissions are defensible enough. It is clear that Hemingway himself considered them apprentice work—work that he had put behind him.

Hemingway's models for those early stories were the fictions in the popular magazines of the time, though even in his early stories we can discover his instinct to experiment and to take new directions. If "The Current" seems most obviously designed for the popular magazine, the story also uses biography in an interesting way. It reflects Ernest's love for his fiancée Hadley Richardson, his efforts to prove himself to Hadley's sister, and his awareness of the differences between Hadley and himself. Above all, perhaps, it suggests the symbolic importance of boxing to Hemingway. He was an extraordinarily handsome man (as his experiences in Italy with Agnes von Kurowsky had let him know, if he needed informing); yet he was willing, even eager, to risk damaging his good looks in the boxing rings of Chicago—and later in the rings of Europe, Key West, and Havana. Hemingway would eventually learn to use the materials of his own life more subtly than he does in "The Current." If plot is too obvious there, Hemingway experiments with setting plot aside in "Crossroads—An Anthology." In its place he substitutes brief portraits of a variety of residents from northern Michigan, including the Indian Billy Gilbert, one of whose daughters, Prudence, would later achieve fame in Hemingway's mature work. The anthology of portraits reminds us of Edgar Lee Masters's *Spoon River Anthology* (1915); an avid reader such as Hemingway would almost surely have known the work of this Chicago poet. But more important than the anthology technique was Hemingway's sense of the value of his Michigan experience as a literary subject. Later it inspired some of his greatest stories, and it was a subject that he never let go.

"Portrait of the Idealist in Love—A Story" also used material from Hemingway's own life. It is, however, not a story in any conventional sense. It does not seem written for any large public audience. Certainly its methods are not those of popular magazine fiction. The idealist of the title is Ralph Williams, a young Chicago newspaperman (apparently), who is trying to win the good graces of the sister of the woman to whom he is engaged. The most obvious counterpart in Hemingway's life was the animosity of Hadley's sister Fronnie toward him and her opposition to his engagement to Hadley. But Ralph Williams's long letter to "Isabelle" transcends that real-life situation. The long letter is framed by a gentle ironic description of Ralph, who is proud that he has composed his letter without recourse to a stimulant: "What he wanted was a good, cool, double lemon coca-cola. It was a good, cool, stimulating drink. A man was better off without stimulants but sometimes they were a good thing. They had their place like everything else and the thing to do was not to abuse them."[5] The narrator's amused glance at Ralph says something about the worth of his letter, which chivalrically claims his "Ideal" is womankind. If anything, the letter reads like a satire of the letters that Hemingway's parents wrote to him.[6] Here Hemingway is satirizing a genre that his own work would eventually help to demolish. But he knew the conventions well. In his third major volume, *Winner Take Nothing* (1933), he would use the epistolary mode in "One Reader Writes" for a very different effect.

Like "Portrait of the Idealist in Love," "The Mercenaries—A Story" has a Chicago setting, one that anticipates later treatments of code behavior in a carefully defined setting of worldly, tough characters. The scene is a café where acceptable clients are served liquor during Prohibition. Especially significant for the fiction that was to follow is the role of the young and unnamed narrator, recently returned from service in World War I. Admitted to the special world of the Café Cambrinus, he listens attentively to the story of a "leather-faced old adventurer" who had "matched his courage against admittedly one of the most fearless men in Europe."[7]

Hemingway sensed that characters outside the law were worth exploring. His "The Ash Heel's Tendon—A Story" recounts the capture of Hand Evans, an especially ruthless hit man. He is outsmarted because Jack Farrell, the "czar" of Chicago's Fifteenth Street police station, discovers that Hand's real name is "Guardalabene." Farrell arranges the playing of a Caruso record one night when Hand visits Wolf's Café. The Italian is so moved by the music that he is easily captured. But, as the narrator admits, his story is "a yarn." Some lessons later, Hemingway would in 1927 give the world an unforgettable story of hired killers in Chicago—"The Killers."

These early efforts by Hemingway are impressive not only for the themes that they anticipate, but also for their variety. The intellectual climate of Chicago in the post–World War I years encouraged experimentation, and Hemingway accepted such a challenge. He was already working very hard at discovering what the short story could do.

He retained that commitment long after he had achieved fame and financial security with his novels. Since his gift was lyrical, the short story was always a genre attractive to him. He began his writing career with the short story and continued to be fascinated by its demands. He knew that he would eventually have to come to terms with the novel as well—and, of course, he did so. But the short story remained for him an important method for viewing the world. He knew that he had achieved some of his most moving results in that genre; this realization helped to sustain him in difficult times.

In Hemingway's vision, small things are often very great things. The title of his first book, *Three Stories and Ten Poems* (1923), is an appropriate beginning to Hemingway's intense wish to say much through a severe economy. After vigorous experimentation and many lessons, some painful, Hemingway could present in book-form three stories—markedly different in subject and technique—but sufficient testimony that an important new talent was at hand. The stories were "Up in Michigan," "Out of Season," and "My Old Man." Their companions were short poems, reminders now of their creator's keen sense of rhythm, his sense of the pause, and his recognition of the importance of silence.

Two of the three stories, "Out of Season" and "My Old Man," made their way into *In Our Time* (1925), a gathering of short stories with a structure that stressed the relationships between the stories. Unlike *Three Stories and Ten Poems*, this book had a commercial publisher. After its publication Hemingway would never relinquish the security of being a commercially desirable writer. He had established that claim with the short story.

Just two years later, *Men Without Women* (1927) confirmed Hemingway's genius with the short story. *Winner Take Nothing* (1933) was his third major collection of short stories. In 1938 Scribner's published *The Fifth Column and the First Forty-nine Stories*, bringing together the stories of these volumes as well as four previously uncollected stories. Since Hemingway never abandoned the short story, from time to time he envisioned other gatherings of his stories. For various reasons another collection never quite materialized during his lifetime. But later other hands gave at least partial fulfillment to Hemingway's plans. In 1969 Scribner's published *The Fifth Column and Four Stories of the Spanish Civil War*. In 1972 Philip Young oversaw publication of *The Nick Adams Stories*, which focused attention on one of Hemingway's most important characters and renewed interest in some of his best stories; additionally, the book included a completed Nick Adams short story never before published plus Nick Adams material discarded or never completed, including a late novel in progress, "The Last Good Country." Then, in 1987, *The Complete Short Stories of Ernest Hemingway* appeared, reminding readers once again of Hemingway's extraordinary contribution to this genre.

The present study, then, pays homage to this achievement. Part 1 explores Hemingway's theories about the genre, largely through looking at some of his later ruminations about the form as reflected in *The Garden of Eden*. Its thesis is that Hemingway followed the pattern that he had established in his early apprentice work: he was always looking for variety of form even though he would repeat important themes and suggestively echo earlier work. Seemingly simple, Hemingway's work is often complex. Although his own life experiences are repeatedly the basis for his stories, the actual experience itself is never the point of a story. Hemingway was a shaper, and the short story as a form continued to appeal to him throughout his career.

In part 1 I explore that shaping process and identify major themes of the short stories. My purpose is not to discuss every short story, or even every great short story—although I do explore some of them as illustrations. I also point out that even the minor stories sometimes have significant dimensions within the context in which Hemingway placed them. Finally, I take special interest in the "new" Hemingway fiction made available in the Finca edition.

Part 2 lets Hemingway himself speak about the short story and his achievement in the genre. His most famous statement comes in his preface to *The Fifth Column and the First Forty-nine Stories*. It is brief but evocative—appropriate to the narrative theory that informs the first forty-nine.[8] If the style of the preface is "tough," it also reveals an appealing human voice and an artist's dedication. The piece, coincidentally, is one that Hemingway recorded, and Caedmon has made it available on record and tape. The companion piece to this preface is a much longer work, previously not readily available to students. Hemingway wrote "The Art of the Short Story" very late in his career. It was to be the introduction to a projected collection of his stories, a volume designed for students. But in 1959 Hemingway found writing of any kind a much more difficult activity than he had found it in 1938. Although getting words down for this preface did not seem a problem, Hemingway found it difficult to take the intended audience seriously. But the more rambling quality of this piece, at times self-indulgent, allowed him to share more aspects about himself and his career than he had for the magisterial collection *The Fifth Column and the First Forty-nine Stories*. The 1959 essay is valuable for allowing a close view of Hemingway in his last years, suggesting the appeal of his personality as well as his late torments. Anything but taut and lean, "The Art of the Short Story" nevertheless makes clear Hemingway's seriousness about the genre, and his statements about his stories repay scrutiny. In 1954 Hemingway told Robert Harling: "I'm a serious writer" and added, "I'm even a serious man. But not a solemn man, I hope."[9] In "The Art of the Short Story" Hemingway proves himself a serious writer, and at least in that regard a serious man. And he emerges as anything but solemn. A version of the essay appeared in 1981 in the

Preface

*Paris Review*. It is a pleasure to include "The Art of the Short Story" in part 2, a version based on the manuscripts of the Hemingway Collection at the John F. Kennedy Library. Since Hemingway first asserted his claims to critical attention with *In Our Time* and *The Sun Also Rises*, the amount of scrutiny given his work has accelerated. We now have some six decades of Hemingway criticism, and whoever would try to read all of it would be kept busy indeed. Part 3 of this book suggests the pleasures to be found in such labor. Pointing to some of the important recent work, it hopes to interest readers in further explorations in Hemingway criticism. The bibliography will help steer readers to books and collections of essays that provide other insights. Anyone wishing a comprehensive listing of books and articles on Hemingway should consult Linda W. Wagner's *Ernest Hemingway: A Reference Guide* (Boston: G. K. Hall, 1977) for items through 1975.

Revisiting Ernest Hemingway's fiction is always an exciting adventure. New rewards as well as re-experienced pleasures are inevitable. It has been especially challenging to return to these riches just after the publication of *The Complete Short Stories of Ernest Hemingway*. So I am grateful for the inspiration that led Anne M. Jones at G. K. Hall to conceive of this series at so propitious a time. Her support and that of Liz Traynor, her successor at G. K. Hall, have been valuable. I appreciate also the skills of Barbara Sutton, manuscript editor at G. K. Hall. It has been gratifying to work under the general editorship of Gordon Weaver, himself a noted disciple of the short story.

I am grateful to Robert W. Lewis and the Hemingway Society for permission to publish "The Art of the Short Story," and to Megan Floyd Desnoyers, Curator of the Ernest Hemingway Collection at the John F. Kennedy Library, for her helpfulness in locating manuscript versions of this essay and the manuscript for "A Clean, Well-Lighted Place." Alan Goodrich, also of the Kennedy Library, assisted in the selection of a photograph of Hemingway at mid-career.

Closer to home, I acknowledge once again the pleasure of talking about Hemingway with students and colleagues. I am especially grateful to Louis Corrigan, who gave me valuable service as a research assistant, proving again his affection for Hemingway and his scholarly excellence. I am grateful to him and to Christine Flora and Susan Marston for their careful readings of work-in-progress. They have made me concentrate harder. Dr. Frank C. Wilson, Jr., also read a portion of the manuscript, and I am grateful to this colleague from the School of Medicine for his continuing participation in the humanities. Charlotte McFall and Jo Gibson have helped me keep on schedule by assisting with proofing and clerical detail. Finally, I have enjoyed watching my sons, all on their own, take a special interest in Hemingway—not because of my interest but because they liked the way he could tell a story.

Joseph M. Flora
*University of North Carolina, Chapel Hill*

# Notes

1. Gregory H. Hemingway, *Papa: A Personal Memoir* (Boston: Houghton Mifflin, 1976), 31.

2. Hemingway's audience has a very broad base, as attested by the Hemingway look-alike contests at Sloppy Joe's Bar in Key West and the annual Hemingway contest for the worst opening sentence to a novel. He would likely approve the fun of these events, but assuredly as well the annual Ernest Hemingway Award contest for the best first novel. A project initiated by Mary Hemingway, the attractive award has been administered through P.E.N.

3. Jackson J. Benson, "Hemingway the Hunter and Steinbeck the Farmer," *Michigan Quarterly Review* 24 (Summer 1985): 441–60.

4. He omitted one of the most interesting, one that is probably Hemingway's first completed story of World War I. Because the story has great biographical interest—especially for his thesis—Kenneth Lynn summarizes it in *Hemingway* (New York: Simon and Schuster, 1987), 130–32.

5. "Portrait of the Idealist in Love," in Peter Griffin, *Along with Youth: Hemingway, the Early Years* (New York and Oxford: Oxford University Press, 1985), 164.

6. The most notorious of these letters was Grace Hall Hemingway's carefully conceived one evicting Ernest from Windemere, the family cottage on Walloon Lake, Michigan. See Michael Reynolds, *The Young Hemingway* (New York and Oxford: Basil Blackwell, 1986), 136–38. Ernest's father pronounced the letter "a masterpiece," but it was a letter that Ernest could never forget nor forgive. Dated 24 July, 1920, the letter was hand delivered on 27 July. "Portrait of the Idealist in Love" was written in the next year.

7. "The Mercenaries" in Griffin, *Along with Youth*, 111.

8. Hemingway begins his preface by discussing the circumstances surrounding the writing of *The Fifth Column*; perhaps he reasoned that it would be useful for the public to have an explanation about his work in an uncharacter-

istic genre. Furthermore, the Spanish conflict provided a basis for a great out-pouring of writing from him. He gives two-thirds of his preface to the play. The final third of that preface points to the gold.

9. Robert Harling, "A Journey to Hemingway," in *Conversations with Ernest Hemingway* (Jackson and London: University Press of Mississippi, 1986), 83. Reprinted from the *London Sunday Times* (19 December 1954), 10.

# Acknowledgments

I am grateful to the following publishers, persons, and organizations for permission to use the indicated materials.

Quotations from the following works of Ernest Hemingway are used by permission of Charles Scribner's Sons, an imprint of Macmillan Publishing Company, and Jonathan Cape Ltd.

*The Sun Also Rises,* copyright 1926 by Charles Scribner's Sons; renewed 1954 by Ernest Hemingway.

*A Farewell to Arms,* copyright 1929 by Charles Scribner's Sons; renewed © 1957 by Ernest Hemingway.

*Death in the Afternoon,* copyright 1932 by Charles Scribner's Sons; renewed © 1960 by Ernest Hemingway.

*Green Hills of Africa,* copyright 1935 by Charles Scribner's Sons; renewed © 1963 by Mary Hemingway.

*For Whom the Bell Tolls,* copyright 1940 by Ernest Hemingway; renewed © 1968 by Mary Hemingway.

*The Old Man and the Sea,* copyright 1952 by Ernest Hemingway; renewed © 1980 by Mary Hemingway.

*A Moveable Feast,* © 1964 by Ernest Hemingway.

*By-Line: Ernest Hemingway,* © 1967 by Mary Hemingway.

*Ernest Hemingway: Selected Letters,* ed. Carlos Baker, © 1981 by Carlos Baker/Ernest Hemingway.

*Ernest Hemingway on Writing,* eds. Larry Phillips and Mary Welsh Hemingway, © 1984 by Larry Phillips and Mary Welsh Hemingway.

*The Garden of Eden,* © 1986 by Mary Hemingway, John Hemingway, Patrick Hemingway, and Gregory Hemingway.

*The Complete Short Stories of Ernest Hemingway: The Finca Vigía Edition,* © 1987 by Charles Scribner's Sons/Macmillan Publishing Company, a division of Macmillan Inc.

Excerpts from "Tradition and the Individual Talent," in *Selected Essays by T. S. Eliot,* copyright 1950 by Harcourt Brace Jovanovich, Inc.; renewed © 1978 by Esme Valerie Eliot. Reprinted by permission of the publisher.

*Part 1*

# THE SHORT FICTION: A CRITICAL ANALYSIS

I'm trying to do it so it will make it without you knowing it, and so the more you read it, the more there will be.

—Ernest Hemingway, *A Moveable Feast*

# Hemingway's Theory of the Short Story

That Ernest Hemingway profoundly affected the course of the modern short story few will deny. Virtually every writer of fiction who began work after Hemingway's *In Our Time* (1925) learned from him. Many of these writers would later find in their teacher much that appalled or saddened them, but the best of them, especially, would remain grateful for the lessons of his craft, for the new directions he gave to the short story, and for the high standard he set for art. Hemingway continues to wield this influence, though some of the instruction comes indirectly from writers who have absorbed what he taught—best by example, but also by pronouncement.

In a wise essay, first published in the *New Republic* of 11 November, 1936, John Peale Bishop pays tribute to Hemingway's extraordinary achievement. To be sure, he has *The Sun Also Rises* (1926) and *A Farewell to Arms* (1929) primarily in mind, but his essay makes numerous references to the short stories as well. Finding Hemingway's vision of life "one of perpetual annihilation," Bishop concludes:

> What is there left? Of all man's activities, the work of art lasts longest. And in this morality there is little to be discerned beyond the discipline of the craft. This is what the French call the sense of *métier* and their conduct in peace and war has shown that it may be a powerful impulse to the right action; if I am not mistaken, it is the main prop of French society. In [Hemingway's] "The Undefeated", the old bullfighter, corrupt though he is with age, makes a good and courageous end, and yet it is not so much courage that carries him as a proud professional skill. It is this discipline, which Flaubert acquired from the traditions of his people and which Pound transmitted to the young Hemingway, that now, as he approaches forty, alone sustains him. He has mastered his *métier* as has no other American among his contemporaries. That is his pride and distinction.[1]

Bishop was a poet, and it was the poet's concentration that made him respond so completely to Hemingway's respect for métier. As Bishop points out, in Paris the young Hemingway honed the prose of his apprenticeship stories under the demanding tutelage of one of the major poets of the century, Ezra Pound. The best place to look for a summary of the lessons that Pound taught is his "A Retrospect" (1918). In this essay Pound reviews the imagist movement, probably the most significant development in poetry as "modern" literature replaced nineteenth-century literature, and he gives practical advice to aspiring poets. At the time, in fact, Hemingway was writing poetry as well as prose—his first small book was called *Three Stories and Ten Poems* (1923). The stories that Hemingway was writing came increasingly to satisfy Pound's imagist credo. "An image," Pound declared, "is that which presents an intellectual and emotional complex in an instant of time." And no matter where we look in "A Retrospect" we will sense the value of Pound's instruction to the young writer. Here is a sampling: "Use no superfluous word, no adjective which does not reveal something" (Hemingway became famous for his lean style). "Don't imagine that the art of poetry is any simpler than the art of music, or that you can please the expert before you have spent at least as much effort on the art of verse as the average piano teacher spends on the art of music" (son of a teacher of voice and himself a cellist in high school, Hemingway would appreciate that caution!). "Be influenced by as many great artists as you can, but have the decency either to acknowledge the debt outright, or to try to conceal it" (Hemingway was an inveterate reader, and his style is much more allusive than his first readers discerned). "The proper and perfect symbol is the natural object" (it would take some readers and critics a while to learn that Hemingway is a symbolist, not a hard-boiled naturalist, precisely because his symbols are the natural object). Finally, a special gem of "A Retrospect": "Good prose will do you no harm, and there is good discipline to be had by trying to write it."[2] Before going to Paris, Hemingway had already had hard training in that discipline. In Paris he found valuable instructors besides Pound, though he did not have the good grace to acknowledge them fully or decently in *A Moveable Feast* (1964). He was quite prepared to take the advice that Gertrude Stein claims to have given him: "Begin over again and concentrate."[3] It is doubtful that either Pound or Stein ever had a more attentive disciple.

He would in a very short time develop a distinctive prose style—praised as muscular, lean, efficient. A brief apprenticeship after his high school graduation as a reporter on the *Kansas City Star* helped him toward that end, teaching him economy and directness. Later, in Europe in the early 1920s, he worked as correspondent for the *Toronto Star*. His assignment was not to report hard news but to write human interest accounts, which he would wire in "cablese," an abbreviated style that challenged the young Hemingway to transmit his ideas using a minimum number of words. Although Gertrude Stein advised Hemingway that he should quit journalism if he wished to be a creative writer, and although Hemingway took that advice as soon as possible, newspaper training had helped to sharpen his skills of observation and to form his style. It also helped to prepare him for the lessons of Pound and Stein.

Not every young reporter could see the possibilities for taut prose that Hemingway did, and his journalistic apprenticeship can carry us only so far in understanding his progress. There are other disciplines that can help define Hemingway's mode. Hemingway himself cited the art of painting as important to his writing goals, calling particular attention to Cézanne.[4] Cecelia Tichi credits Hemingway with bringing engineering values into prose style:

> Dos Passos used structures and machines as the organizational model for the modern novel, but Hemingway enacted the values of engineering in his tight functional prose. His was the efficient modern style for which Ezra Pound had argued. In the era of the anti-waste Efficiency Movement Hemingway's terse, economical lines brought engineering values into the very sentence itself. He reduced the sentence to its essential, functional components. The famous Hemingway style was essentially the achievement, in novels and stories, of the engineers' aesthetic of functionalism and formal efficiency.[5]

Tichi cites Hemingway's apprenticeship in journalism as an important base for his aesthetic, but she also suggests how developments in American literature and American painting were preparing the way for his progress. He was like Thomas Eakins, for example, in showing a covert preoccupation with technics. Hemingway's fascination with bullfights is an extension of his aesthetic of function. His concerns parallel those of another famous son of Oak Park, Illinois: Frank Lloyd Wright. Echoing Wright, Hemingway had said in *Death in the Afternoon*: "Prose is architecture, not interior decoration, and the Baroque is over."[6] Tichi concludes that Hemingway is "full of nostalgia for a preindustrial 'natural' environment, but his sentences are irrevocably of another, a gear-and-girder, world."[7] His style was noticed from the start. In 1981 Martha Gellhorn, a skillful writer as well as Hemingway's third wife, paid accurate tribute to Hemingway as exemplar of that new style: "He was a genius, that uneasy word, not so much in what he wrote (speaking like an uncertified critic) as in how he wrote; he liberated our written language. All writers, after him, owe Hemingway a debt for their freedom whether the debt is acknowledged or not."[8]

The recent reminders by Tichi and Gellhorn of Hemingway's extraordinary skill and achievement are at one with Bishop's praise of Hemingway's mastery of métier, though Bishop's view of métier embraces more than their identification of Hemingway's revolutionary style. If Tichi's goal is to identify the achievement, Gellhorn's primary motive lies elsewhere. She writes with anger and disgust about the dishonesty of the many writers who have created apocryphal accounts of Hemingway, and she laments the cult of personality as demeaning to Hemingway's achievement. She knew well, of course, that he himself had often aided and abetted this cult. John Peale Bishop had, in fact, pondered that tendency in Hemingway in his essay, for homage was not the whole point of it. As Bishop surveyed the recently published *Green Hills of Africa* (1935) he was concerned about Hemingway's future. He worried that Hemingway, in whom he had found "the most complete literary integrity it has ever been my lot to encounter," had become his own legend, much as Lord Byron had become his legend after he wrote *Childe Harold*. The legendary Hemingway, Bishop found, "could not have written Hemingway's early books; he might have written most of *Green Hills of Africa*." Tragically, Bishop concluded, the biggest game Hemingway may have brought down in Africa was himself.

Although the major premise of the present study is that many of Hemingway's short stories are among the literary glories of the century, I must briefly acknowledge the complexity of Hemingway the man. Because his chief literary subject was himself, his readers cannot always escape the difficulties of that self. The legend continues to intrude; it will not lie down. Although the man is gone, his personality continues to perplex and to intrigue. Memoirs about him and valuable biographies continue to appear—sometimes at an astounding rate. Nevertheless, readers dealing with that outpouring may find Hemingway more elusive than Virginia Woolf's Mrs. Brown, who taunted any number of writers to catch her if they could.[9] We come to appreciate more keenly the problems that Carlos Baker, Hemingway's first major biographer, encountered and the virtues of his methodology.

One is likely to hear more brief summaries (and dismissals) of Hemingway the man than of any other writer. Some readers think that they know him all too well. He retains an extraordinary ability to make people angry. One of my colleagues, a teacher of American literature, says that Hemingway has absolutely nothing to say to women, over half of the human race, she adds; to her mind, that reduces his status from major to minor writer. James Jones, author of *From Here to Eternity* (1951) and other war novels and inevitably one of the writers to whom Hemingway must be compared, thought a great deal about Hemingway (knowing, it should be added, that Hemingway was highly critical of Jones's work). A year or so after Hemingway's death, Jones made a trip to Pamplona for the bullfight festival, and he later reported on the event in *Esquire*, spoofing typical scenes from Hemingway's work. He emphasized a reality of Pamplona that Hemingway had skirted over, its overriding smell, especially "a distinct odor of shit." Jones asks, "What had he done to us with his big masculine bullshit? What did it all mean? It meant people still have to have myths to live by, and if you built a better myth the world would beat a path to your door. It meant, to me, that very likely, for quite a while yet, there would still be heroes, great generals, and war."[10] Jones lays a huge burden on the shoulders of Hemingway the writer. Readers are certainly entitled to ponder the cultural significance of the pilgrims who follow "Papa" to Key West to drink at Sloppy Joe's or to Pamplona to run with the bulls—sporting T-shirts to acknowledge their participation in the revels. We may even wonder at the cultural significance of the Hemingway Society. It has an excitement quite unique among literary societies because its members move around the world for their meetings, participating ritualistically in all that Hemingway made exciting. Through him, it is still possible to seek those last frontiers. One can be an academic yet also experience the strenuous life.

There are, happily, a large number of women in the Hemingway Society, and many women scholars continue to find Hemingway a worthy subject for their attention. He does have something to say to them—as, presumably, does Herman Melville, who often portrays a world without women. But the women's movement has rightly led readers and critics of both sexes to look carefully at any number of issues through different eyes. My colleague's accusation, hardly hers exclusively, deserves consideration in this study of Hemingway's short stories. Indeed, the role of women in them is an important part of their power. Certainly Hemingway was much concerned with identifying the proper relationship between men and women. The problem bothered him his whole life, and his stories reveal his concern with the tensions and the ideals of male–female relationships. We must indeed ponder how much "masculine bullshit" soils the stories.

Let us return, therefore, to Bishop's tribute. What happened to Hemingway the short story writer after Bishop paid his homage? At the time of Bishop's writing, Hemingway had already given to the world his third major collection of short stories, *Winner Take Nothing* (1933), and would create only a few more stories, but certainly some of his or anyone's best, for *The Fifth Column and the First Forty-nine Stories* (1938). In his preface to that great gathering, Hemingway wrote: "I would like to live long enough to write three more novels and twenty-five more stories. I know some pretty good ones." He was only thirty-nine on his birthday that year. The aura of mortality had been a noticeable feature of his work almost from the beginning, and there is a suggestion of the pose of the old man in his preface statement about his future writing goals. Nevertheless, he had easily earned the right to a preface—the right to make a survey of his career as master of the short story—and readers at the time must have welcomed his determination to continue to write in that genre.

He was on the mark about what he would achieve in the novel. He lived to complete *For Whom the Bell Tolls* (1940), *Across the River and into the Trees* (1950), and *The Old Man and the Sea* (1952), the latter a novella, originally conceived as part of the long sea novel, *Islands in the Stream* (1970), published after his death. But he never approached the count of the projected short stories (he would publish only seven more), and readers of his work are therefore entitled to speculate about his failure to realize that goal—especially since his work in the genre forms so large a part of his literary importance. Sometimes, of course, writers shift interest from one genre to another. Some fiction writers cut their teeth on the short story and then proceed to devote most of their efforts to the novel. A recent case in point is Doris Betts, a writer first known for her fine short stories. Betts gradually turned from that genre to devote her efforts to the novel, receiving her greatest national acclaim for *Heading West* (1982). Commenting on the shift, Betts said:

# Hemingway's Theory of the Short Story

"I have, I think, reached that age when the short story is no longer as aesthetically pleasing to me. The short story, like the lyric poem, may be the form of youth, when you still believe that people can change in twenty-four-hour periods. Well, you get older, you can't help seeing that the more things change, the more they stay the same, just the way your grandmother told you. And you do become interested, then, in longer structures and also in the things that abide."[11]

Did Hemingway come to find the short story less aesthetically pleasing than the novel? Did he believe that longer structures were more likely to abide? Was that the reason that he created *For Whom the Bell Tolls*, his longest novel, having already cautioned in the long *Death in the Afternoon* about the impulse to write an epic: "all bad writers are in love with the epic" (*DA* 54)? Bishop had already pronounced a verdict on Hemingway's search for "things that abide." Métier, we recall, was a defense against finding nothing that would abide. I have found no statements by Hemingway in which he consciously decided that the short story form was less interesting to him than it had been. Financially, he was free to put his creative efforts where he wanted. Unlike his contemporary F. Scott Fitzgerald, he did not have to look to the short story to support him. His career suggests that he went through some change in his view of himself as short story writer after 1945, when his serious writing efforts went increasingly to long fiction—fiction that he seemed unable to conclude. (In the last decade of his life he was concerned to produce book-length manuscripts for his Havana vault as insurance for his family.) Eventually, much of that writing would be given to the world in the posthumous works. The most successful of them was *A Moveable Feast*. Not technically a work of fiction (although the book's preface invited readers to conceive of it as fiction, and the manuscript declares that it is fiction), it nevertheless proceeded by short units and recalled the great successes Hemingway had had with the short story when he lived and loved in the Paris of the 1920s. But Hemingway did occasionally turn back to the short story even during the post–1945 years. The discipline of the form served him in his dealing with parental angst and in confronting the possibility he was going blind. Less certain than Betts of "things that abide," he never totally abandoned the short story and the comfort of métier. Even when he worked on his longer fictions, he was still conscious of the art of the short story form. Readers of *For Whom the Bell Tolls* will recall that stories within the novel (Pilar's, Maria's) add to its power. A short part of the envisioned sea novel became *The Old Man and the Sea*

(1952). *The Garden of Eden* (1986), the last of Hemingway's posthumous novels to be published, portrays a writer of both short stories and novels. Obviously, he continued to think about the genre. *The Garden of Eden* is set in Mediterranean France and Spain in the post–World War I period. Hemingway began this work in 1946. World War II had just ended, and Hemingway was beginning a new phase of his life with the last of his four wives. In his mid-forties, he had packed the years of his manhood with intense activity (we understand why Bishop had described him ten years earlier as nearing forty). *For Whom the Bell Tolls* was behind him, as was the last spurt of short stories he was to write—stories that grew out of the Spanish Civil War. If the new marriage put Hemingway in a new Eden, the new paradise was a complicated place. And the Eden he was writing about, inhabited by a much younger protagonist living in an earlier time, was also complicated—there was a Lilith in the garden as well as an Eve.

*The Garden of Eden* is worth considering here because David Bourne, the protagonist, is a young writer and his views about writing reflect those of the young Hemingway.[12] Bourne has published two novels, but he is suffering from writer's block. Hemingway's protagonists are usually more attractive persons than David, though David resembles the other heroes in various ways. His redeeming trait is his dedication to his métier, much resembling Hemingway's own dedication. But since David Bourne has restricted himself to that single dedication, he emerges as something of a monster. Although the climax of the novel comes when his wife destroys the manuscripts of stories he has been working on (she is the Lilith of this bizarre Eden), David is more the victim of his self-love and a hardening of his own heart than he is the victim of Lilith or Eve. He is no molder of his destiny—most things, like his women, just happen to him. We do not pity him any more than we pity another essentially passive Adam, Nathaniel Hawthorne's Giovanni in "Rappaccini's Daughter." A great deal of metamorphosis occurs in the Edens of both works, much of it observed in literal mirrors of self-love. Whereas Giovanni is partly the victim of Rappaccini and Baglioni, Hawthorne presents him as a somewhat shallow fellow who fails to trust Beatrice, though her heart is pure. Victim, in part, Giovanni nevertheless ensures his own demise.

As David "revisits" his adolescence in Africa in the service of art, he explores his complex relationship with his father. Disappointed in the way the hunt of an elephant and his role in that hunt had gone, the young David resolves: "I'm going to keep everything a secret always. I'll never tell them anything again."[13] The line expresses more than

10

adolescent despondence in that it identifies a moment of decisive choice, like those moments Hawthorne emphasizes in his fiction. David Bourne (Hawthorne had also used the name *Bourne* for one of his haunted characters, Reuben Bourne of "Roger Malvin's Burial") isolates himself by establishing a rule of inward turning that leaves him ill-equipped to find happiness in any garden. He thinks that his father "knows all about it now and he will never trust me again. That's good. I don't want him to because I'll never tell him or anybody anything again never anything again. Never ever never" (*GE* 182). Like Hawthorne's Bourne he chooses his own isolation and reminds us of that bourne from which no traveler returns. This Adam will not be an easy companion for any Lilith or Eve with whom he may live. To the detriment of Hemingway's novel (or at least to the published version) David becomes too static a figure, sharing with Hemingway's other posthumous protagonists a fault identified by Earl Rovit and Gerry Brenner as a failure to invite multiple responses.[14]

David's inward turning is partly a concomitant of the much-admired resolve of the Hemingway hero to endure. But the courage to endure may lead to a destructive stoicism. Medical thought of our time emphasizes the need for talking out one's problems in order to maintain mental health. Hemingway's heroes are always exceptionally tight-lipped about their pains, and David Bourne's fatal resolution while still a boy to opt for a fierce privacy may offer a strong hint about Hemingway's late problems as well as about David's burdens. The open question at the end of *The Garden of Eden* is simply: will David's commitment to métier sustain him?

His commitment to métier is, to repeat, his redeeming feature. Nothing matters to him more than his writing. Hence, Catherine's act of burning his short stories provides the climax of the novel. David's stories were not stories in the conventional sense of their time. Their intent was partly therapeutic. David will never talk to another person about his problems, but he will write on and around the personal conflicts of his life. Catherine calls them "dreary dismal little stories about your adolescence with your bogus drunken father." Although Catherine describes them as "sketches or vignettes or pointless anecdotes" (*GE* 210), David considers them stories. Typically, he does not attempt to make Catherine understand what he is writing. But he is always reflecting upon the art of fiction:

> Thank God he was breaking through on the stories now. What had
> made the last book good was the people who were in it and the

11

accuracy of the detail which made it believable. He had, really, only to remember accurately and the form came by what he would choose to leave out. Then, of course, he could close it like the diaphragm of a camera and intensify it so it could be concentrated to the point where the heat shone bright and the smoke began to rise. He knew that he was getting this now. (*GE* 211)

Catherine's failure to comprehend his efforts does not cause him any doubts. He tells himself, "But you've worked well and nothing can touch you as long as you can work" (*GE* 211).

What David writes and theorizes about is very similar to what Ernest Hemingway was writing and thinking about in Paris in the 1920s. He was writing short stories, often about his adolescence and about his family. His father was neither bogus nor drunken, however. The point cannot be stressed too vigorously that although Hemingway began to succeed as a writer only after he realized that his best subject was himself, he was no slave to biographical duplication. He was looking for artistic truth. He would present many avatars of himself, but he felt quite free to reconstruct his past, though there was usually a core of biographical fact in most of his stories. (In *The Garden of Eden* Catherine deliberately burns David's stories; in Paris, Hadley Hemingway, wishing to surprise her husband, took them with her on a train as she set out to rejoin him, but when she briefly left her compartment, someone stole the suitcase containing them.)

Hemingway's themes were quite basic. He wrote about the need for independence, yet he could not escape his identity as the son of particular parents. Fiction remained a means for him to explore his relationship with his father, just as it was for David. Hemingway wrote often about the relationship between fathers and sons. He wrote about the splendor of love and its painful loss. He wrote about war and death. He wrote about the loss of traditional values in the Western world. He wrote about aging, the loss of occupation, diminishment. He wrote about writing and about birthing. In complex ways, he combined concerns with the masculine and the feminine.

The power of his writing depended on his remembering accurately a core of detail. Nevertheless, Hemingway did not have much patience with his contemporary Thomas Wolfe, who relied on the window of memory for virtually everything he wrote. For Wolfe, who wanted to forget nothing, to lose nothing, precise and complete recollection was a compulsion. Unlike Wolfe, Hemingway thought about writing as a means of getting rid of reality. Wolfe wanted to make every detail of experience permanent so that he might freeze it and thus conquer time—his mortal enemy. Hemingway was more concerned with the emotion an experience created.

Yet both writers were intently busy gathering experiences so that they could write about them. Both writers had a great deal to say about America, an America they discovered by traveling to Europe. The autobiographical impulse was major in each. But Hemingway and Wolfe took different risks. Wolfe's was the risk of inclusion; Hemingway's the risk of exclusion. In *The Garden of Eden* David Bourne affirms Hemingway's conviction that "the form came by what he would choose to leave out." The risk was that the reader would find the pieces "sketches or pointless anecdotes." Through David Bourne, Hemingway provides a vivid metaphor for the effect he wished to achieve, and it sounds greatly like Pound's definition of imagism, "an intellectual and emotional complex in an instant of time." David thinks of "the diaphragm of a camera . . . concentrated to the point where the heat shone bright and the smoke began to rise." Hemingway's most famous metaphor for describing his method came in *Death in the Afternoon,* and it is apt for describing David Bourne's method: "If a writer of prose knows enough about what he is writing about he may omit things that he knows and the reader, if the writer is writing truly enough, will have a feeling of those things as strongly as though the writer had stated them. The dignity of an ice-berg is due to only one-eighth of it being above water" (*DA* 192). In this study there will be numerous occasions for seeing that theory at work. The emphasis on submerging information is the most revolutionary part of Hemingway's theory of the short story.

As David Bourne is writing his African story, we learn much about his approach to his material, about the demands that the story makes on him, about its insistence on being written, and about his controlling the writing in a measured way. We understand also his insistence on the role of memory as the story becomes discovery:

> The story started with no difficulty as a story does when it is ready
> to be written and he got past the middle of it and knew he should
> break off and leave it until the next day. If he could not keep away
> from it after he had taken a break he would drive through and finish
> it. But he hoped he could keep away from it and hit it fresh the next
> day. It was a good story and now he remembered how long he had

intended to write it. The story had not come to him in the past few days. His memory had been inaccurate in that. It was the *necessity* to write it that had come to him. He knew how the story ended *now*. He had always known the wind and sand scoured bones but they were all gone now and he was *inventing* all of it. It was all true now because it happened to him as he wrote and only its bones were dead and scattered and behind him. It started now with the evil in the shamba and he *had to write it* and he was very well into it. (*GE* 93–94; my italics)

The life of the story can become for the writer more important than his own life, and that can make great problems in his living. Looking forward to the moment of the outpouring of the writing juices, David had thought: "he must remember to be unselfish about it and make it as clear as he could that the enforced loneliness was regrettable and that he was not proud of it" (*GE* 14). The story that comes into being is, then, based on experience but just as certainly invented.

David has given a great deal of thought to his theory of fiction. His writing is not based on any concern for the market. His reader is not Catherine, but some ideal reader who will share the very experience that David undergoes: "It was not him, but as he wrote it was and when someone read it, finally, it would be whoever read it and what they found when they should reach the escarpment, if they reached it, and he would make them reach its base by noon of that day; then whoever read it would find what there was there and have it always" (*GE* 129). Hemingway had espoused the same goal in his speech to the American Writers' Conference in New York on 4 June 1937: "A writer's problem does not change. He himself changes, but his problem remains the same. It is always how to write truly and, having found what is true, to project it in such a way that it becomes a part of the experience of the person who reads it."[15] The belief was one he maintained throughout his writing career.

For the reader and the writer, the great story is a way of finding something he could not lose. David's goal in writing his African story is close to the goal of writing that Hemingway had earlier described in *Green Hills of Africa*. He declares that in prose, if the writer is serious and has good luck, "There is a fourth and fifth dimension that can be gotten."[16] Behind both Hemingway's and David's thinking the reader may hear Joseph Conrad's pronouncement in the preface to *The Nigger of the "Narcissus"*: "My task which I am trying to achieve is, by the power of the written word, to make you hear, to make you feel—it is, before all, to make you *see*. That—and no more, and it is everything. If I succeed, you shall find there, according to your deserts, encouragement, consolation, fear, charm, all you demand—and, perhaps, also that glimpse of truth for which you have forgotten to ask."[17] It is surely there.

The price for such writing is immense. The demand on the writer, the struggle for a fifth dimension, requires superhuman effort, and David Bourne must constantly admonish himself about that challenge: "There is nothing you can do except try to write it the way that it was. So you must write each day better than you possibly can and use the sorrow that you have now to make you know how the early sorrow came. And you must always remember the things you believed because if you know them they will be there in the writing and you won't betray them. The writing is the only progress you make" (*GE* 166). True writing, then, is discovery, the finding of understanding: "The understanding was beginning and he was realizing it as he wrote. But the dreadful understanding was all to come and he must not show it by arbitrary statements of rhetoric but by remembering the actual things that had brought it" (*GE* 182). The remembering recalls Wolfe; the pain involved in understanding stresses the compelling urgency of Hemingway's best work. Later, Joan Didion would express the writer's urgency this way: "We tell ourselves stories in order to live."[18]

The writer, by default, is also a critic and must judge how close he comes to that fourth or fifth dimension. His juices flowing, David finishes his African story in four days: "He had in it all the pressure that had built while he was writing it and the modest part of him was afraid that it could not possibly be as good as he believed it to be. The cold, hard part knew it was better" (*GE* 153). The perfect story, then, results from pressure that carries the writer beyond himself; hence, the magnitude of the climax to *The Garden of Eden*. After Catherine burns David's stories, Marita (at first the friend of the wife Catherine, then her replacement) suggests that he write them again, but David denies the possibility: "When it's right you can't remember. Every time you read it again it comes as a great and unbelievable surprise. You can't believe you did it. When it's once right you never can do it again. You only do it once for each thing. And you're only allowed so many in your life" (*GE* 230). Once right, the story is separate from the writer, who is then only another reader of the story. It becomes the thing that matters. This view is especially evident in Hemingway's reactions to *The Old Man and the Sea*, a short work that Hemingway had written during the time that he struggled with *The Garden of Eden*. He described it as a "strange damn story" that would mean many things to its readers. It affected Hemingway as profoundly as it did his audience. Never had he delighted so much in his sense of being one of his readers.[19] We should, then, pay particular attention to the role of the artist in David's theory; the theory is much like Hemingway's. As I have noted, Hemingway often assumed a boisterous public stance; he himself realized that he had aided and abetted in the cult of personality that followed him. But the artist in truly creating transcends—or overcomes—the public figure. The personality of the writer is subsumed by his art: "You can't believe you did it," said David.

Hemingway's position is remarkably close to that of T. S. Eliot, whom Hemingway liked to spar with, metaphorically speaking. Hemingway's story "Mr. and Mrs. Elliott" is, in part, an infamous put-down of Eliot, the spelling of the last name in keeping with Hemingway's lifelong tendency to misspell Eliot's name.[20] In the case of "Mr. and Mrs. Elliott," Eliot would not mind the distancing, though he and everyone else knew that he was being ridiculed as the essence of everything unmasculine in modern literature. But as was often the case with Hemingway, the put-down masked a profound indebtedness.

In a famous pronouncement, Eliot had declared himself "classicist in literature, royalist in politics, and anglo-catholic in religion."[21] On all accounts, Hemingway was closer to Eliot than he sometimes seems. In a deep sense, he was, like Eliot, a classicist, and his politics were basically conservative.[22] Hemingway was more Catholic than Anglo-Catholic. He converted to Catholicism when he married his second wife, but the old faith had attracted him early on, however a poor practitioner he was. A. E. Hotchner reports Hemingway's saying to him in 1954, after Hemingway had paused for a lengthy prayer in a cathedral, "I wish I were a better Catholic."[23] The sentiment lingered from *The Sun Also Rises* where Jake regretted being "a rotten Catholic" but held it to be a "grand religion."[24] Hemingway's seizing of the iceberg metaphor to describe his theory of fiction has proven so apt that readers have paid insufficient attention to the sentence that precedes it in *Death in the Afternoon*: "Every novel [or short story] which is truly written contributes to the total of knowledge which is there at the disposal of the next writer who comes, but the next writer must pay, always, a certain nominal percentage in experience to be able to understand and assimilate what is available as his birthright and what he must, in turn, take his departure from" (*DA* 192). That sentence should make us think of Eliot's "Tradition and the Individual Talent" (first published in 1919).

Looking at that essay, we find many similarities to Hemingway's theory. Repeatedly, Hemingway paid his tribute to the great writers of the past. He recognized that the writer works from a tradition and contributes to it, rather than creating from himself alone. The artist, Eliot says, "must inevitably be judged by the standards of the past."[25] Hemingway's description of the matter may have been too pugilistic for many as he talked of getting in the boxing ring with various writers, but his essence is much the same as Eliot's. "No poet, no artist of any art, has his complete meaning alone," Eliot contends.[26] That view is writ large in Hemingway's Nobel Prize acceptance speech. And his admonishments to aspiring writers always emphasized the point.[27]

The sense of tradition, Eliot cautioned, "cannot be inherited, and if you want it you must obtain it by great labour."[28] Hemingway got his sense of the tradition through a less conventional and less systematic route than Eliot got his. He entered no college, but he was an eager reader from his earliest years, and he continued to devour books and magazines until near the very end of his life. "Some can absorb knowledge, the more tardy must work for it. Shakespeare acquired more essential history from Plutarch than most men could from the whole British Museum," in Eliot's view.[29] Although Hemingway declined to take the ring against Shakespeare, he was perhaps like him in being a great absorber. He was remarkably adept at storing up fragments from literature and his own intense life that would later become the stuff of his novels and stories.

While the artist works with this material, Eliot informed a public too inclined to praise novelty and "originality," something happens to the artist: "What happens is a continual surrender of himself as he is at the moment to something which is more valuable. The progress of an artist is a continual self-sacrifice, a continual extinction of personality."[30] He called this process "depersonalization," likening the artist to a catalyst in a chemical experiment. He describes the poet's mind as "a receptacle for seizing and storing up numberless feelings, phrases, images, which remain there until all the particles which can unite to form a new compound are present together."[31] The more we learn about Hemingway's life, particularly his inner life, the more apt Eliot's analogy seems for describing the process of creation. Hemingway's mind was a receptacle for storing feelings, phrases, images. And he believed that circumstances had to be right for the new combinations to occur. The chief fascination of Kenneth Lynn's *Hemingway* (1987), the most recent of the Hemingway biographies, is its suggestions of the realities behind the "new compounds." Case in point: "Indian Camp." Hemingway had not, as he said, seen his father perform a Caesarian section on an Indian woman. Readers have been wont to see Hemingway in Nick in the story (much of him is there, to be sure), but he is also present in the Indian husband who slits his throat because his wife's difficult delivery is so prolonged. The story's genesis was not something Hemingway had seen on the shores of Walloon Lake, but his own intense feeling when traveling on assignment for the *Toronto Star* when he received word that Hadley had gone into labor. The news had ignited first his anxieties about Hadley's safety, then later the powerful compound that he called "Indian Camp." Although Hemingway often spoke about the incidents behind some of his stories ("The Sea Change," for instance, grew out of an episode he had witnessed at the beach: a beautiful woman walked away hand in hand with another woman, leaving her husband to ponder her decision), he seldom spoke of the inner realities. He did not comment on his identification with the Indian husband—a husband intensely identifying with his wife in her hard delivery. He did not tell anyone why he found the story of the lesbian woman worth relating. He was, in fact, a good veiler of biographical truths. His life, after all, was his business—even if he often called flamboyant attention to certain aspects of it.

As a critic, he sometimes gave misleading readings, as Kenneth Lynn argues was the case with his comments on "Big Two-Hearted River."[32] Similarly, Hemingway described "The Doctor and the Doctor's Wife" as being about the time that he discovered that his father was a coward, a comment that offers at best a limited reading of the story. He also told his parents that the story had nothing to do with them, and Kenneth Lynn would have us believe that they so read it. (Did all of the Hemingways so read it? Did they ever talk about it? Did the parents ever reread the story?) Nick probably witnesses the scene of his father's humiliation in the confrontation with Dick Boulton, though the narrator never mentions Nick's presence and Nick speaks no words. The narrator pointedly identifies the doctor as "Nick's father" in the beach scene, but he does not use that epithet in the bedroom scene that follows, where Mrs. Adams also humiliates the doctor. Presumably, Nick—stunned that his father does not fight Boulton—retreats to the woods. He will be spared witnessing the doctor's second but more harmful humiliation. But he already knows the emotional truth of his parents' marriage. He reaches out towards his father in love and understanding, choosing him over his mother and giving his father at least for a time good reason not to use the gun he had first taken for consolation. Cowardice is not the major point, though Nick's initial shock over the beach episode is a part of the story.[33]

Poetry, Eliot concludes, "is not a turning loose of emotion, but an escape from emotion; it is not an expression of personality, but an escape from personality."[34] The description is remarkably apt for what Hemingway achieved in the writing of his best short stories and his best longer fiction. For Nick Adams, writing is therapy, and he rid himself of many painful memories by writing about them, he believed. Paradoxically, he is not expressing his personality, but escaping from it. Many of Eliot's readers have found him playful or condescending in the sentence that follows his famous statement about the role of the individual in the literary process: "But, of course, only those who have personality and emotions know what it means to want to escape from those things." Hemingway did know exactly what Eliot meant, and the sentence draws together the theories of the two, neither of whom wanted a biography, or editions of their letters. Both wanted readers to look at their works as expressions of "*significant* emotion, emotion which has its life in the poem and not in the history of the poet."[35] "You can't believe you did it," thinks David Bourne.

Hemingway achieved that ideal in "A Clean, Well-Lighted Place" if he achieved it anywhere. Speaking of this story in his 1959 essay "The Art of the Short Story," he observed: "There I really had luck. I left out everything. That is as far as you can go, so I stood on that one and haven't drawn to that since."[36] "A Clean, Well-Lighted Place" is certainly one of Hemingway's most famous and most evocative stories. It is a story of "significant" emotion, exemplifying what Hemingway believed about the form and the Bourne-Hemingway ideal of writing. Furthermore, it is an excellent example of the challenge of the Hemingway short story, demanding an intense concentration from the reader so that he or she will grasp all that is going on.

First published in the March 1933 *Scribner's Magazine*, it also became the second story of *Winner Take Nothing*, Hemingway's third book of short stories, published in October of that same year. It has since been reprinted in numerous textbooks and anthologies. Its view of the human condition seems particularly appropriate to this century. "A Clean, Well-Lighted Place" portrays man's sense of isolation in an alien universe. The story's most famous lines are the parodies of the Lord's Prayer and the Hail Mary: "Our *nada* who art in *nada, nada* be thy name. . . . Hail nothing, full of nothing, nothing is with thee."[37] *Nada* is Spanish for "nothing," and it signifies the sense of the vast void that modern man discerns—hence his desire for a clean, well-lighted place to help make the darkness bearable.[38]

If Hemingway's life was often noisy, this story is extraordinarily quiet, its action minimal. As is so often the case in a Hemingway story, there are only a few speakers. Four characters speak in the story, but no exchange involves more than two of them. The modulation of these voices is very slight, and the reader is challenged to very careful listening.

The setting of the story is spare; most of the action takes place in an almost empty Spanish café. The opening sentence presents a frozen moment of time: "It was late and every one had left the café except an old man who sat in the shadow the leaves of the tree made against the electric light" (288). We expand our vision to include two waiters who observe the old man sitting in the shadows. Along with the waiters, the reader will explore the meaning of the old man sitting in the shadows, darkness behind him. Although we learn some details about the old man's life, he is left unnamed. Indeed, no character in the story is ever named, heightening the reader's sense of metaphysical exploration, of viewing the old man as an allegorical figure—an old man against a dark sky. Although deaf, the old man "feels" the quiet of the night, and the quiet comforts him.

The simple vocabulary of the story and the simple structure of the sentences are in keeping with the parable-like effect of the story. The rhythms of the King James Bible were a powerful influence on Hemingway's style, and that rhythm is especially appropriate to this story about longing for spiritual meaning. For the older waiter (as well as, apparently, for the last customer of the night) it is important that there exist "a clean, well-lighted place." Somewhat paradoxically, a café is presented here as the place where we find refuge against darkness—refuge Western man once looked for in the church, as the Spanish setting reminds us. The café provides its own ritual, and we sense in the old man the hunger and thirst for transcendence. Finally, as we will see, the story itself emerges as a protest against the dark.

Not everyone feels the darkness or the need to protest it, and the contrast between those who feel and those who do not contributes a large part of the story's meaning. "He that hath ears to hear, let him hear": so Matthew 11:15 reports Jesus saying. That is the particular challenge that readers of "A Clean, Well-Lighted Place" have faced, and Hemingway has made his readers pay extraordinarily close attention to determine what is being said in this "simple" story. As the dialogue of the story begins, the narrator refuses to say who starts talking about the old man: " 'Last week he tried to commit suicide,' one waiter said" (288). The second exchange of dialogue has to do with a soldier and his girl who have walked by the café: "'The guard will pick him up,' one waiter said" (289). Later epithets will identify one speaker as "the younger waiter" and the others as "the older waiter." The reader must look back to decide—or try to decide—which waiter begins these exchanges. By involving the reader, the narrator works to pull him into alliance with the older waiter, who tells the young waiter that they "are of two different kinds" (290). Whereas the younger waiter is eager to close shop, the older waiter is reluctant to leave because "there may be some one who needs the café" (290). Priest-like, he would like to assist that person.

The longest segment of the story involves conversation between the two waiters about the old man's life and their view of its significance. Appropriate to the night setting and the lateness of the hour, the narrator chooses a very effaced stance, which helps to convey the weight of time. The narrator seldom identifies the speakers of specific lines, but does identify precisely the speaker of some key lines. He does not want even the most inexperienced reader to fail to see that the older waiter is sympathetic to the old man and that the narrator shares his view; the younger waiter is rushed, concerned with his own life and comfort, unheedful of the metaphysical anguish of others, at least for the time being because he does not feel any anguish himself. In fact, the narrator's impatience with such insensitivity breaks out in the moment when the younger waiter refuses the old man's request for another drink: " 'Finished,' he said, speaking with that omission of syntax stupid people employ when talking to drunken people or foreigners" (290). The younger waiter is "stupid"—missing a great deal; the reader, emotionally sharing in the indictment, is challenged to define that stupidity.

If one voice is stupid and the other is not, it is curious that readers have had difficulty determining which is which in the discourse. Indeed, critics and readers of the story have not agreed in their assignment of the lines of the dialogue. Some have ascribed lines to one waiter, some to the other, and some have argued that even Hemingway got confused. Wishing to bring order out of the "confused" text, John Hagopian argued for moving a line of text.[39] Surprisingly, his view prevailed. As a result, Scribner's began publishing the story with the Hagopian solution, and the Finca Vigía version printed this emended text. The manuscript of the story at the John F. Kennedy Library reveals, however, that the originally published version is the correct one. The master's story is finer than the one we read in the Finca Vigía version. With the Hagopian text, Hemingway's "luck" with the story was compromised.

In the Hagopian reading, it is the older waiter who has the information about the old man's suicide attempt. But it was impossible to maintain that reading at one point; so Hagopian argued for tidying up the text. Throughout Hemingway's lifetime, readers found these lines:

> "His niece looks after him."
> "I know. You said she cut him down."[40]

The Finca Vigía version, and others in the Hagopian tradition, read:

> "His niece looks after him. You said she cut him down."
> "I know." (289)

If we accept Hagopian's shift, we can now read the text with the older waiter as the consistent provider of information about the suicide attempt, though it leaves us with an embarrassing, not very functional "I know." Hemingway's ear was much finer than that.

Although Hemingway wanted the reader to have to work to determine the speaker of the lines, he provided a consistent and discernible pattern. It is the young waiter who breaks the quiet of watching, a quiet not distressing to the older waiter. The younger waiter, bored with his job and eager for his bed, initiates every segment of the dialogue. That is in keeping with the passivity of the watchful older water (who will become increasingly active as the night advances) and the impatience of the younger waiter. Much of the force of the dialogue comes from the fact that the younger waiter rather glibly provides a topic very much in the mind of the older waiter: "Last week he [the old man] tried to commit suicide" (288). For those who find the basis of the universe to be *nada* the concept of suicide may be attractive; it is certainly understandable. Hence, we may imagine the older waiter's keen interest in the topic. Looking at the old man, the older waiter sees himself. The opening line of the story's dialogue touches a subject the older waiter himself would be reluctant to introduce.

A complex man, the older waiter is not consumed with his own temptation to "despair." He is interested in the younger waiter, too, and reacts to the tone of his voice. Knowing that his colleague doubtless has a lot coming to him, he asks him many questions. The dynamics of the story bear some resemblance to the situation of Robert Frost's "Mending Wall." The older waiter is trying to put a notion in the mind of the younger waiter, just as Frost's narrator is trying to put one in the mind of his traditional neighbor. Perhaps the young waiter, too, may come to sense the reality of the words he matter-of-factly utters: "He was in despair." The older waiter, we increasingly sense, knows a good deal about despair, and he likely wonders if he might last as well as the old man—who appears admirably stoical in his endurance, the suicide attempt notwithstanding. "Look at him" (289), the older waiter admonishes. The younger waiter is not interested in looking, though looking truly at life is the challenge of the story. The older waiter's command takes the reader back to the "picture" of the opening paragraph.[41]

One of the reasons that readers have had difficulty discerning what waiter speaks which lines is that Hemingway twice has a speaker follow himself without a traditional identifying tag. The reader is required to hear the pattern:

> "He's drunk now," he said.
> "He's drunk every night."
> "What did he want to kill himself for?"
> "How should I know."
> "How did he do it?"
> "He hung himself with a rope."
> "Who cut him down?"
> "His niece."
> "Why did they do it?"
> "Fear for his soul."
> "How much money has he got?"
> "He's got plenty."
> "He must be eighty years old."
> "Anyway I should say he was eighty." (289)

The antecedent to the first *he* is the younger waiter. Getting no response to this first "he's drunk now," he repeats the information, with some disgust. The same speaker speaks twice. It is the older waiter who returns to the question of the reason for the suicide; he is not ready to drop the subject.[42] Hemingway could have editorialized the pause, but he would have lost a haunting subtlety. Like a poet, he is making white space work for him. The older waiter continues to probe, continues to try to put a notion in his colleague's mind—and his question about money is designed to cause some deeper reflection, but the younger waiter misses the point. The older waiter looks with some amazement at the enduring old man, marvels that he is eighty. The younger waiter is unimpressed, so the older waiter provides his own response: "Anyway I should say he was eighty." He wonders if he will survive his own despair that long.

The older waiter's story is, of course, a major part of what Hemingway has left out of the story. Probably he, too, once found solace in the arms of a woman, as the young waiter looks forward to doing—though the two waiters identify somewhat differently with the soldier and the girl who rush down the street.[43] The older waiter, like the old man, for reasons that have nothing to do with age, is also a man without a woman. Hinting about the risks of loving, he reminds the younger waiter that the old man once had a wife. But the younger waiter, his view too narrowly sexual, says that "a wife would be no good to [the old man] now." Ever the challenger, the older waiter invites broader vision: "You can't tell. He might be better with a wife." Then comes the line that has led critics astray, but it makes perfectly good sense as the manuscript and first editions have it. When the younger waiter says that his niece looks after him, he implies that she does everything for him a wife could now do. But he misses the point, as the older waiter's response makes clear: "I know. You said she cut him down." I have been listening carefully, he implies, though the younger waiter has not. As the author wrote them, the lines together suggest the older waiter's impatience with his colleague—certainly Hemingway's better ear. The younger waiter immediately conveys just how much he has missed: "I wouldn't want to be that old. An old man is a nasty thing" (289). But not this old man, clearly, and with the older waiter we admire his stoic quality, as we also admire the understanding and compassion of the older waiter.

Hemingway's reader may be reminded of an earlier café scene, that of Hemingway's "Today Is Friday." That story, first published in 1926, was written as a play, the narrator hidden except for minimum stage directions. Its action, like that of "A Clean, Well-Lighted Place," is conversation in a café. One soldier is profoundly impressed with the stoic fortitude of Jesus dying on the cross, but his companion finds the

Nazarene only a faker. Nobody changes anyone's mind, but the reader must decide where to place his sympathies. "A Clean, Well-Lighted Place" is similar in situation, but a deeper work, in part because its religious questions are more subtly, more surprisingly stated, but also because of the intense listening experience it offers.

"A Clean, Well-Lighted Place" does not end with the single café scene, as the play does. The reader needs to sense more of just how long the night is to the older waiter. We need to get inside his mind so that we share his inverted prayers, and recognize the hungers that are behind them. He makes his way to a *bodega*, becoming himself the old man as it were. Not literally an old man, he nevertheless talks like one, in the view of the younger waiter. In the "replay" of the first café scene, a bartender misses the meaning behind his late-night customer's wry humor, thinks him "*otro loco mas*"—a little crazy, if not exactly a disgusting thing. The older waiter's teasing language is a light continuation of his efforts to make an unreflecting listener see more deeply. Understandably, his words are cryptic, bizarre to the bartender who waits on him. The bartender nevertheless offers him a second *copita*. Having been in a sense insulted, as the younger waiter had insulted the old man, the older waiter echoes the dignity of the old man: "No, thank you" (291). Instead, he returns to his room, to wait for the light of morning—feeling the *nada* of the world. The old man, we assume, did not end this night very differently.

If the old man has lost all meaning in his life save for the ritual of his drinking, the older waiter has one meaning left. He lacks everything but work, he tells the younger waiter. To him there remains, then, his métier. As the story makes clear, it is a subtle, sometimes teasing métier. The waiter is like the artist of "A Clean, Well-Lighted Place." For the artist, the work of art protests the void. Yet even as Conrad's credo declares that the artist's vision may also provide an unexpected glimpse of truth, so our waiter offers his own solace: "I am of those who like to stay late at the café. . . . With all of those who need a light for the night" (290). The religious cadence is pronounced. A blend of memorable pictorial detail and haunting dialogue, Hemingway's story is a powerful challenge to understanding and compassion. As he himself observed, in that story he went about as far as anyone could go. We can hope that the next edition of his stories will restore this definitive story to the form that its author so carefully crafted.

# Transcending Autobiography

When Ernest and Hadley Hemingway departed from his parents' home in Oak Park in the autumn of 1923, Ernest gave his newly married sister Marcelline a copy of his first book (privately published), *Three Stories and Ten Poems*, cautioning her not to let their parents see it. Marcelline was not prepared for what she read as her train carried her and Sterling Sanford toward Detroit. She was shocked by the sexual theme of "Up in Michigan" and was especially appalled that her brother had used the names of real people in the story.[44] Like Thomas Wolfe, Hemingway would have to be on guard against lawsuits from persons who objected to their portrayal in his fiction, and his first commercially published book, *In Our Time* (1925), carried the kind of disclaimer that fiction with autobiographical elements usually carries: "In view of a recent tendency to identify characters in fiction with real people, it seems proper to state that there are no real people in this volume: both the characters and their names are fictitious. If the name of any living person has been used, the use was purely coincidental."

Many of the *In Our Time* stories are about Nick Adams, and those that are not make suggestions about his life and help the reader to understand Nick better. Although the book is made up of stories that can be read and understood as discrete works, Hemingway always insisted that the book had "pretty good unity." Nick's character provides much of that unity, just as the character of George Willard helps provide a unity for Sherwood Anderson's *Winesburg, Ohio* (1919).

Jeffrey Meyers, one of Hemingway's recent biographers, suggests that Nick's first name originated with *St. Nicholas*, the monthly magazine for children.[45] The magazine was, indeed, important reading for the young Ernest, and in Hemingway's late, unfinished novel called "The Last Good Country" in *The Nick Adams Stories* (1972) we find Nick reading it. But Hemingway doubtless liked the name Nick for other reasons as well; its tough forcefulness struck just the right chord, and it had allusive possibilities, biographical as well as literary. One of young Hemingway's admired friends in Italy was an officer named

Nick Neroni.[46] When Hemingway returned to the States, he had decided that Italians lived life much more fully than did the Midwestern people he knew, and Italy is for young Nick Adams in Michigan a goal, a symbol for freedom. The name also harkened back to the Indian world, attractive to Hemingway from his boyhood summers on Walloon Lake in Michigan; Nick Boulton, one of the Indians Hemingway knew well, was father to his boyhood friends Rich and Prudence.[47] On the literary side, Hemingway, always an avid reader, had doubtless come across references to the Nick who was not a saint but the devil, and R. M. Bird's *Nick of the Woods* (1837) is the kind of book that would have appealed to the boy who favored books about the active life. Just as *Nick* is appropriate to many sides of Hemingway, *Adams* suggests Adamic and American patterns. *The Education of Henry Adams* was a best-seller in 1919, even as Hemingway was setting about the work that would in time make the Hemingway family the most fascinating literary family of modern America.[48] First and last name, Nick Adams is one of the most aptly named characters of our fiction, only part of him autobiographical—suiting Hemingway's metaphor of the iceberg, only one-eighth of it showing.

Hemingway's fiction begins with the actual, but his goal was not merely to reproduce actuality. Wallace Stegner, novelist and short story writer, pays tribute to Hemingway's skill as a transformer of the actual in the prefatory biographical disclaimer to his novel *Second Growth* (1947): "The making of fiction entails the creation of places and persons with all the seeming of reality, and these places and persons, no matter how a writer tries to invent them, must be made up piecemeal from sublimations of his own experience and his own acquaintance. There is no other material out of which fiction can be made." Stegner explains that he tried to make the New England village of his story so that it could exist anywhere in rural New England, though he placed it in northern New Hampshire: "It should be, if I have been successful, as visible in Carmel-by-the-Sea or Taos or Charlevoix as on the fictitious Ammosaukee River. These people and their village took form in my mind not as portraits but as symbols. There are no portraits, personal or geographical, in the novel." Hemingway would approve Stegner's dictum about the making of fiction, though he would have squirmed at Stegner's statement about characters beginning as symbols. Both of them would agree with Ezra Pound: "The proper and perfect symbol is the natural object."

"The End of Something" is one of the Nick stories in which we see Hemingway using the natural object that becomes symbol. Like most of the stories in *In Our Time*, it is extremely brief, any sense of length partly a function of the paragraph-length interchapters that sandwich it. Called chapters, the sixteen italicized interchapters present episodes of war and violent confrontation with death, giving an edge to the more innocent, more ordinary circumstances of the body of stories that separate them. Certainly "The End of Something" deals with a very ordinary event, the breakup of a young couple's romance. Read in *In Our Time*, the story also borrows some of its meaning from the Nick stories that have preceded it, just as it amplifies the stories that follow.

The story is set in Hortons Bay, an indication that Nick has ventured increasingly far from his parents' world. In "Indian Camp" his father is a tutor-companion, well-meaning, but miscalculating greatly when he allows Nick to be present for a complicated birth in the Indian village. In "The Doctor and the Doctor's Wife" the reader discovers that Nick's parents are not soul mates, and the doctor hangs on desperately to his remaining self-esteem. Nick holds out a redeeming hand to his father, preferring to go into the woods with him rather than into the cottage where his mother waits. "The End of Something" also plays on the end of Nick's companionship with his father, a fact verified in "The Three-Day Blow," the story that follows it. Nick's peers are now more important to him than his parents and family. He has begun to make his way in new settings, increasingly farther from home.

Almost immediately, then, the setting of "The End of Something" takes on symbolic force, as the narrator begins with the lengthy description of the lumber town Hortons Bay and its demise; and as Hemingway wrote it, he may have recalled Gertrude Stein's caution about "mere description." The description carries such force because it focuses on an action: "The schooner moved out of the bay toward the open lake carrying the two great saws, the travelling carriage that hurled the logs against the revolving circular saws, and all the rollers, wheels, belts and iron piled on a hull-deep load of lumber. Its open hold covered with canvas and lashed tight, the sails of the schooner filled and it moved out into the open lake, carrying with it everything that made the mill a mill and Hortons Bay a town." The narrator had begun unhurriedly, much like a traditional narrator: "In the old days Hortons Bay was a lumbering town." But what strikes him and the reader is the seeming suddenness and completeness of that historical ending: "Then one year there were no more logs to make lumber." Ten years later the mill shows only "the broken white limestone of its foundations" (79). The setting made concrete, the rest of the story will actualize it into symbol.

As the action begins, a young Nick Adams is rowing with a girl named Marjorie, and they are looking at the limestone foundations, which Marjorie names "our old ruin." Hemingway carefully leads the reader into the drama of the conversation, which at first seems only the discourse of an early evening fishing date for a couple happy to be together. But it soon becomes evident that Marjorie must carry the burden of the conversation. Nick responds to her, and he seems comfortable only in answering questions about fishing. With the reader, Marjorie realizes that something has changed (Nick's statements become increasingly characterized by the negative; for example, "They aren't striking"). For Marjorie, what Nick is not saying is more important than what he is saying. Nick leaves to her the task of bringing to the front the real issue, that Nick wishes to break off their affair. The reader's sympathies are clearly with Marjorie, who must ask Nick the questions that lead to his admission that for him their relationship is not fun anymore. The reader's sympathies remain with Marjorie, for having been given directly the painful word *No* (81), she behaves with great dignity as she makes her departure, to grieve by herself at the ending of what had been, like the mill of Hortons Bay, a powerful reality.

But our sympathies are also with Nick. The conversation with Marjorie has not been easy, and he has only partly wished to end their affair—and not totally for the right reasons. Although he has not wished to hurt Marjorie (after all, she has done nothing that should result in rejection), he simply is not ready for the kind of commitment she has wished for and has herself made. Nick had anguished about this breaking up before it took place, and he must suffer by himself after it does take place. A part of him does not wish to lose Marjorie. He will be some while working out that pain. Malcolm Cowley is quite right in noting that the end of a Hemingway story typically comes on the next page after the end.[49]

That this is true in "The End of Something" becomes apparent when the third character of the story, Nick's friend Bill, appears to ask if Marjorie went away. The reader then realizes that the events of the fishing trip had not been spontaneous. We find that Nick had talked to Bill about breaking up with Marjorie, and that he has planned to make the break on this particular night—a task made all the more difficult because Marjorie displays all of the qualities that make her such a good companion for Nick. But Nick is still very young, and he fears the loss of freedom that commitment to a woman means. Male bonding is a normal enough part of a boy's growing up, and the reader is reminded of that powerful force as Bill comes out of the woods to see how Nick is. ("The Three-Day Blow" both confirms and mocks the power of male bonding, and it makes clear that Nick's feelings for Marjorie cannot be blown away in a mere three days.)

The power of love and the problems of love are among the major themes of Hemingway. A writer often faulted for his chauvinism, he was able to treat the complexity of human love with marked sensitivity. What makes "The End of Something" work so well is its ability to suggest, its archetypal force. To be sure, the story adds to our emerging sense of the character of Nick Adams, but by itself it creates a story that evokes the memory of the intensity of young love, any young love.

The ending of affairs is a recurrent theme of *In Our Time*, as in "A Very Short Story," a story that reflects Hemingway's first major love affair, with nurse Agnes von Kurowsky, begun as he recovered in Italy from his serious wounding in World War I. In the story, nurse Luz abandons the wounded soldier she had met in the hospital for another man, and she writes him that theirs "was only a boy and girl love" (85). His response makes clear that for him the affair was much more, though "A Very Short Story" does not by itself evoke in the reader the intensity of feeling that "The End of Something" does. Probably, Hemingway created that story with one particular audience, Agnes, in mind. But in "The End of Something"—going back to a simpler place, dealing with adolescent characters—Hemingway found in the ruined mill the right symbol for the ruined relationship. The quiet conversations of the story convey the depths of emotion. The story could speak to readers of many ages who had similarly faced the end of so powerful a something. We think of very young love as a subject of F. Scott Fitzgerald, but no Basil or Josephine story catches so memorably the emotions of what is a common experience as does "The End of Something."

If the phrase "only a boy and girl love" in "A Very Short Story" makes the reader think back to "The End of Something," another story near the end of *In Our Time* may also. "Out of Season," an account of an abortive fishing adventure, was actually written before "The End of Something." Originally published in *Three Stories and Ten Poems*

(1923), it can tell us something about how quickly Hemingway learned the lessons of his craft. He was, in fact, already trying to apply his theory of leaving out and making the reader feel what was left out. Jeffrey Meyers shocks us by saying that the story, like "Cat in the Rain" and "Cross-Country Snow," is "about the disintegration of [Hemingway's] marriage to Hadley."[50] The story, like the others, may reflect certain strains in the marriage, but surely it is "about" other things.

The story is, his first biographer reported, "almost straight autobiography,"[51] but even biographically considered it shows other things than the disintegration of a marriage. As Hemingway's first full-length story after the theft of his manuscripts from Hadley's train compartment, it shows Hemingway as he gets hold of himself as a writer, and even laughs at himself. The narrator calls the unnamed protagonist only "the young gentleman," who borders on the comic as he attempts to deal with a wife who is out of sorts with her man and with a fishing guide who is determined to take the couple fishing, though he will violate the local fishing laws. The husband is as ineffective in dealing with the drunken guide as he is with his unhappy wife, who wishes no part in any out-of-season fishing. The beauty of the story results from what Carlos Baker calls "the metaphorical confluence of emotional atmosphere" as the "out-of-season" metaphor applies both to the fishing expedition and to the marital discord.

What is the nature of the marital discord? The issues may be serious indeed, as the placement of "Out of Season" in *In Our Time* invites readers to speculate. The two stories that precede it and the story that follows it have to do with the desire or the lack of desire for children in a marriage. If marriage by itself is an infringement on personal freedom, having children further restricts the options of the individual. In Hemingway's stories, the males tend to be more aware of those restrictions than do the females—though in *A Farewell to Arms* Catherine Barkley feels even more keenly than Frederic that her baby is an intruder. The wife in "Out of Season" has different emotions. Is the husband inviting her to have an abortion, to break the law in, so to speak, an out-of-season fishing abhorrent to the values of Italian society? She feels cold on a day of rain and threatening rain, and she has difficulty understanding the guide; she tries to pretend that the earlier quarrel with her husband makes no difference. But she is grateful when her husband reaches out to her in a moment of decision that is much more profound than any hasty reading would suggest: "Go on back,

Tiny. You're cold in this wind anyway. It's a rotten day and we aren't going to have any fun, anyway" (138). The permission might end matters, given this reading. But the husband must make his peace also with the decision, and he does so after the incompetent guide can produce no lead for the reels. The fishing cannot go forward this day, and the young gentleman, feeling relieved, quietly tells the guide that he very likely will not go fishing tomorrow. The events of the afternoon lead the reader to believe him, and Hemingway leaves the reader to imagine the reunion of the young gentleman and his wife. Very probably, they had more fun this afternoon than they had thought possible. Very likely, Tiny was suitably warmed.

It must be admitted, however, that in this "autobiographical" story, the hints of impending abortion are few, so few that they were largely missed by early commentators, including Carlos Baker. In an excellent essay, Kenneth Johnston makes the abortion issue the submerged part of the iceberg.[52] The best argument for this reading is the structure of *In Our Time.* Did Hemingway expect his readers to see to the lower depth of this story? We might understand his reluctance to provide more hints on an explosive issue in this early story. Probably the metaphor is not completely effective. Does Peduzzi then represent some incompetent back-alley abortionist? Why does he have no lead? What does the missing lead symbolize? At a minimum, however, Carlos Baker was surely on solid ground when he praised the "metaphorical confluence of emotional atmosphere."

But for most readers, the story does not have the force of Hemingway's greatest stories. Perhaps his symbolism here was too private. Certainly, its suggestiveness does not carry the reader as far beyond the story as does that of "The End of Something." Part of the problem, as we have seen, is Peduzzi, whom the narrator does not understand much better than do the husband and wife. The narrator of "The End of Something," on the other hand, understands Bill and what he is doing. Hemingway later explained that the surprise of "Out of Season" is that Peduzzi committed suicide as a result of his frustrations over the failed expedition. There is no way that the reader could comprehend that Peduzzi was finding unbearable pain in this day's events. If that were clear, we might feel much more deeply about the marital discord than we do. In fact, we do not feel the pain of the young gentleman and his wife as we do the pain of the boy and girl lovers of "The End of Something."

The staging of these two stories controls the degree of emotion. In

"Out of Season" an unsettled private dialogue seeps through the cracks of the public fishing expedition. The strained tone comes from the fact that the couple cannot talk openly about their problem in front of Peduzzi. In his best stories, Hemingway usually focuses on intensely private moments, as in "The End of Something." There are three characters who speak in each of these two fishing stories, but in the more memorable one only two people are present at once. Nevertheless, the restraint of emotion is appropriate to "Out of Season." Although only three characters speak in the story, Hemingway symbolizes the stake of the community in the underlying issue, for the reader visualizes the citizenry: "Groups of three and four people standing in front of the shops stared at the three. The workmen in their stone-powdered jackets working on the new hotel looked up as they passed. Nobody spoke or gave any sign to them except the town beggar, lean and old, with a spittle-thickened beard, who lifted his hat as they passed" (135–36).

In spite of Hemingway's reputation as exemplar of the active life and as portrayer of the violent, a large number of his short stories treat domestic or familial situations. Like Thomas Wolfe, Hemingway came from a complex and fairly large family, given to its own noises and confusions. Whereas Wolfe often renders crowded family scenes, Hemingway does not. Nick has sisters, but only in the posthumous "The Last Good Country" does Hemingway dramatize a scene showing Nick with one; Harold Krebs of "Soldier's Home" has sisters, but Hemingway lets us see only one of them, Harold's favorite sister. Hemingway usually took the private scene of one-on-one as the most revealing of character, perhaps sensing that in those moments human beings do less dramatizing of themselves.

Although we do not get that private, intimate confrontation in "Out of Season," we do get it in "Hills Like White Elephants," a story found in Hemingway's second collection of short stories, *Men Without Women* (1927). In its structure and its use of symbol, the story may remind readers of "The End of Something." In fact, one might ask if the unnamed protagonist is Nick Adams. If so, this story would give us the most unflattering picture of Nick to be found in any of the Nick stories, which characteristically show a perplexed but essentially idealistic character. Hemingway seemed to find returning to that notion of Nick, as he regularly did, fortifying to his own present. But although the narrator is an American, and although several Nick stories portray him having problems with love and commitment, there is no compelling reason to see this narrator as Nick. In fact, the American man seems in marked contrast to the young, perplexed, questioning Nick of "In Another Country," the story that precedes "Hills" in the collection, and the Nick of "The Killers," the story that follows it. Rather than the boy, we get a view of a man, a man rather different from what we hope Nick will become, and rather different from the mature Nick we find in "Fathers and Sons," the story that Hemingway placed last in *Winner Take Nothing* (1933), his third major collection.

Like "The End of Something," "Hills Like White Elephants" dramatizes only a brief dialogue, though neither story seems rushed. Ostensibly nothing happens: the reader simply overhears the conversation of a man and the girl with him, as they sit and drink while waiting to make a train connection in a small Spanish town. Except for the woman who serves the American man and the girl, the reader sees only these two characters. (The story is much like a play, a form Hemingway used for "Today Is Friday" and came close to in "The Killers"—both written on the same day and within months of "Hills.")[53] Both stories begin with a description of setting, a setting that becomes symbol. Just as Marjorie points to the foundation of the mill as "our old ruin," the girl in "Hills" identifies a spot in the landscape and invites an imaginative response from her companion. She is like Marjorie, carrying the initial burden of conversation. Imaginatively, creatively, she observes that the hills in the distance look like white elephants. The man is waiting for the moment to bring the conversation to his topic, the abortion that he would like the girl to have. The reader senses increasingly the symbolic appropriateness of the girl's simile as the characters drink and talk. The narrator makes the moral quality of the story the more intense by never using the word *abortion*, and the characters themselves do not use it either—she because the concept is morally degrading to her, because she would like a home, a family, the sanctioned products of love once dominant in the Western world and exemplified by Spain, and he because abortion is something else if it is not named, something "perfectly simple," he insists.

Although Hemingway shocked his family with his fiction, and many reviewers faulted his subject matter in *Men Without Women*, what he gives in "Hills Like White Elephants" is, in its moral stance, a decidedly traditional story. Hemingway could have been as insistent about the morality of it as he was about the morality of *The Sun Also Rises*, which he counted the most moral book he had written. In 1955 he told Fraser Drew it was almost a "tract against promiscuity."[54] Like that novel, "Hills Like White Elephants" deplores the death of love in the modern world. It is a prose rendering of the kind of episode T. S. Eliot portrays in "The Fire Sermon" in *The Waste Land*. "The Fire Sermon" rather than "A Game of Chess" is the appropriate reference because the characters in the story are unmarried, the identifying tags for the couple being "the American" (or "the man") and "the girl." By calling her *girl* rather than *woman*, the narrator makes her seem all the more vulnerable, all the more victimized by the man who has little regard for her feelings, who believes that reason can satisfy her emotional and spiritual longings. The couple is rootless, wandering, far from home. If she is longing to establish one, he is not.

The Spanish setting underscores the spiritual malaise, for the couple is in the most Catholic of European cultures, a place where abortion is especially abhorrent. Although in transit, the travelers are not pilgrims. They seek new sensations, though even the man realizes that at bottom their uncommitted lives are empty. Trying a new drink, an Anis del Toro, the girl observes that it tastes like licorice. "That's the way with everything," he dispiritedly replies. His companion can only agree: "Everything tastes of licorice. Especially all the things you've waited so long for, like absinthe" (212). The symbol is again the natural object, thoroughly in keeping with these characters, expressing the emptiness of their lives. And the man, despite his easy words, has insights into the futility of their lives. The girl, having decided to accede to his wishes, walks to the end of the station and looks at the Spanish country: "Across, on the other side, were fields of grain and trees along the banks of the Ebro. Far away, beyond the river, were mountains. The shadow of a cloud moved across the field of grain and she saw the river through the trees" (213). But fertility and harvest will not be hers. She and her companion are east of this Eden, but not in any mutual support. Their love has become a white elephant, worthless. There will not soon be occasion for easy banter, for looking at hills, in any vital sense, together.

Although Hemingway frequently treats the theme of endings in the love relationships between his men and women, none of his short stories presents their discovering each other, and "Wedding Day," which describes the wedding day of Nick and Helen, is merely a fragment.[55] When we consider these stories of failed relationships, we are struck by the variety of emotional effects that characterizes those crises and by the variety of fictional techniques Hemingway employs while he relies on the unstated and the understated.

"A Canary for One" is like "Out of Season" in having a resonant metaphorical base, appropriate both to the end of an intense love affair of an American girl during a visit with her mother in Vevey, Switzerland, and to the ending of the marriage of an American couple (who had honeymooned in Vevey in a happier time). The couple now shares a train compartment with the girl's mother, who is taking a canary to her daughter. The daughter still mourns two years after the end of her romance, a romance ended because the mother believed that only American men make good husbands. Although we never see the daughter, some unfortunate Daisy Miller who will not be assimilated into European culture, we feel for her as victim, and we feel the conscious Jamesian overtones to Hemingway's story.

But the story reminds us of other Hemingway stories as well, and Hemingway demands that his readers be aware of contexts, of the effect of story upon story. He had practiced that lesson hard for *In Our Times*, and it became a hallmark of his fiction. He expected his readers to know his earlier work. As is the case with the fiction of James Joyce, readers who recall earlier work will be repaid in their comprehension of later work. Hemingway liked to echo situations and even the language of those situations, a practice he carried into his writing of novels.

Although critics have made less of the unity of *Men Without Women* (in which "A Canary for One" appears) than about the unity of *In Our Time,* the repetition of the theme of marital ending or crisis in love helps give that book unity. Hemingway did not arrange *Men Without Women* chronologically, or by date of composition, or by theme. Disjunctiveness is crucial to his method. For example, the second and last stories of the collection are war stories, dealing with Nick Adams after his wounding. Of the middle stories, "A Simple Enquiry" is set in wartime, but is not about war; it is followed by "Ten Indians," a story set in northern Michigan that recounts Nick's reaction to "betrayal" by an Indian girl as he moves further from the world of his parents. The last story of the collection, "Now I Lay Me," is a first-person story in which Nick Adams worries about many things during his difficult recovery from his war wounds. As he writes, Nick has never married, and he is skeptical of the wisdom his hospital companion has given him: the companion "was going back to America and he was very certain about marriage and knew it would fix up everything" (282). That last sentence of the story is also the last sentence of *Men Without Women*. It touches on the other Nick stories—and on "A Canary for One" as well.

Whereas "The End of Something" portrays a very difficult conversation between a young couple reluctant to make their separation and "Hills Like White Elephants" presents a modern, unmarried couple (words flow much more easily in this exchange) discussing their relationship in view of the abortion, "A Canary for One" presents the married couple after they have had their difficult conversation, after they have agreed on "separate residences," as the narrator admits at the very end of the story.

The talk in this story skirts the basic situation, the impending separation. And the conversation is not between the man and the wife. Rather, we listen to the American lady who shares the compartment with them, and she is a talker! Unnamed, as the couple is unnamed, she seems at first a version of the lady from Dubuque, narrow in her views and insistent on imposing them on others—certainly on her daughter. The portrait is heavily satirical of a type—the destructive American Mom. For a time it seems that the main point of the story is that satire.

But the story has several surprises, one being that this satire is not its main thrust. Another major surprise is that what has seemed a third-person story is not. When, a full third into the story, the narrator takes up his first-person stance, we sense that the story is going in a new direction, that there are yet other ways of considering the American lady. In its opening description of scenes outside the moving train and in the description of the lady as she makes her first pronouncements, the story has seemed third-person. "All night long the train went very fast and the American lady lay awake and waited for a wreck" (259). Since she is alone, we seem to be relying on an omniscient third-person narrator. But the story is well along before an "I" identifies himself: "For several minutes I had not listened to the American lady, who was talking to my wife" (259). Coming at the end of a paragraph, the sentence is especially forceful in calling attention to the realities that have to that time been avoided. The narrator has been hidden from the reader, but so has his wife.

Descriptions of numerous catastrophes that the narrator has seen outside the train take on new force, as does the urgency of the moving train. If the man has been looking outside the window and not talking to the American lady, he has also not been talking to or looking at his wife—the reality is that he is like Nick in "The End of Something," not wanting to talk, needing to talk, but omitting things that he is feeling and would not trust himself to say. It is easier to observe the passing scenery and to take the measure of the American lady, who is the most oppressive image of destruction in the story.

What the narrator comprehends—and the American lady does not—is that the essence of love is risk and that its demands can be difficult and unexpected. The American lady wants life to be risk-free. She does not welcome change, but love must adjust to it. Perhaps the hardest truth is that love involves listening, and the narrator reports that the American lady is "really quite deaf." Despite all the talking between the man and the girl in "Hills Like White Elephants," the man is not really attentive to the girl's meanings; they are left for the reader to discover. But the man in this story is a skilled listener and—as his careful reporting of scene that becomes symbol also suggests—he approaches material in the way a writer of fiction observes it. We sense that he catches the deeper meaning of his wife's question after the lady reports that she took her daughter away from Vevey after she fell madly in love:

> "Did she get over it?" asked my wife.
> "I don't think so," said the American lady. "She wouldn't eat anything and she wouldn't sleep at all. I've tried very hard, but she doesn't seem to take an interest in anything." (260)

Love dies slowly. The romance had taken place two years ago.

The unnamed husband of this story is, then, a much more attractive figure than the unnamed man of "Hills Like White Elephants." He seems caught up in forces he cannot control. He does not like the destination he has arrived at, though the turning point seems definitive. If *abortion* is the harsh word not mentioned in "Hills Like White Elephants," here *divorce* is the harsh word, part of the iceberg implied: "We followed the porter with the truck down the long cement platform beside the train. At the end was a gate and a man took the tickets" (261). No, the American lady is not the point, though we may wonder if there was some other outside agent of destruction involved in the end of this marriage, as there was an outside agent in "A Very Short Story."

We may wonder also why this couple remains unnamed. Hemingway was wonderfully skilled at naming his characters, but he often made the not naming of them an important device of his stories. In "Hills Like White Elephants" the couple seems all the more transitory, representative of the wasteland they define because they remain unnamed, uncommitted to place or to marriage (though she hungers for that commitment). Her nickname *Jig*, unlike "the girl," moves us toward the personal, heightens our sympathy for her. The characters of "A Canary for One" seem less culturally representative. The first-person narrator moves the story from that representativeness. The not naming here stresses the numbness of the narrator and his wife. The exchange of names between beloveds is an important part of their privateness. (In *A Farewell to Arms* Catherine repeatedly calls Frederic "Darling"; the world's name for him is not one we hear her use. He often addresses her as "Cat.") But there is no communication between husband and wife in this story, and if they did speak, the language of intimacy would no longer be quite appropriate.

Could it be that Hemingway wishes us to identify this unnamed man as Nick? The story, after all, follows "Ten Indians," which concludes with the boy's awakening to a new day after his disappointment in the news that Prudie has been unfaithful to him: "he was awake a long time before he remembered that his heart was broken" (257). There are no specific details about other events in Nick's life that would allow for a certain identification, though, as we have seen, the narrator of the story does present his material with the instincts of a writer. He looks for his symbols in the natural objects. He shows the kind of sensitivity in that observation that we associate with the mature Nick, and he is obviously in great pain as the story ends, trying to keep a stiff upper lip (and his art helping him to do so) as he faces a future without the wife.[56]

The preface to *A Moveable Feast* ends with a statement that the reader is free to consider the book fiction: "But there is always the chance that such a book of fiction may throw some light on what has been written as fact."[57] Although there is some doubt that Hemingway wrote those words, the reader of this memoir will be reminded of the many links between fact and fiction in Hemingway's work, and the ending of *A Moveable Feast* will take him back to "A Canary for One," for both end with memorable scenes in a Paris train station. Here is the scene from *Feast* describing Hemingway's remembered feelings as he recalls Hadley's meeting him at the station, where he arrives much later than he had promised because he had been with his new love:

> When I saw my wife again standing by the tracks as the train came in by the piled logs at the station, I wished I had died before I loved anyone but her. She was smiling, the sun of her lovely face tanned

by the snow and sun, beautifully built, her hair red gold in the sun, grown out all winter awkwardly and beautifully, and Mr. Bumby standing with her, blond and chunky and with winter cheeks looking like a good Vorarlberg boy. (*MF* 210)

Some biographers prefer to dismiss the memory, judging that Hemingway idealized Hadley in his late book. Are we embarrassed at having him deal with the softer emotions? Why must we deny these emotions to Hemingway? In truth, the stories abound with them. The fact of the passage above can emphasize the biographical truth in the fiction.

Gertrude Stein would not be surprised by the paragraph. She found a large streak of what she called the Rotarian in Hemingway. He could be, she found, surprisingly conventional. Michael Reynolds, in his fine study *The Young Hemingway*, makes much of the fact that Hemingway never portrayed Oak Park, his conventional, suburban hometown, in his writing. Reynolds's observation is both true and untrue. Oak Park is a major part of the iceberg, and we need not oversimplify it—judging it only as something to be dismissed. Oak Park also represented a manifestation of a cultural heritage that goes back to Europe and the long history of the Christian faith.

When we consider the many influences on Hemingway the short story writer, we need to count that heritage as one of his important sources. Before Theodore Roosevelt, before Kipling, before Sherwood Anderson, before Gertrude Stein, before Joseph Conrad, before James Joyce, there was the King James Bible. I can hardly overemphasize its importance in Hemingway's arsenal. It is there not only in the title but in his naming of Jacob Barnes in *The Sun Also Rises*; it is there in his naming of Santiago in *The Old Man and the Sea*. It is present in the prose rhythms of that novel and in the Christian symbolism, more natural to Hemingway than to many of his current interpreters, living in a time when its influence is much less than it was in Hemingway's. The Bible stories likely confirmed Hemingway in his preference for the minimalist story. He knew paintings with biblical motifs from his youth when he would go to the Chicago Art Institute, and he looked even more closely at such paintings in the museums of Europe. That he would write a play giving a modern version of the Crucifixion ("Today Is Friday") is not surprising. Hemingway's Oak Park heritage prepared him for looking at a larger Christian heritage even as that broader perspective helped him to see the inconsistencies and failings of Oak Park mores. Many of the assumptions of the heritage would, however, be an important aspect of much of what he wrote. They would help prepare him to understand *The Waste Land*, which influenced him as profoundly as it did any writer. He might not warm to Eliot the person and might cast aspersions on him, but at bottom he judged him "a damned good poet and a fair critic."[58]

In his famous interview with George Plimpton for the *Paris Review*, Hemingway listed both Dante and John Donne as among his most important literary forebears. It is pleasant to think that Hemingway took from Donne more than the title for a major novel. Like Donne, Hemingway believed in passionate romantic love, what an earlier age called profane love. Donne was a poet and preacher who loved the sacred with as much passion as he ever loved his earthly lovers. Hemingway was never so fortunate as to fuse the two visions as Donne had, but the ideal is one that he could understand. Hemingway could read both sides of Donne with comprehension and with sympathy. He was often tormented because he failed to fulfill the ideal of love, sacred and profane, that Donne portrayed. "I wished I had died before I ever loved anyone but her." Hemingway's fiction—short and long—prepares us for that admission.

A case in point is "Cross-Country Snow," another story Jeffrey Meyers identifies as "about" the disintegration of Hemingway's marriage to Hadley.[59] That is a curious oversimplification of the story. The story is about Nick's coming to terms with his wife's pregnancy. (There is no doubt that Hemingway was unhappy about Hadley's pregnancy. Gertrude Stein is quite convincing about his response.)[60] Nick had been advised by his friend Bill in "The Three-Day Blow" that "Once a man's married he's absolutely bitched" (90), but Nick had been reluctant to accept Bill's verdict. In *In Our Time*, "Cross-Country Snow" lets the reader know that Nick has taken the risks of loving and marrying.

The story takes place after World War I, as the reader knows by the story's placement in *In Our Time* in a grouping of postwar stories and by the fact that Nick's leg is damaged. The story is quiet and visual, restful after the turbulent interchapter that precedes it. Nick Adams and his friend George (we get Nick's last name, but not George's—one of the marks about who is more important in the story) are in the last day of a skiing trip in the Swiss Alps. The narrator first describes the challenging skiing motions of the two men (made difficult for Nick because of his bad leg) and then takes them inside a Swiss inn, where they enjoy a bottle of wine and each other's company.

Knowing Hemingway's practice of employing the natural symbol, Meyers makes a great deal of the empty bottle, seeing it as the major symbol of the story and cause for equating Nick's response to his wife's pregnancy with Frederic Henry's and Catherine Barkley's response to her pregnancy in *A Farewell to Arms*—making both events examples of a single biographical interpretation. But the cases are very different, the symbolism more complex in "Cross-Country Snow" than Meyers indicates. Indeed, the major symbol of the story is not the empty bottle but the snow of the title, made verb almost, certainly made exhilarating.

"Cross-Country Snow" is about pleasure—and about responsibility. And responsibility is not necessarily something every person accepts immediately. The passage that Meyers selects as pivotal is indeed important, but it has more ambiguity than Meyers posits—and he breaks it off at a misleading point. The conversation between the two friends gets to the real topic, Helen's pregnancy, only after rituals of drinking and eating and other talk (reminding us of talk between Nick and Bill in "The Three-Day Blow"). But there is no indication from the narrator that Nick is muttering (as Meyers states) his responses to George's questions. The most important of these is the one about Nick's response: "Are you glad?" Nick does not hesitate, and he is completely honest: "Yes. Now." (By contrast, in *A Farewell to Arms* Frederic and Catherine are never glad about Catherine's condition.) The uncertainty in Nick's response has more to do with how they will handle it. He "guesses" that they will go back to the States for the baby's birth, though neither he nor Helen is eager to return to America to live (they seem harmonious on more than one point!). The narrator then focuses on George, who has not made the kind of commitments that Nick has made, whose life is simpler: "George sat silent. He looked at the empty bottle and the empty glasses" (146). For George, not Nick, the empty bottle is the measure of Nick's new life, prompting him to say, "It's hell, isn't it?" Unfortunately, Meyers ends his quotation of the exchange with George's question.[61] But Nick specifically denies George's interpretation. Fatherhood is also something to look forward to. In looking at the empty bottle, George may begin to ponder the reality of his own life.

Nick and George have not been alone in this tavern. Swiss woodcutters have entered and left during the time that they have been there. They symbolize the world of work and responsibility that George has not accepted but that Nick has, and with increasing assurance. The story is not sentimental about that acceptance. There is no promise about an easy future, but there is a sense of Nick's realism and newfound maturity, pronounced when we look back to "The Three-Day Blow," where Bill's experience exceeded Nick's, where the story ends by mocking Nick's illusion that he could always still go into town and find Marge. In "Snow" George is the one desperate to hold on to the world of male camaraderie, but the last line of dialogue belongs to Nick and it stresses his realism: "There isn't any good in promising" (147). Bill is the leader at the end of "The Three-Day Blow"; Nick is the leader here as he and George leave the inn and prepare to ski home. The final image is the skiing, not just for its exhilaration, but for the control that Hemingway has been careful to associate with it. Nick appears to have an impressive degree of control over his life as the story concludes, and there seems to be nothing threatening about the penultimate and deliberate world of the last sentence of the story: "Now they would have the run home together."

When one of the nymphs of Edmund Spenser's "Prothalamion" sings blessing for the forthcoming marriage, she sings:

> Let endlesse Peace your steadfast hearts accord,
> And blessed Plentie wait upon your bord,
> And let your bed with pleasures chast abound,
> That fruitfull issue may to you afford,
> Which may your foes confound,
> And make your joyes redound,
> Upon your Brydale day, which is not long:
>     Sweete Themmes run softlie, till I end my Song.

To good purpose, T. S. Eliot alluded to Spenser's poem with its classic statement of Christian married love as he portrayed the decline of this ideal in the Western world. Hemingway was a good ally for Eliot in much of his short fiction. As we have seen, "Hills Like White Elephants" is something of an exemplum. In "Homage to Switzerland" we encounter a trio of increasingly dark episodes involving American men who are traveling in Switzerland, each for different reasons a man without a woman, each incapable of loving or cut off from the kind of blessing Spenser's lines evoke. Collectively the episodes pay homage to Switzerland or what Switzerland represents, not the spectacular, but the ordinary in life: love, marriage, fruition—just as the Swiss woodsmen in "Cross-Country Snow" represent these things. In "Homage to Switzerland" the American writer Mr. Johnson is being divorced, a state one of the porters tells him is not common in Switzerland. When Mr. Johnson asks a married porter if he likes being married, the porter replies, *"Oui. C'est normale"* (327). Many of Hemingway's stories reveal deep longing for that normalcy and for a blessing like that in Spenser's wedding poem. In some of his stories, there is a good measure of that blessing.

Perhaps the gentlest of Hemingway's stories, and one of his most underprized, is "A Day's Wait." To good purpose Hemingway placed it right after "Homage to Switzerland" in *Winner Take Nothing.* Here is a story rendering "the normal." It has, of course, peculiar Hemingway turns. At first seeming merely a report of an actual event in Hemingway's life, it relates to his most important themes, to love and marriage, to fathers and sons, to zestful realization of the active life, to coming to terms with the certainty of death.

The narrative line is spare. The dialogue defines the relationship between the two speaking characters, the father and his nine-year-old son. There is also a third character in the story, her exact identity kept from the reader. Knowing Hemingway's biography, the reader may be tempted to fill in gaps (in life the boy would be Bumby, the sleeping figure his stepmother), but the narrator lets the reader know all the reader needs to know. Here it is enough to recognize that the narrator is not like Mr. Johnson or the other Americans of "Homage to Switzerland." The woman does not speak in the story, not because the narrator wishes to show her inept or uncaring, but because he is defining a relationship between a father and a son. As he usually does, Hemingway prefers very simple exchanges, putting as little of the iceberg above water as possible.

The reader's first responsibility is to view the events of the story in the confines of the fictional world. Equating any character exactly with Hemingway is risky. Here Hemingway evokes home, a sense of a secure world for the child, who knows he is loved and knows where to go for assistance and comfort. Philip Young has identified the story as being about Nick Adams, and all of the details of the story do fit the pattern of the adult life of Nick. Accepting that, the reader gleans that the role of father to which Nick had to adjust in "Cross-Country Snow" provides him with a great deal of pleasure.

The first-person narrator, unnamed, has found much pleasure in his life. He has the pleasure of the marriage bed, the first given of the story. He is sleeping nude. "You go to bed. I'll see you when I'm dressed" (332), he tells his son, who has come into the bedroom, shivering and ill. His offspring does give the speaker pleasure, is not an unwelcome intrusion into his morning comfort. He greets the child with an affectionate "Schatz" and certainly will give him his time, as we see in his natural suggestion that he read to the boy: reading is a means of pleasure, a means of getting outside oneself, a means natural to the man and growing in the son. The first-person narration has the shape of the written word as opposed to an oral rendering or stream of consciousness, linking the story further with Nick, who became a writer and was also a constant reader. It is not amiss to see the writing as also a part of the narrator's means to pleasure. Writing is not only a means of getting rid of things, it is also a means of preserving them. Finally, the narrator takes his pleasure in the world outdoors, in going hunting and in relishing his senses during the hunt. Pursuit, Hemingway declared in *Green Hills of Africa,* is a means to happiness. Here the narrator takes it, thinking that he has tended to his son, that his obligations are fulfilled.

But in Hemingway fiction, as in the poetry of Robert Frost, the narrator is more concerned with inner than with outer weather. When he returns from the hunting, he learns what has made Schatz so tense. The boy has been waiting for death: having interpreted a Fahrenheit temperature reading as centigrade (the child also thinks in kilometers rather than miles, signifying that his education has been European), he has had a long day's wait, a day in which his father has not until late in the day realized the son's inner state. If the boy has misinterpreted, the father has misread some signals, too. But comprehending that ordeal—and admiring the boy's fortitude and bravery—the father understands what it has cost: " 'You poor Schatz,' I said. 'Poor old Schatz' " (334). The relieved boy's easy tears that follow are natural, and the father understands them completely.

The stoicism is decidedly a key Hemingway value. And as always it is hard won, and it may date Hemingway as a "square," or as an exemplification of frontier values. As Wallace Stegner reminds us, Hemingway stands at an opposite pole from the urban novelist Saul Bellow, who "specifically and angrily and repeatedly" repudiates that frontier stoicism.[62] But we may count Hemingway square on other matters as well. As we have seen, "A Day's Wait" celebrates many aspects of the "*normale*"—the ordinary, the wholesome.

Hemingway emphasizes the stoic attitude in several stories. It is the strongest element in "After the Storm," which he placed first in *Winner Take Nothing*. He also emphasizes the stoic in the epigraph that he invented for that collection: "Unlike all other forms of lutte or combat the conditions are that the winner shall take nothing; neither his ease, nor his pleasure, nor any notions of glory; nor, if he win far enough, shall there be any reward within himself." But in the final story of *Winner Take Nothing* Hemingway returned to the values of "A Day's Wait." "Fathers and Sons" is one of Hemingway's major stories—and in it Nick Adams is holding on to a great deal. Stoicism is not the only Hemingway value.

Anyone expecting the clipped, staccato sentences of Hemingway's early fiction in "Fathers and Sons" will not find them. The prose rhythms of the story are decidedly different from the rhythms of such stories as "The Battler" or "The Killers" and the short sentences of the interchapters in *In Our Time*. In the stories that portray Nick's shocked bafflement at the world, we often find a jumpy rhythm, appropriate to nerves at the raw. Often Nick is trying to blunt his thought, to hold on to an uncertain equilibrium, which he sometimes loses. "Fathers and Sons" portrays a middle-aged Nick, a ripe thirty-eight year old, comfortable in his thoughts, dealing with his past with perspective and a good deal of pleasure. The story takes place in mid-autumn, evoking harvest and reward. Its rhythms are appropriately mellow, the sentences tending to be long and even languid. Afternoon moves on toward evening as Nick drives his automobile, creating finally something like evensong.

Reflecting in *Death in the Afternoon* on his early struggles as a writer, Hemingway observes: "I found the greatest difficulty, aside from knowing truly what you really felt, rather than what you were supposed to feel, and had been taught to feel, was to put down what really happened in action; what the actual things were which produced the emotion that you experienced" (*DA* 2). Presentation of emotion is the goal of this evensong, and the narrator of "Fathers and Sons" moves skillfully from motion to emotion, letting us know what awakens the emotions and memories in Nick. The story tugs between past and present and ends by taking a glimpse at the future.

Nick has been driving for a long time. He has arrived in country very different from the country of his own boyhood. The small Southern town through which he passes makes him feel a stranger. Those who read the fiction as if it were biography call out Piggott, Arkansas, and we indeed know that in November 1933 Hemingway drove his son Bumby from Key West to Piggott, Arkansas, to be with his stepmother Pauline and his half-brothers for Thanksgiving. But "Fathers and Sons" should have us thinking of Nick Adams and his life. The narrator does not identify Piggott. Indeed, the town with which he opens his narrative is called "this town"; its suggestiveness is what the narrator observes. He is not at journey's end, but knows that this day's journey's end is nearing, "knowing the town he would reach for the night," a different town from "this town." There is biographical fact here, but its end is modified for the end of art. To good purpose, Hemingway is not precise about this journey's immediate end. The story has a larger purpose than presentation of a biographical moment. Nick again becomes archetypal—he can represent many fathers and many sons. Similarly, the journey becomes many journeys and finally the last journey.

Through the town, back into open country, Nick observes the fields carefully, hunts them in his mind. The hunting is not the tense activity that fishing the streams of his mind was for Nick in "Now I Lay Me," and inevitably his pleasure in the hunting makes him think of his father, the great hunter of keen eyes who taught him to hunt and to fish. In the many years since Nick learned those lessons, he has remained grateful to his father: the activities his father taught him have remained his passions, things that cannot be lost. They are certainly a tie between past and present.

The meditative story easily invites Nick to give his judgments on the past, and on his father, whose suicide Nick can now ponder with some understanding—and he looks forward to the time when he will write about it. Thinking about death is also thinking about life, and Nick pulls toward life, to memories of his first sexual experiences, which took place with an Indian girl in the woods of northern Michigan. Representativeness of setting gives way to exactness of setting; past becomes, for a time, more vivid than present. Although the narrator has given us ruminations about his father's death, he has given no dramatizations about it. The writer's mind is not yet ready for those, but it falls easily to zestful re-creation of scene as Nick relishes recollection of early sexual adventure. However accurately or inaccurately he remembers, he also remembers the sense of responsibility that pulls him away from Trudy when the sexual adventure is over. He cannot be as free as Trudy. No, he tells Trudy, he will not come out after supper. The adult has faulted his doctor father's extreme sexual puritanism, but even while a boy Nick shares in the values of his father's world. Eddie Gilby had better not try to copulate with Nick's sister Dorothy!

Having pulled toward responsibility, Nick's mind again explores the lost world of his childhood, moving into deeper waters as he recalls other conflicts with his father, even owning to the son's Freudian wish for the father's death. Angry that his father had sent him to the woodshed for telling a lie, he had drawn a bead upon him from his window in the shed. His sense of sonhood (his rising sense of adult responsibility) caused him to put the gun aside. Mark Twain often lamented the burden of the moral sense, just as Huck Finn found conscience a nuisance. However inconvenient, its burden is necessary. License means chaos. The worthless Pap Finn is not burdened with conscience, but it is the quality that makes Huck so valuable.

Two-thirds of "Fathers and Sons" is memory and reflection, qualities that also characterize the adult mind. The final third of the story is dialogue—intimate and quiet—between Nick and his son, a one-to-one exchange so common in Hemingway's stories, though not usually this tender. Nick's young son has also been soothed by the easy rhythm of a long drive in uncongested country, his sleep further freeing Nick's mind for his fancy. When the boy awakens, Nick does not even notice—so vivid has been his remembrance of life past. But the boy is also a part of the story's aura of harvest and fruition. Hemingway evokes warmth and security in the relationship between Nick and his son, many of the details inviting sure identification with the characters of "A Day's Wait."

Some of those details and the unstated facts about the journey take on new meaning, however. If Nick and his son now have strong bonds, maintaining them will not be easy. The challenge to Nick is to make stronger ties with his son than his father had made with him, and we are not sure that Nick will be any more successful in doing so, though he will try to give his son the same model of happiness in hunting that his father gave him. The son's first words as he awakens startle Nick, for they are a challenge (though the boy cannot realize it) to Nick's role as father. The boy asks what life was like among the Indians, giving Nick opportunity to discuss sexual matters more fully than his father had. But such discourse across the generations is not easy—not for Nick, nor for his father, who had given Nick the information and advice he thought best for a young man—half of it wrong, the other half incomplete. Although Dr. Adams had been successful in training Nick to appreciate the pleasures of fishing and hunting, he had been noticeably inadequate in conveying much about the possible joy of human sexuality.

That failure calls attention to the absent mother of the present moment in the automobile as well as to the absent mother of Nick's reveries. The female who is dramatized in the story is Trudy Mitchell, and she performs openly, unashamedly, paganly in the center of the story as Nick's sexual partner. But Hemingway's art of concealment becomes immensely powerful as we contemplate the other women of the story, the women who are excluded from the presentation. Hemingway makes us feel the first, Nick's mother, by using his doubling, or echoing device. As I noted, the story begins with presentation of the progress of Nick and his son in an automobile through terrain native to neither. That description is paralleled with another lengthy description of a journey—Nick's walk from the family cottage to the hemlock woods behind the Indian camp. In actual distance, the journey is not great, but metaphorically it is. Rather than the modern world of automobiles and paved highways and traffic lights, we are carried to a pre-civilized world, where people move on bare feet through forest and swamp. By its length, the vivid description of Nick's remembered journey through the woods emphasizes the distance between the sexual values of Nick's home and mother (her only dramatization comes in "The Doctor and the Doctor's Wife," and that story makes clear the sexual distance between Nick's parents) and the values of the adult Nick. The young Nick has been traveling not only to a destination, but from one. He travels away from a female as well as toward a female.

As the sexual dimensions of the story become paramount, the reader will more likely find Nick's immediate destination of significance. What has the narrator been concealing? As the conversation between father and son makes clear, it will be hard for these twentieth-century people for whom travel is so simple a thing to maintain the continuity and traditions of earlier generations. If Nick growing up knew intimately the life of Indians and the recurrence of summers near them, his son has lived in France, in ways has been formed by that culture, though now he travels in America. Living in France has helped make the boy understand tradition, and that experience intensifies a natural longing for familial tradition. If they were French, the boy believes, he would be able to visit and pray at the tomb of his grandfather—the father about whom Nick thinks so constantly. Like "Wine of Wyoming," "Fathers and Sons" yearns toward the traditions of older European civilization, and also like "Wine of Wyoming" it shows American culture as too transient to maintain those values very satisfactorily. Both stories long toward earlier faith. Appropriately, the allusion of Hemingway's title is to the work of a European writer. Moreover, Turgenev's *Fathers and Sons* also has as one of its themes the difficulty of the generations in discussing or understanding the sexual dramas of the other. Nikolai Kirsanov cannot explain to his grown son Arcady that he has taken a mistress, sensing that children hold ideals of sexual behavior for their parents even as parents have them for their children.

Although Hemingway's narrator never states it directly, the son at his side is going to visit a stepmother (probably the woman we see on the pillow next to Nick in "A Day's Wait") as well as to spend time with his father. The boy is growing up in France; the father lives in the United States, but in a different part of the country from that where his father is buried. Although the middle-aged Nick Adams is reaping pleasures in his role of father as he travels with his son, his own domestic life has been complex. If anything, he will have to strive even harder than his father did to keep discourse between father and son open. He succeeds warmly, touchingly in this story, but his son is not yet twelve years old. By his own admission, Nick, by the time he was fifteen, shared nothing with his own father.

Clearly, "Fathers and Sons" represents a powerful yearning toward tradition and continuity, toward faith and forgiveness. If the family life of Nick's parents and their children was complex and sometimes disturbing, there are also disturbing and complex elements in the life of Nick and his son. "Don't you think we might all be buried at a convenient place?" (377) asks Nick's son, who argues for that continuity. Nick understands that longing; hence he declines the suggestion of being buried in France. He claims his American and familial heritage even as he has been exploring his past in memory and forgiveness in the reveries of an autumn afternoon. He understands exactly what his son means when he says, "Well, I don't feel good never to have even visited the tomb of my grandfather" (377). And although Nick acknowledges in the final line of the story that they will have to make such a visit, the placement of the promise and the story's honesty make the reader doubt that they ever will. Nevertheless, we do not forget Nick's homage to his father—his frequent visitations to sights and scenes of their past. Although for Nick praying may now be different from what it is for his son and the tradition his son evokes, there is a sense in which the story shows Nick praying at that tomb.

Even as "Fathers and Sons" finds Nick looking forwards and backwards, it invites the reader to look forwards and backwards into Nick's life. It is possible to view Nick Adams's life in its progress, but Hemingway did not write about him in a neat chronological progression, and his last effort on Nick is the unfinished "The Last Good Country," which shows Nick as an adolescent, almost ready to break forth from the authority of his parents. It is appropriate, therefore, that we juxtapose this reading of "Fathers and Sons" with a look at the final story of *In Our Time*—"Big Two-Hearted River." Both are intensely personal stories that should strongly influence our sense of the books they help define. I have noted the importance of the role of tradition in "Fathers and Sons." The role of tradition also contributes to the dynamics of "Big Two-Hearted River," the story that confirmed the genius of the young Hemingway.

The story is the classic fishing story in the English language. Looking at the story after looking at "Fathers and Sons," we can see the story, in part, as tribute to Nick's father—who was very sound about fishing. We have no doubt of that skill as we share in the precise detail of fishing and the code that goes with exact fishing:

> He [Nick] had wet his hand before he touched the trout, so he would not disturb the delicate mucus that covered him. If a trout was touched with a dry hand, a white fungus attacked the unprotected spot. Years before when he had fished crowded streams, with fly fishermen ahead of him and behind him, Nick had again and again come on dead trout, furry with white fungus, drifted against a rock, or floating belly up in some pool. Nick did not like to fish with other men on the river. Unless they were of your party, they spoiled it. (176)

Protesting the messiness of careless fishermen, Nick reveals his belief about the way life should be lived. "Big Two-Hearted River" is nothing if it is not a longing for, a search for order. Nick's fishing, as readers have long noted, contains many elements of the ritualistic. So does Nick's approach toward camping, and readers have relished the many specific details of Nick's hiking and camping as he goes about his affairs. The ritualistic aspects underscore the metaphysical dimension to the longing for order. The precise details have often made readers consider the story as in part a "how to" story. But behind those details, there are echoes of a tradition to which the reader should also respond. "Order is Heaven's first law," Alexander Pope declares in *An Essay on Man* (Epistle 4, line 49). Hemingway may not have known that line, but he may well have remembered Saint Paul's admonition: "Let all things be done decently and in order" (1 Corinthians 15:40). He knew the ideal, and for him sports were a means both for exemplifying and for stating the ideal. He learned a great deal about the code of fishing and hunting from his father—and those details in the story are a link to him, a part of the unstated, of the submerged iceberg of the story.

Although memory is in the foreground of "Fathers and Sons," the reader of "Big Two-Hearted River" will discover that it also is a story of memory. The difference is that the mature Nick of the one story can allow recall to engage him lengthily and constructively, while the younger Nick of the earlier story is reluctant to let memory engage him for very long. Although he does not have, apparently, his father's suicide to think about, he knows that there are aspects of his father's life that he must yet come to terms with—as made clear by such stories as "Indian Camp," "The Doctor and the Doctor's Wife," "Ten Indians," and "The Three-Day Blow." But those memories are not realities that Nick can deal with in the time present of "Big Two-Hearted River." It is surely true, however, that Nick is holding on very tightly to lessons about field and stream that his father had taught him, and he would like to find behind those lessons the values that his father had also taught.

We may also find Dr. Adams in the careful attention to food in "Big Two-Hearted River." That story calls into play all of the senses, and the sense of taste as memorable as any:

> Nick laid the bottle full of jumping grasshoppers against a pine trunk. Rapidly he mixed some buckwheat flour with water and stirred it smooth, one cup of flour, one cup of water. He put a handful of coffee in the pot and dipped a lump of grease out of a can and slid it sputtering across the hot skillet. On the smoking skillet he poured smoothly the buckwheat batter. It spread like lava, the grease spitting sharply. Around the edges the buckwheat cake began to firm, then brown, then crisp. The surface was bubbling slowly to

porousness. Nick pushed under the browned under surface with a fresh pine chip. He shook the skillet sideways and the cake was loose on the surface. I won't try and flop it, he thought. He slid the chip of clean wood all the way under the cake, and flopped it over onto its face. It sputtered in the pan. (174)

We share the making and the eating of Nick's food, wondering just what the onion sandwich dipped first in the cold stream tastes like. But the happy sign of the story is that Nick handles the details of food with as much skill and efficiency as he does the other details of his hunting. Something of that, too, is tribute to his father. In "Ten Indians," after an all-day Fourth of July excursion with the neighboring Garners, young Nick returns at night to the family cottage, where his father has waited up for him. Dr. Adams has prepared for Nick a late-night snack of cold chicken and a glass of milk, with huckleberry pie, the berries fresh from the Michigan woods. The big piece his father cuts him is a gesture of affection. Nick is at the time of sexual awakening when ties with his father are snapping. The father senses that the relationship is in transition, and the reaching out with food is an effort toward fellowship. Although there is no family celebration around the ritual of food in this family on the big holiday of the summer (such as Mrs. Garner has provided her family, we assume, or such as Madame Fontan of "Wine of Wyoming" would abundantly provide), the doctor knows food as an important value and symbol. In any case, Nick is quite adept at providing tasty food on this journey to the Big Two-Hearted River. Its quality is part of the affirmation of the story, and if Nick risks thinking about his mentor in the brewing of his coffee, below the surface there are surely memories of his father's culinary skill.

Although one of the chief dramas of the Nick Adams stories portrays Nick moving from his parents' world into a larger one, that larger world is often perplexing. In returning to more carefully controlled activities such as hunting or fishing, he looks for ideal circumstances. "Unless they were of your party, they spoiled it," Nick remembers, in a story of extremely fine discriminations and one of Hemingway's most intensely private stories.

The longest story of *In Our Time*, "Big Two-Hearted River" is unique in having just one character. But the sense of the larger world that challenges and sometimes frightens Nick is never far from the reader's consciousness, or from Nick's. It breaks through in occasional, essentially casual references to a very few persons Nick has met, never to stated references to family or lover. It hovers in the realities of the violence of the modern world, chiefly in the devastation of war, that have defined life in the book and that have profoundly challenged Nick's idea of himself and the world.

The privateness of Nick's fishing trip takes on special force also because of its placement in *In Our Time*. It follows "My Old Man," a story that portrays one of the most public of sports—horse racing. Like bullfighting, horse racing exists essentially and almost exclusively in an arena where a crowd looks on. The observers' response to the death of the narrator's father allies "My Old Man" with the bull-fighting interchapters, which place strong emphasis on crowd behavior.[63]

In chapter 14, one of those interchapters, we watch the bullfighter Maera as he lies in the sand, having just been gored. The action (unlike that of "Big Two-Hearted River") is fast-paced and leads to Maera's fatal wounding. Maera is carried into the infirmary: "There was a great shouting going on in the grandstand overhead. Maera wanted to say something and found he could not talk. Maera felt everything getting larger and larger and then smaller and smaller. Then it got larger and larger and larger and then smaller and smaller. Then everything commenced to run faster and faster as when they speed up a cinematograph film. Then he was dead" (161).

In "Indian Camp" the boy Nick had asked his father if dying was hard. With Maera's death, so strategically placed in *In Our Time*, we find something of an answer in Hemingway's description of the sensation of Maera's dying (that rhythm and the rhythm of sexual intercourse he would attempt repeatedly in his fiction). By the time of "Big Two-Hearted River" Nick has seen a great deal of death. Indeed, he has come very close to it himself. How well he performed in battle or thinks he performed is part of the concern of stories that Hemingway wrote afterwards—"In Another Country" and "Now I Lay Me" in *Men Without Women* and especially "A Way You'll Never Be" in *Winner Take Nothing*. And although the surface of "Big Two-Hearted River" is often calm and assuring, interchapter 15 interrupts it to remind us of the complicated world that Nick wishes to escape, or at least to understand better. Its subject is meeting death, and for mobster Sam Cardinella (whose prison execution the interchapter describes) the dying is a very hard thing indeed. Fears about meeting death and making judgments against the highest standards of behavior are important parts of the submerged iceberg of "Big Two-Hearted River." But the judgments will be private in this private fishing story. Interchapters 14 and 15 prepare us for understanding some of the implications of the dark swamp that Nick turns from at the end of the story. "Big Two-Hearted River" does not reveal its many secrets on one or two readings. Its readers will discover them as they heed the stories of *In Our Time* and the Nick Adams stories of *Men Without Women* and *Winner Take Nothing*. Nevertheless, Hemingway provides many clues to the meaning of Nick's private journey, and many readers have quite meaningfully first encountered Nick in this story.

In part 1, as Nick climbs a hill with a heavy burden on his back (actually the terrain around Seney is flat), he is like some later incarnation of Bunyan's pilgrim: "The road climbed steadily. It was hard work walking up-hill. His muscles ached and the day was hot, but Nick felt happy. He felt he had left everything behind, the need for thinking, the need to write, other needs. It was all back of him" (164). The specified need is for writing, and the story sharply conveys that its protagonist is a sensitive observer of the world and will have something to say, some secrets to reveal. The determination and the optimism of the ending of the story lead us to believe that he will indeed fulfill that need.

But what are the other needs? The most specified is the need to think. "Now I Lay Me" lets us know the kinds of things that Nick had to think about, and that story lets us know that the issue of courage in the face of death (Nick recalls his lack of courage in "A Way You'll Never Be") has been only a partial cause of Nick's sleeplessness. Nick's fears have more to do with living than with dying—and Hemingway's placement of "Now I Lay Me" as the last story of *Men Without Women* should remind us of the last story of *In Our Time*. Not only are both stories about Nick, but both are fishing stories. In "Now I Lay Me" Nick keeps hold of himself by fishing and refishing in his mind the various streams he has fished in former days. He also visits and revisits certain memories of his life. Mainly, these memories have to do with his past and his family, wherein he sees his father as victimized by his mother's domineering destructiveness (fire is her weapon). The title, alluding as it does to the child's prayer, lets us know that Nick has been traumatized in some deep sense by events of his childhood.

The child's prayer is not, however, the prayer that Nick tries to pray in "Now I Lay Me." On nights when his thinking is most disturbing and he prays the Lord's Prayer (the fishing not working those nights), he can get only as far as "On earth as it is in heaven." Why can't he go on? Not because the next petition is "Give us this day our daily bread" but because of the harder petition that follows: "And forgive us our trespasses, as we forgive those who trespass against us." Nick is too inward turning, much like David Bourne in *The Garden of Eden*. Nick cannot share very much of himself with his friend John in the hospital bed next to him. Rather John gets to talk about himself. Only in the act of writing (appropriately "Now I Lay Me" is a first-person story) can Nick share his inner turmoil. Writing can be an urge to confession, which is part of the iceberg of the story. Nick seems to be unable to go beyond the single line that he gives his mother in the story: "I've been cleaning out the basement, dear" (278). Nick cannot forgive the mother who controls this house from its basement to its attic, where the wedding cake rests in the tin box that hangs from the rafters. Nick is therefore not inclined to believe that John has very good advice for him: that marriage will take care of his problems. In truth, Nick is very fearful that marriage would only compound his problems.

The reader of "Big Two-Hearted River," even the first readers of the story who did not yet have "Now I Lay Me" as a point of reference, would have a strong indication of Nick's perplexing problems with women. The story ends with Nick's assurance that "There were plenty of days coming when he could fish the swamp" (180). The swamp represents every dark aspect of Nick's psyche, and it conveys a great deal about the unresolved tensions in his family background and his fear that Bill's warning in "The Three-Day Blow" about the destructive reality of marriage is justified.

The swamp invites the reader of "Big Two-Hearted River" to reflect again on "The Battler," a story placed near the middle of *In Our Time*, though it was the last written story of *In Our Time*, created specifically for that book after "Up in Michigan" was judged too strong for inclusion. Hemingway declared that the late addition strengthened the considerable unity of his book. The final image of "The Battler" is Nick's view of two men without women—Bugs and Ad Francis—"in the clearing" but surrounded by the threatening swamp along the railroad track where Nick had been hiking.

Characteristically, Hemingway puts the reader in Nick's place, probably uncertain about what to conclude about the strange happenings of this evening. The story starts with Nick's having been deceived by one voice, that of the brakeman who knocked him off the train. Readers have been uncertain if the voice of Bugs (who tells Nick the strange story of Ad Francis's bizarre marriage to a woman who looked like his sister) is to be trusted. In part, Ad is as victimized by Bugs as he could possibly have been by his wife, but at least the existence of the two misfits from society shows a way of coping. If Bugs speaks truth, then Nick may ponder further about unexpected twists in the relationships between men and women, between husbands and wives, who live out their dramas in a social matrix that challenges their happiness and helps to destroy it. Yet there seems to be something enduring in marriage. Ad's wife still helps to support her defeated boxer. It is an easy step from Ad's prophetic line that Nick, never before crazy, has a lot coming to him, to "A Way You'll Never Be." The line also links Nick to his own immersion in what Chaucer's Wife of Bath describes as the "woe that is in marriage."

Is the Nick of "Big Two-Hearted River" married? If we are reading about Nick's life chronologically in *In Our Time* (and chronology does emerge as one of the principles of the organization), then so we must take him. The event that was the basis for the story did in Hemingway's life predate his marriage to Hadley, but Hemingway changed a great deal when he fictionalized the account: the original journey was not a single-man trip, the river was not the Two-Hearted River nor the Little Two-Hearted River, but the Fox. We know that he excised references to Nick's married life, though the excision did not necessarily return Nick to bachelor status. The story does, after all, follow "Cross-Country Snow," which shows Nick not only married, but also nearing fatherhood.

It is clear, however, that Nick does not wish on this fishing trip to think about women. In large part, the story evokes an Adam reaching for the simplicity of pre-Eve days. To get to where he wants to go, to be the writer he wants to be, Nick must here take a psychological journey that starts very far back—in a world with as much innocence as he can find, with as few complexities as possible. Hemingway, in fact, calls our attention to the extraordinary absence of the female on this venture. Even the trout Nick catches are male, as the narrator carefully notes.

The only time on this fishing trip that Nick lets memory deal with women comes near the end of part 1. Nick has had his long journey through the Michigan woods and has found he can recapture all of the old feeling. He has created for himself a satisfactory camp, a "home" as he appropriately names it, employing in that process the lessons of the woods that he has learned from his father. Nick is happy, exulting in a mood that is religious: " 'Chrise,' Nick said, 'Geezus Chrise,' he said happily" (168). It is the third and last time he speaks in the story.

Feeling this much assurance, confident that he can choke off any unwanted thinking, Nick lets the single direct reference to women surface as he makes coffee at the end of a very satisfactory meal. Making the coffee makes him think of his friend Hopkins, with whom he had camped in earlier days: "They called Hop's girl the Blonde Venus. Hop did not mind because she was not his real girl. Hopkins said very confidently that none of them would make fun of his real girl" (169).

This is the tip of the iceberg—a reference to Hop's girl, not Nick's, though the kidding motif of a girl not really yours is major in "Ten Indians," where Carl Garner kids Nick about Prudence Mitchell, the tenth Indian of the story. As the ending of that story emphasizes, Nick's affair has been of the flesh; he will rebound quickly from the news of Prudence's infidelity. But if Hop has a Venus in his past, he also has had a "real girl"—and so has Nick, and not only the Marjorie of "The End of Something." He has learned more about the intense agony of lost love. "A Way You'll Never Be" gives us a nightmare rendering of Nick's complicated love affairs, closely associated with images of destruction:

> [A]nd he could see that hill every night when he dreamed with Sacré Coeur, blown white, like a soap bubble. Sometimes his girl was there and sometimes she was with someone else and he could not understand that, but those were the nights the river ran so much wider and stiller than it should and outside of Fossalta there was a low house painted yellow with willows all around it and a low stable and there was a canal, and he had been there a thousand times and never seen it, but there it was every night as plain as the hill, only it frightened him. (310)

Images and memories like these are precisely what Nick has programmed out of his postwar fishing trip on the Big Two-Hearted.

Obviously, the Nick of "Big Two-Hearted River" has come some distance from the insecurity he shows in "A Way You'll Never Be." But he works very hard to keep much of his past under his emotional control, as the rhythms of the story repeatedly emphasize. The more recent past involves another woman, the Helen of "Cross-Country Snow." Nick had made some kind of reconciliation with his wife's pregnancy, I noted, but if we read many Nick stories we understand his fear that domesticity might emasculate him. Helen's pregnancy (in terms of the dynamics of *In Our Time*, not of any simplistic equation of events in the stories to precise counterparts in Hemingway's life) is likely one of those events with which Nick is still coming to terms. Had the trout Nick caught been female, he would have been reminded of the production of eggs and offspring. He will have to struggle again with the possibility of parenthood in his life, perhaps to discover that offspring need not destroy his life as a writer, but might enhance his work and strengthen him as a writer and a person.

Nick is not ready to deal with the possibility of parenthood on this trip, though the dynamics of "Big Two-Hearted River" give readers ample reason to believe that he will fish the swamps on another day, that eventually he will deal fully with life and death. The story itself is a celebration of Nick's successful effort to live deliberately, giving us a twentieth-century version of Thoreau's retreat to Walden Pond. (Thoreau's account offered no suggestion of man's sexual needs, but, as we have seen, Hemingway deliberately left them out yet hinted at them in male trout and in the memories that begin to seep through the narrative.) Hemingway's story is not, of course, an effort to awaken his neighbors to fuller living, as Thoreau professed he wanted to do. Rather, Hemingway deals with the emotions of a character who has been traumatized by war but has also to face several unresolved conflicts that are unrelated to war, a character striving for meaningful retreat. Nick seeks meaningful recovery by returning to the source of earth and water, retreat now so that there might be progress. Hemingway has made no easy promises about Nick, showing us both the precarious state of his nerves and his many strengths. In *In Our Time* Hemingway interrupts the story with chapter 15 to remind us of the changed world in which Nick must live. "*L'Envoi*" serves the same purpose. There the Greek king and queen are trying to comprehend the realities of the new world that revolution creates; so is Nick. *In Our Time* ends with this line about the king: "Like all Greeks he wanted to go to America" (181). Nick has just returned to a changed America, but he still pursues happiness (his basic American impulse) and understanding, understanding that will come through his art, the art we have strong reason to believe he will achieve.

The reader of Hemingway's stories, then, must be attentive to the relationship of story to story. By ending *In Our Time, Men Without Women*, and *Winner Take Nothing* with a story about Nick Adams, Hemingway emphasizes the relationship among the collections, challenging readers to reflect further on what is hidden and seemingly made minimal. In that regard, his stories are different from those of his great contemporaries—Faulkner, Wolfe, Porter, and Fitzgerald. Even though Porter wrote several stories about Miranda and Fitzgerald several stories about Basil Lee, those characters served them differently from the way Nick served Hemingway. The new story did not serve as a challenge to revisit an earlier story; rather we have the sense of a continuing saga, a new direction in the character's life. Hemingway achieved something unique in the American short story by refishing old streams.

That Hemingway ended each of his first three major short story collections with a Nick story underscores the affirmation that kept reappearing in his work. Nick Adams was a recurring means for Hemingway to conquer the darker vision of human experience explored in stories such as "The Killers," "A Clean, Well-Lighted Place," and "The Gambler, the Nun, and the Radio." "Big Two-Hearted River" ends with the kind of courage the young writer needs, with the conviction that "there were plenty of days coming when he could fish the swamp." "Now I Lay Me" recounts a time in Nick's life when he did not have such assurance; told in first person, the narrator is making the kind of acknowledgement in his writing that he could not relate otherwise. "Fathers and Sons" portrays a Nick for whom memory is no longer so threatening, and it shows him with adult understanding of some difficult realities of his past. He expresses some measure of the forgiveness that he could not request in "Now I Lay Me."

# The 1930s: New Directions

Noting that *Winner Take Nothing* includes several inferior stories, Kenneth Lynn judged "One Reader Writes" an embarrassment and described "Fathers and Sons" as the splendor of an essentially undistinguished collection.[64] Reviewers of Hemingway's third collection of stories had also been less impressed with it than they were with the first two. It was not as avant-garde as *In Our Time*, and although it sold well, the consensus was that *Winner Take Nothing* did not have the emotional force of *Men Without Women*.

To what extent was Hemingway's artistry with the short story in serious decline? Carlos Baker reminds us that in 1932 Hemingway experienced "a big revival of belief in the short story,"[65] and Hemingway's correspondence with Maxwell Perkins makes clear that Hemingway took great pride in the volume. What was he doing, then, in "One Reader Writes"? Baker called it probably the easiest story that Hemingway ever wrote, and commentators have usually been silent about it. Indeed, it may well be Hemingway's most dispensable short story—if we take it by itself.

But as is the case with so many of Hemingway's short stories, which sometimes echo beyond the volume that contains them, "One Reader Writes" reaches beyond itself. A more famous example of a short story that reverberates throughout the collection that contains it and into later work as well is "A Very Short Story" of *In Our Time*. It was not immediately seen as a pivotal piece of the book, but its importance for *A Farewell to Arms* is now widely recognized. Increasingly, also, readers have found the story an important part of *In Our Time*: in the context of the book, it comments on other stories, calling attention to the minimal surface treatment of women in "Big Two-Hearted River," for example.

"One Reader Writes," the story in the exact middle of *Winner Take Nothing*, is the very short story of that volume. It is not a piece that attracts anthologizers. But in context it is a story of more than passing interest. It should, as I have suggested, remind the reader of "A Very Short Story," a piece that had its first incarnation as one of the brief

61

chapters of *in our time*, the 1924 book consisting of the chapters that were soon modified into the interchapters of the 1925 *In Our Time*. This echo of the earlier minimalist method calls attention to the technical variety of *Winner Take Nothing*, a volume that was in no wise a duplication of the structure or methods of *In Our Time*. The variation is certainly made evident in the rendition of Nick Adams in *Winner Take Nothing*. "A Way You'll Never Be" is unlike the other Nick stories in that it takes us to the war's front, and Hemingway portrays directly the chaos of Nick's wounded psyche, treating the thinking process quite directly. As I have observed, in "Fathers and Sons" Hemingway shows Nick many years later. The internal life of the character is again at front stage, though here the mood is languid, autumnal, beneficent. Hemingway was moving toward the longer unit, as the final three stories in *Winner Take Nothing* indicate. Hemingway was ever a seeker of new forms. The challenge to make a thing new was one he never ignored. Tonally and technically, this volume of stories is different from the two that precede it, and "One Reader Writes" helps to assert that difference by reminding readers of the early method.

"One Reader Writes" also calls attention to this shifting perspective. *In Our Time* puts emphasis on the shock of idealistic youth in confrontation with the violence of the world, and it relates that violence to a young man's uncertainties about the security of love and family; it calls attention to the disjunctiveness of the world by interweaving interchapters between the stories. *Men Without Women*, declaring still the violence of the world, gives numerous examples of men who learned to cope with the world in various ways in the face of various losses; they were men without women. In almost every story the influence of the female is kept removed, causing Virginia Woolf to object that for women readers Hemingway was, like Norman Douglas, James Joyce, and D. H. Lawrence, too self-consciously virile.[66]

"After the Storm," the opening story of *Winner Take Nothing*, might also invite that accusation. Its narrative voice is that of the tough, hard-boiled male—the dominant note in the short stories that went into the making of what may be Hemingway's weakest novel, *To Have and Have Not* (1936). By accepting Maxwell Perkins's advice to place this story first in *Winner Take Nothing*, Hemingway appropriately gives us an image of a figure who embodies the stated theme of the book's epigraph. But in the succeeding stories there is not another such protagonist as the tough narrator of "After the Storm." And although Hemingway continues to have male protagonists in most of the stories, he admits more of the female perspective. The one story that is presented from the woman's point of view is "One Reader Writes."

She is not, to be sure, a developed character. Her importance is primarily thematic. Her plight, in ways, reverses the situation of "A Very Short Story." In the earlier story the male is unable to understand the change of heart of his first love, Luz, and he contracts gonorrhea from a salesgirl in the back seat of a taxicab while trying to convince himself that sex is only a commodity. The wife of "One Reader Writes" does not find sex a commodity, nor does she assume that her husband does. She has, instead, something like the fierce devotion to her man that Marie Morgan of *To Have and Have Not* exemplifies. The wife has written to a physician newspaper columnist about her fears that her husband cannot be cured of the syphilis he contracted during a three-year military assignment in China. Her father said a cure was impossible, she writes, "but I want to believe my Husband most" (320). What the narrator presents finally is not the woman's naiveté, but her pain, her love, her hunger, her victimization. He takes us directly into her thought processes:

> It's such a long time though. It's a long time. And it's been a long time. My Christ, it's been a long time. He had to go wherever they sent him, I know, but I don't know what he had to get it for. Oh, I wish to Christ he wouldn't have got it. I don't care what he did to get it. But I wish to Christ he hadn't ever got it. It does seem like he didn't have to have got it. I don't know what to do. I wish to Christ he hadn't got any kind of malady. I don't know why he had to get a malady. (321)

The repetition may remind the reader of "Up in Michigan" and the disillusionment of Liz Coates. The story is Hemingway's announcement (really, his reminder) that although he sometimes buries the woman's viewpoint, he is always aware of it. By the time he gets to the stories of *Winner Take Nothing* he has had a great deal of experience that would cause him to be mindful of that perspective, though it was most often a part of his submerged iceberg. By reminding the reader of "A Very Short Story," Hemingway suggests that he has not forgotten the method of the early work, but that he is interested in other short story techniques; especially he is interested in longer stories. In *Winner Take Nothing*, following "One Reader Writes," Hemingway placed a series of stories that call attention to absent wives, and hence to the idea of the solid marriage that "One Reader Writes" depends upon. As the absent mother has a powerful effect in many of the Nick Adams stories, the absent or scarcely visible wife has a powerful effect in the later stories of *Winner Take Nothing.*

Both the title and content of the story that follows "One Reader Writes" pay tribute to the wife's ideal. In "Homage to Switzerland" Switzerland represents home and stability, and through portraits of three traveling Americans Hemingway pays his homage to the solid values of middle-class Switzerland, and, in a sense, to the best qualities of Oak Park. Tributes often come in a three-part salute, and Hemingway not only breaks his story into three parts, he also emphasizes his experimentation by labeling those parts: "Portrait of Mr. Wheeler in Montreux," "Mr. Johnson Talks About It at Vevey," and "The Son of a Fellow Member at Territet." Each section takes place in a station café, and the method of each section is dramatic. Each individual episode is realistic, but the effect of the three is close to the method used by the absurdist playwrights of the 1950s and 1960s, such as Eugene Ionesco and Edward Albee: repetition emphasizes absurdity, talk emphasizes the vacuum. Hemingway catches a tone at once light and sinister by repeating certain items of dialogue. For example, Mr. Wheeler, Mr. Johnson, and Mr. Harris each offers the waitress a cigar. Similarly, the setting of each dramatic scene echoes the other; although the episodes take place at different stations, the scene is essentially the same. And each contrasts inner and outside temperatures. Tellingly, the setting of each catches a detail of "One Reader Writes." It is snowing in Virginia as the wife writes her letter to the syndicated columnist, and it is also snowing as the three men face their particular forms of loneliness.

Mr. Wheeler is the least sympathetic of the three men. He distrusts women. He is, in fact, rude—even sadistic—capable of making only the most superficial ties with other people. Careful about his money, he is also careful about his sexuality. He has taken no risks, unlike the wife of "One Reader Writes." Mr. Johnson has taken his risks, and he is aware of his present loneliness. The Vevey location should remind the reader of "Canary for One" and the sad train ride of a couple who have lost the happiness they knew earlier at Vevey. Mr. Johnson tells the porter that his wife has decided to divorce him. The cause is unknown, but doubtless she has her reasons. Mr. Johnson is having difficulty dealing with that pain; he considers nostalgically the concept of life that the Swiss porters around him embody:

"You like being married?" Johnson asked one of the porters.
"What?"
"You like the married state?"
"*Oui. C'est normale.*"
"Exactly," said Johnson. "*Et vous, monsieur?*"
"*Ça va,*" said the other porter.
"*Pour moi,*" said Johnson, "*ça ne va pas.*" (327)

He regrets that failure greatly, and he would like to blunt the pain.

The absence of the normal is also Hemingway's topic in the story of Mr. Harris. Like the two other American travelers, Mr. Harris is middle-aged, an expatriate who has been away from America a long time. The pain that occupies him is the recent suicide of his father, who shot himself. The kindly old man who has been talking with Mr. Harris about the National Geographic Society does as well as anyone might in responding to Harris's news: "I am very truly sorry. I am sure his loss was a blow to science as well as to his family." Humor is one means of coping, and Mr. Harris observes that "Science took it awfully well" (331). This is another way of saying, "*Pour moi, ça ne vas pas.*" Set in multilingual Switzerland, the story emphasizes the uses of language and the inadequacies of language to blunt pain. When the wife writes in "One Reader Writes," she is like Faulkner's Benjy Compson of *The Sound and the Fury* "trying to say," but she succeeds hardly at all in saying what she feels.

*Winner Take Nothing* moves very appropriately from "Homage to Switzerland" to "A Day's Wait," a story that contains a great deal of the beauty of the normal, as this study has shown. It also calls attention to the importance of the sleeping wife, whose story might be kept for a later time. The scarcely perceived, scarcely acknowledged wife is an important aspect of "Wine of Wyoming," another story wherein Hemingway makes clear that the married state is one of his most important subjects. The writer-protagonist looks admiringly at the life of the Fontans, the French couple who live in Wyoming and who take a keen interest in him. The Fontans represent the best of the Old World traditions. They believe that the married state is indeed the best course of life for most people, and they worry that American culture has undermined it, that their sons will be hard pressed to duplicate what they have found through marriage. The Fontans are religiously conservative, Catholic in a part of America where there are few of their faith. They believe in good food and good fellowship. Only at the end of the story does the narrator indicate that he is married, though he never uses the word *wife* and never speaks of his wife by name. His muted treatment of his married state is revealing. The history of the Fontans and their various losses in Wyoming is the visible part of "Wine of Wyoming," but by story's end we ponder not so much the unhappiness of the married Fontan son or even the condition of the elder Fontans as we do the state of the narrator. On one level the story reflects on the closing of the American frontier and the present state of American life; on another it looks suggestively at the narrator's marriage. The narrator is conspicuously silent about his wife, but the reader of *Winner Take Nothing* is looking at her story in a context that invites no easy responses, that invites compassion and tentativeness.

"The Sea Change," among the shortest stories of *Winner Take Nothing*, had also announced the more tolerant note of the third volume. Based on a conversation Hemingway had overheard in a bar between a young man and the woman who was leaving him for another woman, the story strikes many of the motifs that would be part of Hemingway's thinking when he worked on *The Garden of Eden*. Metamorphosis is the keynote of the story. The suntanned young man learns about the change in the "girl" (the narrator's designation is consistent with the practice in "Hills Like White Elephants," tending to make the woman seem vulnerable). But it is the change in the young man that the narrator emphasizes. Befuddled by sexuality, he moves from the desire to murder his competitor to a realization that the girl is caught up in a force that she can't seem to control. He sends her off to her new lover at the story's end, but he knows he will take her back, if indeed she wishes to return.

A book that looks at several women characters with compassion, *Winner Take Nothing* succeeds in placing before the reader some of Hemingway's most vivid female portraits. In addition to the Trudy of "Fathers and Sons," there is the wonderful Madame Fontan of "Wine of Wyoming," whose voice more than any other creates the successful tension with the voice of the narrator and the haunting contrasts of the story. *Winner Take Nothing* also has the lovely voice of the huge whore Alice of "The Light of the World." We know that this story was a favorite of Hemingway's; it is certainly one of which he could be justly proud. In fact, he had wanted to place it first in the collection, but was dissuaded by Maxwell Perkins, who argued that its subject matter would draw the fire of the critics. It is the one story of the volume in which youthful innocence is the hallmark; it is the one story told by an adolescent, in marked contrast to the middle-aged angle of vision that characterizes most of the other stories. The teenager narrator is, presumably, Nick Adams, who recounts a recent excursion with Tom, a slightly older friend.

Although throughout his career Hemingway found Nick Adams an important fictional persona, he approached Nick differently each time, varying his narrative methods and emphases as he considered Nick's experience. Late in life, Hemingway was still trying to get Nick inside a novel. In "The Light of the World," using first-person narration and never using Nick's name, he suggests that Nick is trying, but with mixed success, to deal with a dark and deceitful world by being "tough." The implied narrator looking at events beyond Nick's surface presentation asks the reader to view the story as much more than the unadorned account it might seem to be. The title is the first indication of the complex method. It does not come from the storyteller, but from the author beyond. The title has several analogs that reinforce each other and emphasize the story's complexity. First, the title is scriptural, though even in biblical terms the title has more than one reference. In Matthew 5:14 Jesus declares in the Sermon on the Mount: "Ye are the light of the world. A city that is set on a hill cannot be hid." In John 8:12 Jesus says: "I am the light of the world: he that followeth me shall not walk in darkness, but shall have the light of life." The words were well known to Hemingway. Both verses are oft-quoted portions of the scripture. Hemingway's title is also the title of a popular Protestant hymn by P. P. Bliss, and chances are good that he was familiar with it. He was certainly very familiar with Holman Hunt's painting by that title, a fact that lets us know that Grace Hall Hemingway would read this story somewhat differently if the story had been titled otherwise.[67] Rather than the sentimental version of Jesus in Hunt's picture, Hemingway's story creates the legend of a contemporary Christ figure, a dead boxer. In the words of a peroxide whore: "He was the greatest, finest, whitest, most beautiful man that ever lived, Steve Ketchel, and his own father shot him down like a dog" (295). Finally, the reader will be uncertain of the truth about Ketchel, but the reader will be certain that Ketchel has remained a vital force in the lives of at least two of the women who had known him. His legend lives on.

The analog that Hemingway had identified for the story was Maupassant's "La Maison Tellier."[68] Hemingway's story of an excursion of five whores is a darker tale than Maupassant told, and his title prepares his readers for the difficult challenge of deciphering ambiguous lights and shadows. "The Light of the World" does not begin with the whores but with Nick and Tom in a Michigan saloon, in a setting and atmosphere that owe much to the popular western. Although Hemingway does not mention *Alice in Wonderland,* Lewis Carroll's classic tale also entered into his thinking: the whore who gets Nick's sympathies is named Alice, and Hemingway surrounds her with a baffling world of chimerical vision, from the shimmering dresses of the whores to the inexplicably disappearing but silent Indians who share the train station setting. The reader may credit the shifting details to the inexperience of the first-person narrator, but they are more accurately attributed to the implied, very sophisticated narrator looking over Nick's shoulder.

Either way, Alice (perhaps her real name, perhaps her chosen name) is a memorable character. The largest whore that Nick has ever seen, indeed one of the largest women he has ever seen, Alice is the most attractive character in the story, save only the innocent narrator. Until the reader hears Alice's voice, the several voices of the story are mainly hostile, reflecting a dark world in need of a great deal of light. Accustomed to insults, as the young Nick is not, Alice responds to the insults and aggression around her with laughter, a means for coping that Hemingway increasingly recommended. The narrator keeps reminding us that Alice has a nice voice. One of the challenges of Nick's growing up has been learning which voices to trust. In "The Battler" Nick finds himself knocked off a train he has hopped because he has mistakenly trusted the deceiving voice of the brakeman. Later, he is struck by the smooth, velvety voice of Bugs. At best, Bugs is an ambiguous character. He does save Nick from trouble, but Bugs knows how to use his voice to manipulate his companion. The possibility is real that Bugs has also manipulated Nick. In the dark of future nights, Nick may puzzle over the reliability of the information Bugs has given him.

There is no way for Nick to know, either, if Alice has given him any incorrect information, but his inclination is to trust her. As his friend Tom leads him away from Alice at the end of the story, Nick recalls her voice: "She certainly had a nice voice" (297). It is significant that he bids her good-bye. The reader wants to trust her, too, for like Alice the reader will probably dislike the peroxide whore, who has indulged herself in excessive rhetoric while describing her life and love with Steve Ketchel. The Indians at the station, apparently, never believe that Peroxide has any truth in her speeches, and they walk out in the midst of her high rhetoric. Through Alice, the reader can protest this excess, this playing to an audience. Hemingway's most sensitive characters have always believed that if you talk about a thing, you lose it. Alice makes only the claim of a woman who is good at her work as she describes her relationship with Steve Ketchel: "He said, 'You're a lovely piece, Alice.' That's exactly what he said" (296).

Should we believe this voice? Tom does not pay it much heed, and the cook challenges it. The cook is right that the boxer from Cadillac was *Stanley* Ketchel. Both Peroxide and Alice have confused Stanley and Steve. The older Tom recognizes Nick's inclination to believe Alice and acts to remove Nick from her influence, but Tom misses much. The most important truth about Alice is not her size, her pretty face, or her nice voice. What the pretty face and nice voice signify is a character within, a character that is capable of affection and realistic assessment. Alice makes no pretense to be other than what she is, a prostitute who enjoys men, who wishes to serve them, and who makes no unwarranted claims on them. Probably most prostitutes have a low sense of self-esteem, but Alice emerges as a character with true nobility, one who assesses the world and herself with some accuracy. She has learned to live better in it than do most, the story implies.

Alice's realistic assessment of herself is like that of another of the admirable professionals of *Winner Take Nothing*, Cayetano Ruiz, the wounded gambler of "The Gambler, the Nun, and the Radio." Having endured great pain from the gunshot wound that has left his leg paralyzed, he tells Mr. Frazer, also a patient in the Hailey, Montana, hospital, "I am a cheap card player, only that" (365). Mr. Frazer, a writer who suffers more from "tricky nerves" than from the broken leg that has had to be reset, has great need of the example Ruiz provides, an admirable example of how to live, that recurring concern of Hemingway's fiction: "'I am a poor idealist. I am the victim of illusions.' He laughed, then grinned and tapped his stomach. 'I am a professional gambler but I like to gamble. To really gamble. Little gambling is all crooked. For real gambling you need luck. I have no luck'" (365). Like Mr. Frazer, he waits for his luck to change, for his pain to subside. He does so with stoical dignity (a stoicism that nevertheless permits weeping when the circumstances are right). He manages through a sense of humor (he is a man who laughs and grins), and his wry humor characterizes Hemingway's story. But the story embodies several kinds of humor. The humor results partly from irony of circumstances: the gambler will not reveal the identity of his assailant; the Mexicans summoned to console and comfort Ruiz are the friends of that assailant; Mr. Frazer's doctor, adjusting the patient's bed for a good view of the

world outside the window, overturns the lamp and knocks him uncon-
scious. The humor results especially from the play of the dialogue—as
characters speak beyond the comprehension of a listener or in an open
naiveté that contrasts with the analytical mind of Mr. Frazer, whose
angle of vision controls the story. In the opening scene, the official
interpreter gives highly inaccurate translations of Ruiz's response to the
detective's interrogation. Much of the naiveté comes from the discourse of the nun.

But the nun of Hemingway's story is far more than a source of humor. She is the character in the story who makes things happen; she is
essential to plot and theme. Hemingway's title emphasizes her importance, giving her equal billing with the admirable Ruiz, revealing her
function as transition between Ruiz and the third item of the series,
the radio—an item that checks the emphasis on profession that the first
two items put before us. The nun is interesting as an example of her
profession just as the gambler is important as an example of his. For
Hemingway, professions help define people, as the professionals exemplify their professions admirably or inadequately. The radio of the
title helps to conceal for a time the importance to the story of Mr.
Frazer, the writer who responds sympathetically to the gambler and
the nun, both of whom will help him to return to his work with greater
understanding.

Having experienced the comedy of the dialogue between Ruiz and
the detective in the opening scene of the story, the reader first en-
counters Sister Cecilia in a passage of indirect discourse. Sister Cecilia
brings Mr. Frazer news of Ruiz each morning. The paragraph that reports her news is a conglomeration of many mornings and reflects Mr.
Frazer's pleasure in her talk, which he is pleased to recall. That remembrance reveals several things about the nun. First, much more
than the other characters in the story, she is a talker. She speaks with
energy and speed; words come easily to her. Through them, she is
trying to make the world a better place. She is keenly aware of the pain
of the world; she is most sympathetic to its keenest sufferers. But her
talk is as much to herself as to others, and it spurs her always to action:
"Poor Cayetano, he's having a dreadful time and he doesn't make a
sound. What did they have to shoot him for? Oh, that poor Cayetano!
I'm going right down and pray for him." A one-sentence paragraph
follows the paragraph of indirect discourse, punctuating Cecilia's gen-
uineness: "She went right down and prayed for him" (358).

When the reader next meets Cecilia, the narrator provides an ex-

The 1930s: New Directions

tended scene that confirms the values of the earlier passage. The comedy follows a long section that reveals Mr. Frazer's sleepless night and his attempt to deal with the darkness through the ritualized practice of listening to the radio as his stations move from the Midwest to Seattle, Washington. The nun's brightness and vivacity change the mood dramatically. Notre Dame is playing on the West Coast, and the nun is beside herself with excitement. Mr. Frazer invites her to listen to the game with him on his radio:

> "Oh, no. I couldn't do it. The world series nearly finished me. When the Athletics were at bat I was praying right out loud: 'Oh, Lord, direct their batting eyes! Oh, Lord, may he hit one! Oh, Lord, may he hit safely!' Then when they filled the bases in the third game, you remember, it was too much for me. 'Oh, Lord, may he hit out of the lot! Oh, Lord, may he drive it clean over the fence!' Then you know when the Cardinals would come to bat it was simply dreadful. 'Oh, Lord, may they not see it! Oh, Lord, don't let them even catch a glimpse of it! Oh, Lord, may they fan!' And this game is even worse. It's Notre Dame. Our Lady. No, I'll be in the chapel. For Our Lady. They're playing for Our Lady. I wish you'd write something sometime for Our Lady. You could do it. You know you could do it, Mr. Frazer." (359)

Cecilia yearns for a Notre Dame victory out of loyalty to Our Lady, not from any understanding or appreciation of the game of football. She may know a bit more about baseball than she does about football, but she experiences the game with her emotions, not her mind. Nevertheless, her excitement over this particular game with Southern California is understandable, as most readers of the story in 1933, the year it was published in *Scribner's*, would have recognized. When Notre Dame played at USC on 6 December 1930, the Irish were the defending national champions, going after their nineteenth straight victory. By trouncing the Trojans 27–0, the Irish retained the national title. Although the score at the end of the first quarter was 13–0, not 14–0 as in Hemingway's story, readers would recognize the rhythm of the game. Knute Rockne, Notre Dame's coach, called the game the "greatest" of the year.

Cecilia admits that she always likes the "bad" patients; she is something of a rebel, as Hemingway lets us know in an amusing joke. In the World Series that fall she had cheered for the Athletics and against the Cardinals, preferring Philadelphia, the City of Brotherly Love, over

71

St. Louis, the city of the "Cardinals," who have power over nuns. (Philadelphia won the World Series against St. Louis in 1930, but St. Louis won in 1931 as the two teams faced each other again—an agony Cecilia had yet to face. She would also have to face that year the end of Notre Dame's reign as the monarch of college football. At South Bend on 22 November 1931, a field goal in the last two minutes gave Southern Cal a 16–14 victory and the national championship.) With her World Series prayers answered, she declines the invitation to listen to the Notre Dame game with Mr. Frazer, for a Notre Dame victory would mean even more: "It would be too much for me. No, I'll be in the chapel doing what I can" (360). That is her chief characteristic, doing what she can. So insistent is this theme in the story, one might easily be reminded of a famous story of Mark's Gospel. After certain authorities rebuked the woman who had anointed Jesus' head with precious spikenard ointment, He replied, "Let her alone; why trouble ye her? She hath wrought a good work on me. For ye have the poor with you always, and whensoever ye will ye may do them good: but me ye have not always. She hath done what she could: she is come aforehand to anoint my body to the burying" (Mark 14:6–8). In the context of male treachery, Mark's story interposes the intuitive feeling of the "female," and she is welcomed by the protagonist of Mark's story, just as Ruiz and Frazer admire and respect Cecilia's faith and compassion.

Just as the doctor's good intentions bring a lamp down on Mr. Frazer's head, Cecilia's good efforts can produce ironic results. Believing Ruiz lonely, she brings a party of Mexicans to the hospital to visit the gambler and to play their musical instruments. Their visit is not cheering to Ruiz because the visitors are the friends of the man who shot him. The most objectionable guest at the party is a strident Marxist who is in bitter opposition to Cecilia's church.

The Marxist Mexican wonders if Cecilia is "a little crazy" (362), but it is just that state of "craziness" that helps ally her with the intellectual Mr. Frazer, who is coping with tricky nerves, and not for the first time. She is at one with the Nick Adams of "A Way You'll Never Be" and "Big Two-Hearted River." She is at one with the waiter of "A Clean, Well-Lighted Place" who ponders the world's *nada*. Seeing *nada*, she instinctively pulls in another direction. It is, of course, one of the chief ironies of the story that her sympathy for Ruiz causes her to bring his enemies to the hospital to see him—not once but twice. That is part of the risk of doing what you can, and it is worth noting that Ruiz understands the motivation of her gesture just as Jesus understands the motivation of the woman who anoints him.

Although some readers have found Cecilia's "craziness" off-putting, she brings Mr. Frazer pleasure. "She was very handsome, and Mr. Frazer liked to see her and to hear her talk" (363). The verve of that talk I have already noted. Cecilia has the ability to surprise in her speech, a trait delightful to any writer, one assumes. Mr. Frazer is surprised to hear her say, "This morning I feel as though I might be a saint" (364). Her explanation helps to provide insight into her simplicity and to stir the reader into admiration for her resolve to continue in her religious life:

> "Yes," Sister Cecilia went on. "That's what I wanted to be. A saint. Ever since I was a little girl I've wanted to be a saint. When I was a girl I thought if I renounced the world and went into the convent I would be a saint. That was what I wanted to be and that was what I thought I had to do to be one. I expected I would be a saint. I was absolutely sure I would be one. For just a moment I thought I was one. I was so happy and it seemed so simple and easy. When I awoke in the morning I expected I would be a saint, but I wasn't. I've never become one. I want so to be one. All I want is to be a saint. That is all I've ever wanted. And this morning I feel as though I might be one. Oh, I hope I will get to be one." (364)

Like Alice's voice in "The Light of the World," this voice is memorable. Ruiz, who waits for his luck as a gambler to change, would understand the nun's longing and her determination, even as the thin Mexican, who distrusts all nuns, priests, and monks, would not . understand.

Cecilia has a saint's name, but not the reality of sainthood. That name, like that of Alice, is suggestive, recalling Saint Cecilia's roles as patron saint of music and light-bringer—motifs that merge strongly in the conclusion of the story as the Mexicans return with their musical instruments to play the Cucaracha. If Cecilia meets failure along the way, she does not always recognize the failure. Assuredly, she has her successes as well. Perhaps her pleasure in the phenomenal success of her teams this fall (1930 was indeed her year) has buoyed her confidence about other goals. In doing what she can, the nun sometimes achieves a great deal. Finding Mr. Frazer deeply depressed, even with dismissal from the hospital imminent, she convinces him that seeing

Ruiz would be a good thing. As the two men discuss their pain and the means of coping with it, the nun observes them "happily," and well she might. Mr. Frazer recognizes the kindred spirit and moves beyond his own pain, impressed with the way Ruiz copes with his. Because Mr. Frazer understands the drive of the gambler and the nun, he is led to his deepest thinking, understanding better than he had the nature of opiums and of the political slogans of his own times. "Revolution, Mr. Frazer thought, is no opium. Revolution is a catharsis; an ecstasy which can only be prolonged by tyranny. The opiums are for before and after. He was thinking well, a little too well" (368). Mr. Frazer will not write about Our Lady, but because of his contacts with the gambler and the nun, he will probably write very well about his radio, his newly discovered opium.

Hemingway's longer stories in *Winner Take Nothing* anticipate two of his most famous short stories, the world's biggest dividend from his first safari to Africa. One of them, "The Short Happy Life of Francis Macomber," became the lead story in *The Fifth Column and the First Forty-nine Stories* (1938)—one of the most impressive collections in the history of the short story. "The Snows of Kilimanjaro," the greater of the two, was placed third. The extraordinary fame of these two stories—both long short stories by Hemingway standards—is reflected in their both being made into major motion pictures.

Although Hemingway's African adventure did not produce a novel, it did produce a book—*Green Hills of Africa* (1935). As I have observed, that narrative of the safari was not hailed as a success, and it raised doubts among many observers about Hemingway's career. It should be stated that the African short stories themselves are so good as to answer the charge. If in the 1930s Hemingway was not writing the kind of material a proletariat-oriented intelligentsia wanted, nor novels that were of the stature of *The Sun Also Rises* and *A Farewell to Arms*, he was writing some memorable literature—and he was best during the 1930s in the genre of the short story. The stories that he tried to merge into *To Have and Have Not* (1937) were greater than that novel. So, of course, was *Winner Take Nothing*, a collection that reveals Hemingway's continuing wish not to repeat himself and to continue experimenting with form.

That intention is clearly revealed in the African stories, stories that may profitably be viewed as companion pieces. Their first readers doubtless took them that way. "The Snows of Kilimanjaro" first appeared in the August 1936 issue of *Esquire*. The next month "The

Short Happy Life" appeared in *Cosmopolitan*. In both stories the protagonist dies at the end; both are studies of living and especially of the
act of dying as the quintessence of living. The subjects are as old as
Western thought, and these two stories exemplify many of the traditional motifs in Western art. We can profitably consider the stories with
the paintings of the Western world in mind—an approach especially
appropriate since Hemingway had been greatly influenced by great
painters.[69] (That the protagonist of *Islands in the Stream* is a painter can
hardly be surprising.) We might, for example, think of William Blake's
"The Death of the Good Old Man" and "Death of the Strong Wicked
Man," designs created to illustrate Robert Blair's poem "The Grave."[70]
I do not claim Blake's etchings as Hemingway's inspiration for the African stories; rather, I emphasize the relevance to these stories of this
Western mode of contemplating death.

"The Short Happy Life of Francis Macomber" easily qualifies as a
study of a fortunate death. Hemingway's title appears to play against
Tolstoy's title *The Death of Ivan Ilyich*. (Tolstoy was much on Hemingway's mind as he wrote his African stories.)[71] Hemingway's title makes
clear, however, that he wishes to celebrate the life of Macomber. Macomber's death is, to be sure, a major part of the story. He dies confident in his manhood. His death is clean and neat. The last words
Macomber speaks in the story emphasize the triumph of his life. After
Margot Macomber says, "You've gotten awfully brave, awfully suddenly," her husband replies with "a very hearty laugh": "You know I
*have* . . . I really have" (26). Although his wife suggests that the bravery is "sort of late," Macomber declares, "Not for me." Macomber is
"cheerful" about going into the brush after the wounded bull. He has
discovered the feeling of happiness about action to come, one of the
important motifs of *Green Hills of Africa*.

Usually Hemingway's stories do not deal with the process of decisive
change so much as the fact of that change, which is another way of
saying that "The Short Happy Life" is not a typical Hemingway story.
Its concern with manhood may be familiar to his readers, but his stories
usually present much quieter moments, portraying internal action more
than external action. In "The Short Happy Life," in contrast, physical
action is of the essence. The story falls into several discrete episodes,
and the very words on the page appear to rush the reader on to the
next episode—in contrast to "The Gambler, the Nun, and the Radio,"
in which single line spaces separate the various segments of the story.
Appropriate to the title of the story, speed characterizes the narrative

method. Hemingway has given us other protagonists who like to hunt, but this short story is his only story in which the action of hunting is also the action of the story.

The difference may stem in part from the genesis of the story. Jeffrey Meyers identifies as the germ of the Macomber story a true story of adultery and suicide during a 1908 safari embarked on by John Henry Patterson with Mr. and Mrs. Audley James Blyth.[72] Hemingway was much taken with the history of Patterson and the Blyths. Usually, he started with events closer to his own experience, "The Gambler, the Nun, and the Radio" being typical in this regard: in 1930 Hemingway spent several weeks in a Hailey, Montana, hospital, the consequence of an automobile accident and a broken arm. But his imagination appropriated the Patterson adventure, and he overlaid that scandal with material from his own life. Margot Macomber—one of the most famous of Hemingway's characters and one of the most notorious women of American fiction—owes much to Jane Mason, a beautiful and wealthy resident of Havana, with whom Hemingway had carried on an adulterous romance. Robert Wilson owes something to the husband of Isak Dinesen, Bror von Blixen, who led safaris. Inspired by Hemingway's safari, Jane Mason went lion-hunting with Blixen. Perhaps on some level Hemingway viewed this action as a betrayal of himself. Robert Wilson was also partly based on Philip Percival, the English game hunter who led Hemingway's safari. But Wilson, reflecting Hemingway as well, speaks his favorite lines from *Henry IV, Part 1*. "By my troth, I care not; a man can die but once; we owe God a death and let it go which way it will, he that dies this year is quit for the next" (25).

One might also argue that Hemingway is found mostly in Francis Macomber even though the name *Francis* is a clear hint that the immediate reference is to F. Scott Fitzgerald. Whenever Hemingway wrote about Fitzgerald, he would inevitably write about himself. Fitzgerald was never far from Hemingway's thoughts, especially in the middle and late 1930s—as the African stories emphasize. Hemingway had been dismayed to read Fitzgerald's confessional essay "The Crack-Up" in the February 1936 *Esquire*. Hemingway had always worried about Fitzgerald's masculinity, and he considered Fitzgerald a victim of an emasculating wife. But when Fitzgerald made public his judgment that he had been "only a mediocre caretaker of most of the things left in my hands, even of my talent," Hemingway felt that a fundamental rule had been violated. As Robert Wilson tried to make Macomber realize, there are some things one does not say.

Despite his considerable achievement as a writer in the 1930s, Hemingway feared that he, like Fitzgerald, might not be taking good care of his talent. He was aware that Fitzgerald was battling depression, alcoholism, and writer's block. Having viewed the dramatic decline in Fitzgerald's reputation and promise, Hemingway feared the model. He knew that he was battling some of the same monsters that Fitzgerald was confronting.

Scott Fitzgerald veiled the *Francis* of his name. By American standards it was effete; so he signed himself F. Scott Fitzgerald. But he would have recognized that Hemingway was touching on their relationship when he named the hero of his African story "Francis." Not only does Hemingway boldly display the name in the story's title, but he emphasizes it in the story. The narrator uses the full "Francis Macomber" several times (as we have seen, though Hemingway often uses names sparingly, he sometimes chooses to emphasize them). Although Wilson never addresses Macomber as Francis, Margot does frequently, and in one of her most damaging lines she uses the name to contrast her husband with the professional and brave Wilson. She asks, "How is the beautiful red-faced Mr. Wilson? Are you feeling better, Francis, my pearl?" (9). The pearl is white, lily-livered, she implies. The *Macomber* is obviously Scottish, contrasting with the English *Wilson* just as an Irish *Fitzgerald* would contrast with it. If Hemingway knew that Fitzgerald would be attentive to "The Snows of Kilimanjaro," he surely knew he would catch the more overt allusion in "The Short Happy Life."

The references to Fitzgerald fit nicely Hemingway's preferred mode of operation. He would write about his own demons, but always approach them obliquely. He himself had long feared the power of the emasculating woman. How much more fortunate to die Macomber's death than to "survive" in the condition of Dr. Adams in "The Doctor and the Doctor's Wife." How much more fortunate to die quickly after the blissful discovery of his manhood as Macomber does than to endure the lingering death of an Ivan Ilyich, who also faces the reality of his superficial marriage. Except, of course, one does not necessarily get to choose one's death. It may be lingering, caused accidentally, as Ilyich's is, as Harry's is in "The Snows of Kilimanjaro." Hemingway's African stories warn against death-in-life, and the sequence in which he presented them to us in *The Fifth Column and the First Forty-nine Stories*, with "Snows" following "The Short Happy Life," suggests that the less dramatic, lonelier scenario is more typical.

But the larger statement about living and dying has sometimes been lost, and many readers have judged the story as Hemingway's bitter statement about women. Many have seen Hemingway's view as that of Robert Wilson, who judged American women "the hardest in the world; the hardest, the cruelest, the most predatory and the most attractive and their men have softened or gone to pieces nervously as they have hardened" (9). In a stimulating review of *The Garden of Eden*, E. L. Doctorow pairs Margot Macomber with Frances Clyne of *The Sun Also Rises*, "the kind of women the author has before [*The Garden of Eden*] only detested and condemned."[73] Jeffrey Meyers calls Margot "the real villain" of Hemingway's story. For him she is both betrayer and murderer.[74]

But Hemingway's study of Margot is much more complicated than Doctorow or Meyers allows. "The Short Happy Life of Francis Macomber" is fascinating not only in its fast-paced action (beginning in medias res, its action is contained in a twenty-four hour period), but as a revelation of Hemingway again working toward the new thing. His handling of point of view in this story is different from that in any of his other short stories. Typically, his narrator is very effaced, scarcely allowing himself a judgment. But in "The Short Happy Life" he is but one of several consciousnesses that the reader enters. Since one of those consciousnesses is that of the wounded lion, we may be quite sure that Hemingway the artist has given careful attention to his handling of point of view. An important part of the challenge of the story is that the narrator takes the reader into Macomber's consciousness and especially into Wilson's but never into Margot's. As narrator he is not as detached as the usual Hemingway narrator; he is capable of irony, of sarcasm. He says that the Macombers "had a sound basis of union. Margot was too beautiful for Macomber to divorce her and Macomber had too much money for Margot ever to leave him" (18). It is a cynical view that counts this a "sound" foundation for a marriage. The narrator knows that truth is a complex matter. He knows that the truth about Margot is complicated, and he does extend sympathy toward her, telling us "she had done the best she could for many years back and the way they were together now was no one person's fault" (26). Margot has her side, as the narrator understands even if he does not take us into her consciousness.

Many readers, then, have condemned her unfairly, though over the years Virgil Hutton and a few other critics have come to Margot's defense.[75] The most recent of Margot's attackers is Meyers. After pronouncing the ending of the story "ambiguous," he says that Hemingway "conclusively" resolved the ambiguity. In a 1953 interview Hemingway said, "Francis' wife hates him because he's a coward. But when he gets his guts back, she fears him so much she has to kill him—shoots him in the back of the head."[76] Robert Wilson would have accepted this late reading by Hemingway, made some fifteen and more years after he completed the story. But this was not Hemingway's last word on the matter. In the 1959 "The Art of the Short Story," he takes a different stance: "No. I don't know whether she shot him on purpose any more than you do. I could find out if I asked myself because I invented it and I could go right on inventing. But you have to know where to stop. . . ." The reader will be better advised to trust the tale than the teller, who, after all, liked to tease, even mislead, his readers.[77]

Why did he create an ambiguous ending, as Meyers asserts he did? Was it artistic failure? Or was it because the narrator knew that there was some truth in Robert Wilson's original surmise that Margot "seemed to understand, to realize, to be hurt for [Macomber] and for herself and to know how things really stood" (9)? Wilson reflects about Margot on the morning after he has cuckolded Francis, "What's in her heart God knows" (21). The narrator does let us know Margot's intention when she shoots at the end of the story: "Mrs. Macomber, in the car, had shot at the buffalo with the 6.5 Mannlicher as it seemed about to gore Macomber and had hit her husband about two inches up and a little to one side of the base of his skull" (28). Can the narrator be clearer? Mrs. Macomber shot "at the buffalo." If she wants Francis dead, she need do nothing; the buffalo will do her work for her. But at least a large part of Margot wants Francis alive. The narrator is careful to identify her in the shooting scene as "Mrs. Macomber" and to call Francis "her husband." At this point, these are the identities that the narrator stresses.

Wilson does not, of course, know what the narrator knows and what even Hemingway may have forgotten. Perhaps for his own reasons Wilson is relieved to be able to beat Margot back, as he brutally does. Emphasizing that Margot shoots while she is "in the car," the narrator reminds us of the tangled relationships among this trio, especially of Margot's knowledge that the expedition led by the brave Wilson has not followed all of the rules. Chasing buffalo from cars is illegal; he would lose his license if it were reported. But we also recall Wilson's pleasure in Macomber's transformation. "I'd begun to like your husband" (28), he tells Margot. There is no reason to doubt that he did, but he is certainly missing some of the truth about Margot Macomber at the story's conclusion.

Robert Wilson is the most self-confident character of the story. He is given to broad judgments. And he does know something about handling fear. He believes in courage and admires bravery. But he breaks the rules of his trade when it suits his purpose. He is also an incomplete man—unable to merge his life successfully with that of another person. Throughout the story the narrator reminds us not only of the redness of his face, but also of his "flat, blue eyes." Macomber associates him with a swine. If the story provides abundant evidence of Margot's skill in using cutting words, Wilson's barrage that ends the story shows him equally adept in the art of "bitchery." Furthermore, Wilson can be dead wrong. Before the bull charges in the climactic scene, Wilson had just pronounced the bull dead. The reader should be wary of accepting his verdict about Margot.

In numerous ways, the story invites the reader to ponder Margot's viewpoint. After the incident of the lion, the narrator reports that Macomber "did not know how his wife felt" (18), challenging the reader to try to fathom those feelings. The clues to the feelings are found not only in what Margot says, but in the actions she takes. Wilson finds a keen mind behind her skillful insinuations and cutting remarks, but even the great hunting guide intuits a sensitivity as well: "she seemed a hell of a fine woman. She seemed to understand, to realize, to be hurt for him and for herself and to know how things really stood" (9). Macomber thinks that she is through with him after his disgrace, and her excursion to Wilson's cot that night seems to be an act of punishment. Margot probably did not ponder much the results of that excursion, but her action has important consequences. Macomber becomes angry with both Margot and Wilson. The hatred proves an important ingredient in Macomber's transformation. In the chase for the bulls, Wilson shouts at him not to shoot from the car, and the narrator reports that Macomber "had no fear, only hatred of Wilson" (22). The car stopped, Macomber is quickly out and doing his best shooting, finding the most exhilarating moment of his life. Without Margot's betrayal, could this have happened? Like Macomber, she was victim of the expectations of her class, victim of her great beauty, trapped in a marriage of convenience. Because she is highly intelligent, she wishes for more. On some level, her adultery is not just a punishment but a prod to make Macomber be something else.

Having pushed Macomber to a decisive action, Margot is unprepared for her own feelings, but their expression is completely convincing and serves to emphasize the Macombers' growth. The scene seems worthy of D. H. Lawrence:

"By God, that was a chase," he said. "I've never felt any such feeling. Wasn't it marvellous, Margot?"
"I hated it."
"Why?"
"I hated it," she said bitterly. "I loathed it."
"You know I don't think I'd ever be afraid of anything again," Macomber said to Wilson. "Something happened in me after we saw the buff and started after him. Like a dam bursting. It was pure excitement." (25)

Margot is barred from the exhilaration, but something has happened to her too. Certainly, life with this man Francis is going to be different from her life with the boy Francis. Great change requires great adjustment. Margot is fearful, but not because she fears Macomber will leave her. Certainly, we find him here reaching out to her. Shaken, when the buffalo attacks Macomber she again takes an instinctive action, an action to save her husband, as the narrative stance emphasizes. She misses her intended target, and as the story ends we see her as the victim of a hunting accident, crouched and crying in the corner of the car.

There is, then, a memorable ambiguity at the end of "The Short Happy Life of Francis Macomber." Francis has died in the moment of his triumph, happiness at last his; furthermore, he is never to be tested further. *His* dying has been very easy. But Wilson does not take any consolation from the fine lines from *Henry IV, Part 1*, and the fact that the cowardly Falstaff speaks them may be culminating irony. The aftermath to a death can be immensely painful, and the truthful narrator lets the reader see more than Wilson does.

"The Snows of Kilimanjaro" is a study in a different kind of death. If "The Short Happy Life of Francis Macomber" shows us Hemingway writing a very different kind of story from any he had previously attempted, so does "The Snows of Kilimanjaro." Whereas the Macomber story is fast-paced and teeming with physical action, "The Snows" is a static piece, a single scene really, though in present time both stories are confined to something like a twenty-four hour period. "The Snows" emphasizes thought, perhaps because the protagonist of the story, on his deathbed, can no longer avoid thinking. Ironically, the end result of this African hunt has been reflection and judgment— something the African safari had been designed to keep at a distance. Numerous Hemingway protagonists have tried to refrain from thinking, or have rigidly controlled the direction of that thinking, as Nick

Adams does in "Big Two-Hearted River." On his hospital bed, Mr. Frazer has had to give time to thinking. In "The Snows" Hemingway lets thinking and memory serve as the story. As we have seen, thinking and reflection account for most of "Fathers and Sons," but there the thinking demonstrates confidence and measures gains and reflects fruition.

The epigraph of "The Snows" helps to prepare the reader for a story in which thinking and analysis are stressed. Hemingway invented an epigraph for the title page of *Winner Take Nothing,* but he had not used one previously for a story. He knew from his reading of T. S. Eliot that the device could serve useful purposes, and in this story Hemingway approaches Eliotic material. Surely, the great African stories show Hemingway like John Webster and John Donne, who, as Eliot cites in "Whispers of Immortality," were "much possessed by death." "The Snows" is a meditation on death, and it strikes us both by its catalogs of memory, so representative of Hemingway's desire to distill experience into a paragraph, and by the power of its images. The epigraph helps prepare us for the great visual power of the story that follows. It also prepares us for the breaks of the segmented parts, for the italicized sections of memory and the purposeful use of white space common to poetry.

The images of the story have ample counterparts in Western art. I have already recalled two etchings by William Blake. We might go back much earlier than Blake. A woodcut in the 1470 *Art of Dying Well* shows the good man dying on his deathbed. A ministering woman—his wife, probably—sits at the side of the bed. At the bottom of the bed and across the lower part of the woodcut, monstrous-looking creatures of sin and temptation wait to pull the dying man down. But his conscience sits on his shoulder, looking upward at a band of angels. The good man on his death-bed will find succor and his release in that other good man, who is nailed to a cross, set off by white space and a company of adoring saints who have followed him. To look at an example of a similar work later than Blake, one might consider the painting of the American John McGrady, *Swing Low, Sweet Chariot.* Here the dying good man is a rural Southern black, but the symbolism is much the same as that of the medieval woodcut.[78]

Although Hemingway provides his dying protagonist with many details for a precise biography, one that provides variations on several of the episodes of his own life, "The Snows" has the numerous allegorical dimensions of such paintings. Hemingway had originally named his protagonist Henry Walden, but he dropped the too-obvious reference to Thoreau for a simpler *Harry*, last name unspecified. The simple *Harry* is sexually appropriate to the self-indictment of the protagonist, who faults himself for having "sold vitality" (45), and the name increases the allegorical suggestion of the story.

The major allegorical dimension of the story is that of death—a force that most easily invites the form of the allegory. It is visualized for us in the opening image of the story, the birds of prey. The hyena that slinks around the camp is companion to the mysterious force that Harry is preparing to confront: "It came with a rush; not as a rush of water nor of wind; but of a sudden evil-smelling emptiness and the odd thing was that the hyena slipped lightly along the edge of it" (47). Later, looking at his wife's pleasant smile, "he felt death come again. This time there was no rush. It was a puff, as of a wind that makes a candle flicker and the flame go tall" (49–50). Death as an allegorical figure becomes palpable as Hemingway describes in some detail Harry's death:

> . . . just then, death had come and rested its head on the foot of the cot and he could smell its breath.
>
> "Never believe any of that about a scythe and a skull," he told her. "It can be two bicycle policemen as easily, or be a bird. Or it can have a wide snout like a hyena."
>
> It had moved up on him now, but it had no shape any more. It simply occupied space.
>
> "Tell it to go away."
>
> It did not go away but moved a little closer.
>
> "You've got a hell of a breath," he told it. "You stinking bastard."
>
> It moved up closer to him still and now he could not speak to it, and when it saw he could not speak it came a little closer, and now he tried to send it away without speaking, but it moved in on him so its weight was all upon his chest, and while it crouched there and he could not move, or speak, he heard the woman say, "Bwana is asleep now. Take the cot up very gently and carry it into the tent."
>
> He could not speak to tell her to make it go away and it crouched now, heavier, so he could not breathe. And then, while they lifted the cot, suddenly it was all right and the weight went from his chest. (54)

Numerous renditions of the moment of death show the dying person contending with demons and drawing on the best spiritual resources, and Hemingway's story is structured with a similar tension. The epigraph presents a compact allegory of the story in its vision of the leopard who has inexplicably climbed into the snowy heights of Africa's highest mountain, its western summit called "the House of God." From this loftiness, the story alternates between sections focusing on the present rottenness (literal and figurative, as Harry, dying of gangrene that resulted from careless inattention to a minor scratch, abuses his wife with cruel words, more to entertain himself than to make her suffer) and italicized sections of precise and clear memories. The italicized sections make clear what a rich reservoir Harry's memory is, his keen ability to respond to life, the glory of his gift. "*He had seen the world change; not just the events*" (49). Although he had not written it, he was well-equipped to portray life in our time.

If "The Short Happy Life of Francis Macomber" lets the reader see a woman skilled at verbal insult, "The Snows" portrays male bitchery. Harry's wife tries valiantly to ease his pain, to make their conversation pleasant, but she must endure a great deal from him. He calls her a "bloody fool" (40), he taunts her for her "bloody money" (41), and, at the end of the first section of the story, he tells here that he does not love her and that he never has. Like Harold Krebs of "Soldier's Home," he will later retract his denial of love, and like Harold he is not truthful in the retraction.

Why does this "comforting" wife suffer so greatly? Not, it is clear, because she deserves to, and the dying Harry knows that she does not deserve the ill-treatment he heaps upon her. Many readers have found it easy to dislike Margot Macomber, but Harry's wife has not elicited anything like the interest that Margot has, nor the sympathy she might warrant. Indeed, in recent years Margot has probably received a good deal more sympathy. In the companion African stories, where the principle of contrast is so important, the "good" wife of the one story is a foil to the "bad" wife of the other.

Margot Macomber's individuality is stressed in many ways—in her accent, in the frequent use of her name, in her active role (she makes things happen). In Harry's wife, Hemingway is presenting a different kind of woman. She admonishes that Harry should not drink, that he should not give up hope, that he should be kind to her. She is the compliable woman. What Harry wants to do, she will do. She is responsive in bed; she has learned to hunt—save for Harry's accident, she has been happy in Africa. She is happy to be with Harry. He is the center of her life. But although she speaks many lines in the story, only once does her language show any daring. "'If you have to go away,' she said, 'is it absolutely necessary to kill off everything you leave behind? I mean do you have to take away everything? Do you have to kill your horse, and your wife and burn your saddle and your armour?'" (43).

Although "The Short Happy Life" reminds the reader frequently that Francis and Margot are man and wife, the speech just quoted contains the only use of the word *wife* in "The Snows." Certainly, the marriage of "The Snows" is not a marriage of true minds, though it is probably legally sanctioned. The narrator uses Harry's name, and the wife uses it frequently in addressing him. Harry, however, never uses the wife's name, and the narrator habitually calls her "the woman." The narrative stance emphasizes that she does not mean much to Harry. She is a companion, an object (and Harry lets her know that for him she serves as sex object, as end rather than as inspiration or soul mate). Harry feels himself a kept man, not a husband, and that is the emotional truth of their relationship though not the legal truth.

The narrator lets us know that this wife has had a difficult life in many ways. She had lost her first husband while she was still a comparatively young woman. For a time she gave her attention to her two just-grown children, but they did not need her. Without direction, she consoled herself with drink, then with a series of lovers, until she found Harry, who again made her life worthwhile. But she is most pitiable in the story because she is dull. As Harry lies dying, he reflects that if it gets no worse he can manage, "except that he would rather be in better company" (53). Harry, be it remembered, has taken Scott Fitzgerald's province as his own, and as a spy in their country he had planned to write about the very rich. Through his wife and her circle, he has learned that "the rich were dull and they drank too much, or they played too much backgammon. They were dull and they were repetitious" (53). Just before Harry feels the final approach of Death, he summarizes his condition, using an image from *The Great Gatsby* that the reader will recognize: "The party's over and you are with your hostess now" (54). His hostess is the story's principal means of portraying the dullness of the rich. If Harry has been cruel to her, he has been so to relieve his boredom with her.

Despicable in many ways, Harry would seem to be exemplar of the bad man on his deathbed. Certainly his death is harder than Francis Macomber's, but Hemingway grants Harry the grace of a good, even an exceptional death. We sense it in the ending of the portrayal of allegorized Death completing its work: "suddenly it was all right and the weight went from his chest" (54). The alternating sections would lead the reader to expect that the next section would be italicized, but Hemingway breaks the pattern, retaining Roman type as Harry is granted transcendent glory—the buzzards of prey that opened the story give way to the airplane, the band of angels, so to speak, that will carry Harry to Kilimanjaro, to "the House of God."

Earl Rovit and Gerry Brenner discuss this surprise section as a "trick," and they rightly point to Ambrose Bierce's "An Occurrence at Owl Creek Bridge" as a progenitor.[79] But by breaking the alternation of Roman section (time present) and italicized section (memory), Hemingway signals a major transition in the story—the moment of astonishing transcendence, parallelling Macomber's discovery of manhood and happiness. Although the reader at first believes that the section relates events in the world rather than in Harry's mind, the passage has several hints before the powerful reference to Kilimanjaro and Harry's destination. Hemingway describes carefully the ascent of the airplane, its swinging low like the chariot of the spiritual, before its smooth landing, and the appearance of the pilot come to take Harry home. The pilot is not dressed as a pilot, but as some sort of friendly guide, some beneficent Charon. Dressed comfortably in slacks, a tweed jacket, and a brown felt hat, the pilot is known to Harry. Harry recognizes him as "old Compton," though the reader recognizes an embodiment of Grandfather Death. Compton's manner is cheery, as Hemingway emphasizes. "What's the matter, old cock?" (55) Compton asks, his address reassuring to Harry's pride in his sexual prowess, his vitality. "There's only room for one" (55), he says in a line that could hardly be more allegorical. Often portrayed in literature as a gentleman, Death is to be treated with utmost respect. Harry at first offers Compton breakfast, then is concerned that Compton take tea. As "Compie" gets Harry into the plane, he is efficient and gracious, always concerned for the comfort of his passenger.

One of the most striking elements in this astonishing section is in the role of the woman. The narrator lets no worrying or gently nagging voice break the genteel aura. As we have noted, in this story Harry never addresses his companion by name; he never addresses her with any endearing substitute. But the woman in this vision at last has a name. Rovit and Brenner, like other critics, have assumed that the Helen of this section is the rich wife from the safari. But we know that in earlier days Harry has looked in vain to regain his first great love, always looking for her double. "*How when he thought he saw her outside the Regence one time it made him go all faint and sick inside, and that he would follow a woman who looked like her in some way, along the Boulevard, afraid to see it was not she, afraid to lose the feeling it gave him*" (48). The use of the name *Helen* in this Bierce-like section may well signal that Harry in death reclaims that earlier woman, the Helen of his life. Hemingway plays with doubles in much of his fiction. "The Snows" and "The Short Happy Life" are obvious instances, but the alternating sections of "Snows" emphasize their role in that story. The pairing of the two women is also a part of the technique.

Like many other male writers, including Poe and Fitzgerald, Hemingway was attracted to the name *Helen* for its classical associations. Helen signifies idealized beauty. It was the name Hemingway gave Nick Adams's first wife; it was also the name of Krebs's favorite sister in "Soldier's Home." In this story, in which snow is an important motif, we may be reminded of "Babylon Revisited," one of Fitzgerald's most moving stories. In that story Charley Wales's wife, Helen, has died, a casualty of the vast carelessness of their time and class, but she is much remembered as he returns to Paris, reassessing the snows of yesteryears. Hemingway may have had Fitzgerald's story, first published in 1931, in the corner of his mind as he wrote "The Snows." Harry's life in Paris and the loss of his wife are among the haunting memories that he has to fault himself for not writing about.

That the woman of the penultimate section of "The Snows of Kilimanjaro" is not the woman of the safari seems clear in the final section of the story. Just as "The Short Happy Life" ends with our attention focused on the wife of the dead man, so does "The Snows of Kilimanjaro." The narrator calls her "the woman." She is awakened from her sleep by "a strange, human, almost crying sound" (56). Her dreaming had taken her back to yesteryears as well. It was the night of her daughter's debut. Somehow the woman's father was also there, and he has been rude to her—a convincing transferral in light of the treatment she has had from Harry this day. She seems more a victim of her class than ever, ill-equipped for the reality of the death before her. She cannot look at Harry's leg, which has come undressed. Her last words parallel the helplessness of Margot, and she utters the *please* that was so satisfying to Wilson. "Harry! Please, Oh Harry!" (56)

What does Hemingway achieve in this double ending? In giving Harry a death with a large measure of grace, Hemingway raises the question of Harry's ultimate worth. There is grace in Harry's death in part because he has been a stern judge of himself. If he has many faults, no one is more aware of those faults than he. While his wife is off shooting, he thinks:

> She shot very well this good, this rich bitch, this kindly caretaker and destroyer of his talent. Nonsense. He had destroyed his talent himself. Why should he blame this woman because she kept him well? He had destroyed his talent by not using it, by betrayals of himself and what he believed in, by drinking so much that he blunted the edge of his perceptions, by laziness, by sloth, by snobbery, by pride and by prejudice, by hook and by crook. (45)

Harry's defects also reveal his strengths. His verbal abuse of his wife springs from his revolt against the boring. Harry is above all a person of imagination. As a writer, his goal is very high. He contemplates demanding tasks: "it seemed as though it telescoped so that you might put it all into one paragraph if you could get it right" (50). A failure in so many ways, Harry nevertheless has hold of the redeeming idea. Writing is for him the ultimate pull toward life. Following his mental recapturing of his first marriage, he says, "I want to write" (49), and just before his death he has indeed been writing. How much we cannot say, but the idea redeems.

The final section pulls us back the other way and will not let us sentimentalize Harry's death or overlook his shortcomings. His smell is rank. We are reminded of his weakness in choosing this wife for the wrong reasons, though we commend the honesty that will not let him lay the blame for his failure on his wife. He has written on this last day of his life, but surely not a great deal. His gift will never be shared with the world. The reader knows that Harry has failed the duty he believes his talent placed upon him. On a biographical level, "The Snows" was Hemingway's warning voice to himself. He recognized it also as the greater of the African stories.

# The Stories of the
# Spanish Civil War

In 1938, when Hemingway reflected on his achievement in the short story for *The Fifth Column and the First Forty-nine Stories*, most of his "favorites" (these included "The Short Happy Life of Francis Macomber," "The Snows of Kilimanjaro," "A Way You'll Never Be," "A Clean, Well-Lighted Place," and "The Light of the World") were stories of the decade that had not yet ended—a decade that he could count as major for his contributions to the short story. Indeed, before the 1930s ended, he had made a good beginning on his promise to give readers another twenty-five short stories. If "The Snows of Kilimanjaro" were written in part as self-admonishment, Hemingway had good reason to judge that he was heeding the admonishment. On 7 February 1939 he wrote to Max Perkins with preliminary plans for another collection of stories. Three of them—"The Denunciation," "The Butterfly and the Tank," and "Night Before Battle"—had already been published in *Esquire*. "Nobody Ever Dies" was scheduled for March publication in *Cosmopolitan*, he advised Perkins. (In October *Cosmopolitan* would also publish Hemingway's "Under the Ridge.") Hemingway told Perkins that he had another story completed, "Landscape with Figures," that he had not yet sent out. "I know how to work," he told his editor, and he proceeded to mention three "very long" stories he wanted to write, one of which eventually became *The Old Man and the Sea*.[80]

For Hemingway, getting the work done was indeed a constant goad. The 1930s would end with his intense drive to complete *For Whom the Bell Tolls*, his novel set during the Spanish Civil War. That work was his longest novel; in it he again set new artistic challenges for himself. For this war novel, he did not need the long gestation that *A Farewell to Arms* had required. It was ready for publication soon after the end of the Spanish Civil War. For the purposes of this study, however, it is necessary to emphasize Hemingway's extraordinary contribution to the short story in the decade, an achievement sometimes slighted in the light of his triumphant return to the novel. It has been slighted also because the short story project he had envisioned and had explored with Perkins was not realized, though after Hemingway's death it would have partial fulfillment when Scribner's published *The Fifth Column and Four Stories of the Spanish Civil War* (1969). Although publishing the previously uncollected stories with the play was a useful service to readers, the collection did not include "Landscape with Figures," also a story of the Spanish conflict, nor "Nobody Ever Dies," which though not set in Spain has a male veteran protagonist who has just returned to Cuba after fighting in the Spanish war. Had those stories been published together, perhaps with "Old Man at the Bridge," the public would have had a stronger sense of Hemingway's continuing interest in the short story—and a stronger sense of his achievement in the genre during the 1930s.

In *Green Hills of Africa* Hemingway declared that a writer who had experienced war had an advantage over other writers. Furthermore, he thought civil war the "best" type of war, "the most complete" (*GHOA* 70–71). Not too long after Hemingway made that declaration, he would have his own opportunity to study this "best" circumstance, and the short story would be a means for his portrayal of a civil war possessing profound international implications that heightened its value as a subject. Hemingway had found the short story his first appropriate means for using his World War I experience. (He did not use his World War I experience in a novel until several years afterward.) With the Spanish conflict, there would be a much greater sense of immediate use of the material, and the short stories he wrote about it bear little resemblance to the World War I stories. The Spanish short stories make a more direct use of events in Hemingway's life, and the prose is not as suggestive as that of his more imagistic stories about World War I. One important reason for the difference is that he was developing plans concurrently for an ambitious novel about the Spanish Civil War—*For Whom the Bell Tolls*. His hardest concentration went into the novel, and the Spanish stories were partly a warm-up for that work. By contrast, when Hemingway wrote the stories of *In Our Time*, those stories absorbed virtually all of his creative effort.

The first of the Spanish stories to be written was "Old Man at the Bridge"; originally a news dispatch, it appeared in 1938 as one of the first forty-nine stories. It recalls Hemingway's ability during the Greco-Turkish war to capture human emotions while describing war and destruction. The first-person narrator speaks to an old man who sits at the side of the road near a bridge while refugees march across. The old man is too tired to cross, and the narrator questions him about his inaction since the Fascists are advancing toward the Ebro. The old man had been taking care of the animals, but that duty taken from him, he has lapsed into lassitude. The best efforts of the narrator are to no avail, and the narrator looks with pity toward the old man: "It was a gray overcast day with a low ceiling so their [the Fascists'] planes were not up. That and the fact that cats know how to look after themselves was all the good luck that the old man would ever have" (58). Brief as this vignette is, it is considerably longer than the vignettes that became the interchapters of *In Our Time*. It signals how vastly different the stories of the Spanish Civil War would be from Hemingway's earlier war stories.

Each of the Spanish stories, like "Old Man at the Bridge," is a first-person story. The narrator is identified in three stories as Edwin Henry. As he so often does, Hemingway plays with his protagonist's name. In "The Butterfly and the Tank" the narrator is unnamed, but circumstances of profession and tone ally him with the "I" of the other stories. Some readers have taken the address of the Greek known as John in "The Denunciation" as accurate. He calls the narrator Mr. "Emmunds," but John speaks broken English, which helps add color to the story. He is probably giving his version of "Edwin." Two Spaniards in the same story call the narrator "Enrique," which translates as Henry—like Edwin, also a first name. In "Night Before Battle," where the narrator's last name, Henry, is specified, the tankman Al Wagner addresses him in a private moment as "Hank." Clearly, Hemingway was requiring that his readers look carefully at this protagonist—and that through his handling of his name we be reminded of his fine art of concealment. Readers have been quick to note that Edwin Henry carries the same initials as Ernest Hemingway; moreover, that Henry has the same last name as the protagonist of *A Farewell to Arms*. Like Hemingway, Edwin Henry is an American writer, committed to the Loyalist cause, present in Spain for the purpose of filming the conflict. He is present, then, for the purpose of seeing. True, his work may prove useful for molding public opinion and promoting specific actions, but as "Old Man at the Bridge" anticipates, this writer is interested in showing several faces of war. He is not the calloused or uncommitted observer he at first seems in "The Denunciation."

Although Hemingway shows us several dimensions of the character Edwin Henry, Hemingway's depiction of Henry is not nearly so important or problematic as the cumulative effect of the many stories that create Nick Adams. When Hemingway returned to Nick, he would inevitably show us something of Nick's shocked innocence and vulnerability. Nick's inability to handle tough circumstances or his difficulty with them was usually what interested Hemingway in that persona. We are not invited to view Edwin Henry in those ways, however. We see Henry as a man experienced in his art, and mature and realistic about war and the affairs between men and women. Because a good deal of the narrator's sensitivity to the human condition that we find in "Old Man at the Bridge" is part of Edwin Henry in the other stories, we are sympathetic to him, but his mysteries do not become ours, as Nick Adams's mysteries usually do. That may account for the failure of these stories to move us as deeply as the more suggestive Nick Adams stories do. Nevertheless, there is much to admire in the Spanish Civil War stories as we experience a variety of events that show us several aspects of war.

Compared to most of Hemingway's other stories, the Spanish stories are very crowded, embodying anything but the simplicity of "Old Man at the Bridge." The major setting for two of the stories is Chicote's bar. Edwin Henry and his friends like to gather at Chicote's, formerly "one of the best bars in the world" (420). Because of the war the good liquor is all gone, but despite the war Chicote's retains some of its old character and is usually a cheerful place; the noisy conversations there reflect a diverse and discriminating clientele.

Almost all of the action of "The Denunciation" takes place at Chicote's; indeed, the story is something of a paean to it. The story harkens back to the mood and theme of Fitzgerald's "Babylon Revisited" since both stories recall the happier days of the bars and the happier days of a culture, and both portray barmen who help "make a place" (420). The great change at Chicote's occurs not just because the country is at war, but because its war is a civil war. Previously, Chicote's was like a club where customers gathered to talk about many subjects, though not often about politics. Now politics is under the surface of almost every conversation at Chicote's, and the drama of the story occurs because a former patron (a Fascist in the strife) and friend of Edwin Henry risks coming to Chicote's for the sake of old times. The narrator admires the gambling instinct of Luis Delgado, but he understands the Loyalist commitment of the waiter who feels compelled to notify the authorities of Delgado's whereabouts. The narrator abets the waiter's plan, he confesses, "in one of those excesses of impartiality, righteousness and Pontius Pilatry, and the always-dirty desire to see how people act under an emotional conflict, that makes writers such attractive friends" (426). The story ends with the narrator's calling Delgado's captor to request that Delgado be told that Henry, not the waiter, reported him. Our "hardened" narrator is paying tribute to the old idea of communality at Chicote's. Hemingway's "wow"—his prescribed method for ending a story—is sinisterly ironic.

Little of the former quality of Chicote's is evident in "The Butterfly and the Tank." The stage is congested, noisy, and unpleasant. Outside it is raining, and the narrator, world-weary and war-weary, seeks brief respite from the arena of death. Almost immediately he wishes he had not stopped at the bar, his feeling about the atmosphere caught in his response to an unattractive woman and her companion who are seated near him: "Life is very short and ugly women are very long and sitting there at the table I decided that even though I was a writer and supposed to have an insatiable curiosity about all sorts of people, I did not really care to know whether these two were married, or what they saw in each other, or what their politics were, or whether he had a little money, or she had a little money, or anything about them" (430).[81] But the writer will be aroused before this evening is over, as the strain caused by the war overrides all other concerns.

A young Spaniard, seeking a touch of prewar gaiety, begins spraying people with perfume from his flit gun. But his joke backfires and some soldiers beat "the flit king" and one shoots him dead. Now the narrator thinks he has found a story. Although "the forceful girl" advises him not to tell the story because it might seem prejudicial to the Loyalist cause, the narrator thinks that the "comedy" has a real point to it. He believes that it is not his function to write stories that invite political responses, but rather to tell the whole truth. The narrator does, in fact, tell the story back at the Hotel Florida, and to good response. Chicote's manager urges him to write it and to call it "The Butterfly and the Tank." In the final paragraph of the story, "on that bright cheerful morning" Chicote's becomes more like it used to be, and the narrator reveals his compassion as well as his understanding: "I took a sip of the gin and tonic water and looked out the sandbagged window and thought of the wife kneeling there and saying, 'Pedro. *Pedro,* who has done this to thee, Pedro?' And I thought that the police would never be able to tell her that even if they had the name of the man who pulled the trigger" (436).

"Night Before Battle" takes the reader close to the battlefield, close to the war that lurks behind the scenes of "The Denunciation" and

"The Butterfly and the Tank." Edwin Henry's role as part of the team seeking to capture on film "the very shape of battle" provides the opening motif of the story. It has been difficult for the crew to get the camera close enough to the fighting, and Henry laments the failure of the Loyalist offensive as well as the failure of the crew to "get the shape of the battle." But Henry's craft, as we have seen, is not first as filmmaker. He is a writer, and through conversation, through words, he succeeds in taking his readers close to some grim battle scenes involving both tank and air warfare. His method is to work by indirection as he lets us listen to conversations with Al Wagner, an American tankman, and Baldy Jackson, an American pilot who has had to parachute from his burning airplane. "Night Before Battle," one of the longest short stories in the Hemingway canon (with a large cast of characters), is easily the longest of the Spanish war stories. What is surprising given the length is that it is a story almost exclusively of talk—the talk of an evening and night before battle.

Waiting is one of the primary actions of war. One way of dealing with the waiting is through talk. Often the Hemingway protagonist eschews talking about what is worrying him, but talking in "Night Before Battle" serves a decided therapeutic value for Al Wagner, who faces overwhelming odds in the battle of the next day—and knows it. Furthermore, the talking is also a means of conveying duration, and the story attempts to give the feel of a night's duration, much as Eugene O'Neill attempted to do in his play *Hughie* (1958). Al Wagner commands outmoded tanks and only a few capable helpers; he judges the other tankmen as at best only well-meaning. "I know what I'm fighting for and I'm not worried. But I'd like things to be efficient and used as intelligently as possible" (445), he tells Edwin Henry. His situation is, of course, very similar to that of Robert Jordan, the protagonist of *For Whom the Bell Tolls*, though Jordan did not have anyone like Henry with whom to talk.

Chicote's frames the best talking of the story, and the reader feels it to be a version of "a clean, well-lighted place." Although Al and Henry indeed talk of politics, the atmosphere (especially the respectful waiters) provides the right circumstances for the drinking and the conversation. The challenge to Al is "not to talk too wet about getting killed" (445).

The privacy of Chicote's contrasts markedly with the scene in Henry's room at the Hotel Florida, where men and women gather to drink, to gamble, and sometimes to take a bath. Edwin Henry resembles Jay

Gatsby at one of his parties when he and Al join the party in progress. One of the crapshooters asks him, "You haven't seen this guy Henry around that owns the place, have you?" (448). Like Delgado of "The Denunciation," Al is also an unlucky gambler, as he later reports to Henry as they meet for dinner at the Gran Via restaurant. The Gran Via understandably has bad food and mainly bad wine, and unsympathetic waiters again make the reader mindful of the ideal of Chicote's.

That ideal provides Hemingway with an appropriate way to close his story. From their dinner, Henry and Al do not return to Chicote's, but go back to the Hotel Florida, where they meet a very drunk and very verbose Baldy in the elevator. With Baldy in Henry's room, there is plenty of "wet talking." In the vignettes of *In Our Time* Hemingway had portrayed the part liquor plays in dealing with war, especially the waiting before battle, but he had not portrayed liquor as a means of dealing with the aftermath—as he does here through Baldy's account. Listening to Baldy, Al Wagner regains his perspective and declares his intention of returning to his room for some sleep in the remaining few hours before battle.

> "See you tomorrow night at Chicote's," I said.
> "That's right," he said, and wouldn't look me in the eye. "See you tomorrow night at Chicote's."
> "What time?"
> "Listen, that's enough," he said. "Tomorrow night at Chicote's. We don't have to go into the time." And he went out. (459)

The promise is like Robert Jordan's promise to Maria at the end of *For Whom the Bell Tolls*. Henry, of course, understands and respects both Wagner and Baldy.

The compassionate eye of the narrator—and the necessity that his eye capture accurately every aspect of the war—governs "Under the Ridge," which takes the reader to a failed artillery tank offensive. Edwin Henry chooses to begin his account during the retreat from the failed battle. He himself is, at least for that day, free from the ominous sense that haunted Al Wagner. On "a sudden distrust" he had moved the cameras from their location. When the shelling justifies his instinct, he feels confident about that day, but his writer's instincts are sharp for the sights about him and for the conversation about him. Although he realizes that the Loyalist government would wish him not to report everything he sees and hears, the first-person narrative is itself his resolution to be an accurate camera, a truthful writer. The most haunting parts of his account concern the executions of Loyalists by Loyalists. Edwin Henry is moved by the story of the young boy Paco. After Paco had attempted to avoid battle by shooting himself in the hand, the Loyalists gently nursed him back to recovery and reformation, but then shot him as an example. The Frenchman who walks out of the battle to make his separate peace walks to his execution—not from fear, but simply because he sees "clearly the stupidity of dying in an unsuccessful attack" (465). Although Henry cannot write about these events now, the story ends with the general's passionately urging him to "write it all afterwards" (469).

Curiously, the fifth short story about the Spanish Civil War, "Landscape with Figures," did not make its way into the 1969 volume. Hemingway, though he had not yet sent the story out to a magazine, had let Perkins know in 1939 that it was ready for publication with the other stories. Hemingway's plan would have placed it last in the book, right after "Nobody Ever Dies"—his intention being, apparently, to move the reader gradually to scenes of actual battle.

Hemingway's title is splendidly appropriate to his method of showing the reader actual battle. Its referent is the art of painting (one of Hemingway's characteristic ways of observing a scene) rather than the art form of the cinema, the endeavor that engages Edwin Henry. Because the film crew captures panoramic scenes, the notion of landscape has appropriateness, but it also assumes an ironic edge: the carnage is the opposite of the pastoral or romantically grand. As in the other Spanish stories, the principle of contrast governs Hemingway's writing. The Spanish sequence takes us gradually into battle, but Hemingway varies tone and staging arrangements in each of the stories.

"Landscape with Figures" emphasizes another aspect of Henry's character—his ability to make jokes as a means of surviving the stress of war, a trait suggested but not underscored in the other stories. The desire for the joke, we recall, had not served the flit king well in "The Butterfly and the Tank." But Hemingway had insisted on the value of the joke to his own life, and he ends his portrait of Pascin in *A Moveable Feast* declaring: "They say the seeds of what we will do are in all of us, but it always seemed to me that in those who make jokes in life the seeds are covered with better soil and with a higher grade of manure" (*MF* 104). A joke Henry plays on the Spaniard Johnny who is working on the film is one of the inciting incidents of "Landscape with

Figures," but Henry's portrayal of events also exemplifies his belief in the joke.

"Landscape with Figures" is also different from the other Spanish Civil War stories because one of its central figures is a woman. Brief portrayal of Pedro's wife added to the effective conclusion of "The Butterfly and the Tank," and "the forceful girl" was useful for creating the changed atmosphere at Chicote's. The sexually provocative Manolita is present at Henry's room in "Night Before Battle" to make clear that sexual intercourse will not be one of the opiums Al Wagner chooses that night. Mainly, war stories provide limited opportunity for female characterizations. But a woman turns out to be especially useful in creating the major dramatic impact of "Landscape with Figures."

Close friend of Henry and his film crew, an American woman journalist finds that her hotel room increasingly serves as a gathering place for kindred spirits; it is affectionately known as the Club. We see her as kin to Dorothy Bridges of *The Fifth Column* and to Martha Gellhorn. What strikes us about her in the story is her great intelligence and sensitivity. Edwin Henry as character calls her "daughter"; as narrator he typically addresses her as "the American girl" or, more simply, as "the girl." We learn her name, Elizabeth, only when another character addresses her. She is different from "the girl" of "Hills Like White Elephants," however. Hemingway emphasizes not her vulnerability, but her professional curiosity and intelligence: "So that's war. That's what I've come here to see and write about" (595). Although the narrator, who has filmed many battles, describes the scene that is the landscape of the title, it is through the emotional impact of the "landscape" on Elizabeth that the reader sees; the difference between Henry's experience and her inexperience is crystallized by her reaction.

> The girl held the field glasses to her eyes. Then she put them down.
> "I can't see any more," she said. The tears were running down her cheeks and her face was working. I had never seen her cry before and we had seen many things you could cry about if you were going to cry. In a war everybody of all ranks including generals cries at some time or another. This is true, no matter what people tell you, but it is to be avoided, and is avoided, and I had not seen this girl doing it before.
> "And that's an attack?"
> "That's an attack," I said. "Now you've seen one." (593)

Henry is, of course, instructing the reader as well as Elizabeth. The other stories downplay Henry's role as instructor or authority. In "Night Before Battle," for example, he listens to Al Wagner as a sympathetic, if knowing, equal. A part of the humor of "Landscape with Figures" comes from Henry's mockery of an unnamed British "authority" who seeks admission to the Club. His condescending dignity annoys Henry, and Henry tries vainly to instruct the British officer, whom he never identifies by name and usually mocks with the epithet "the Authority." The British officer's obtuseness, in fact, leads to a shelling at the house from which the film crew is working. Henry had warned him that reflections from his steel helmet and his glasses would cause the Fascists to think they had located the commanders of the battle, but he had ignored Henry's warning.

Elizabeth and the reader see Henry as the real "Authority." Upset at what she has seen and what the British officer had carelessly caused, Elizabeth tells him that she is going back to the hotel with Edwin Henry. Affecting a British accent, Henry informs the Englishman that he no longer belongs to the Club. But the tables get turned once more. This American journalist is able to reassess and come to her own conclusions. She does not act stereotypically. She continues to listen and learn from Henry, but she brings her own feelings to the scenes she observes. Watching the British officer walk away from his embarrassing dismissal, she rescinds and invites him back to the Club. Moreover, she decides to ride with him in his car. Edwin Henry is left to travel with Johnny, who has forgiven Henry the bad taste of the joke that began the story. Elizabeth and Johnny give Edwin Henry some needed instructions on the care of the feelings of others. The reader may be able to detect many traits of the public Hemingway in Edwin Henry, but the reader may also find the private Hemingway to be critical of those traits.

The one story Hemingway had planned for his new collection not told in the first person was "Nobody Ever Dies." The Enrique of this story is not Edwin Henry, but a young Loyalist badly wounded and now back in Cuba, where he, nevertheless, is not safe from Franco's forces. The secret police hunt him down, shoot him, and capture his girlfriend. She will be facing torture and perhaps death. Carlos Baker describes the story as being in Hemingway's "worst vein of tough sentimentalism."[82] Most readers would agree that the political romance was not Hemingway's forte, for the story is greatly inferior to the more distanced stories that come to us through the mature experience of

Edwin Henry, who does not speak politics from the book. "Nobody Ever Dies" is probably the least convincing short story that Hemingway ever wrote. Stephen Cooper compares it to "The Revolutionist" of *In Our Time*, much to the advantage of the earlier story where the narrator's conscious irony gives the story a convincing resonance.[83]

The story did, however, give Hemingway a chance to practice the handling of romantic love in wartime. Hemingway took risks with point of view, switching from the consciousness of Enrique and ending by focusing attention on Maria. This Maria is not as vivid as the Maria of *For Whom the Bell Tolls*, but the narrator is most interested in the transformation that is taking place inside her, and he dares to insist on her heroism. He ends by being sentimental and propagandistic and unconvincing as he compares her to Joan of Arc. "Nobody Ever Dies" makes clear the advantage of the angle of vision Edwin Henry provides in the other stories. The Cuban story now has, at best, some minor critical value because of the similarities between it and *For Whom the Bell Tolls*, but the Edwin Henry stories—though certainly not the equal of the African stories—reveal a Hemingway still committed to the short story and achieving some commendable results with it.

Because of the excellence and fame of *For Whom the Bell Tolls*, Hemingway's seven (counting "Old Man at the Bridge" and "Nobody Ever Dies") stories of the Spanish Civil War will cause most readers to think first about the several themes that the stories share with the novel: the conflict between the political implications of the war and the writer's duty to tell the whole truth as he sees it, the absurdity of going out to face death in battles where there is no chance of victory, the ways in which war-weary patriots pass the tedium of waiting, the possibility of finding romantic love in such circumstances. We should not, however, let those concerns keep us from appreciating the individual structures of the stories, their strengths (and limitations) as stories in their own right. For Hemingway had conceived a meaningful progression in their order and was indeed attempting some new effects in the form.

Most noticeable is his use of first-person narration. He had, to be sure, written numerous stories using the first person, but never before had he written a sequence of stories about a single character in first person. Since the events of those stories cover a fairly short time span, continuing in first person once he had begun in it probably seemed natural enough. The risk is that with the somewhat war-hardened journalist providing the angle of vision, the stories may seem thrown together, the easy thing, mere reportage. More and more Edwin Henry may seem Hemingway the mythic man of war, even to his calling Elizabeth "daughter" in "Landscape with Figures." The choices are not as concentrated as they are in the stories of *In Our Time, Men Without Women,* and *Winner Take Nothing*—or in the great African stories he had so recently completed.

Yet there is something to be said for the boldness of the first-person sequence. It is as if the author of "The Snows of Kilimanjaro" were making inclusion a principle. Unlike Harry, he would not waste the material of the Spanish Civil War. Although Brenner and Rovit find the Harry of "Snows" the most convincing of Hemingway's writer-protagonists, Edwin Henry is convincingly a writer—and more than a journalist. His duty as a writer is never far from his thinking, and he is always functioning as a writer-observer. The controlling thread of the stories is as much his response to the war as the war itself. The problem Henry faces is *what* he will write about the war, and this problem challenges him in many directions. The waiter in "The Butterfly and the Tank" exhorts him not only to write the story of the flit king, but tells him what to name the story. Later, other Loyalists tell him that he must not write about certain events that will appear unflattering or detrimental to the cause. The general in "Under the Ridge" wants him to tell it all. The duty that he accepts in "Landscape with Figures" is portrayal of the reality. Part of the reality is his own character, which slowly emerges in the stories. He is not nearly the romantic figure that Robert Jordan is, in part because Jordan is more the apprentice in war than Henry is, but also because writing is not as consuming a duty for Jordan, a college teacher. In "Nobody Ever Dies" Maria rebukes Enrique three times for talking "like a book." That is something that Edwin Henry is determined not to do, and the first-person stories, even as they reveal his weaknesses as a human being, also reveal important strengths. Writer's block, however, will not be his problem.

Although the Spanish stories do not match the African stories for power, a backward look at a very early Hemingway story, one written before he learned the lessons of Anderson and Pound and Stein, is instructive for highlighting the skill of the Spanish stories. "The Mercenaries—A Story" is not to be found in *The Complete Short Stories of Ernest Hemingway,* nor are four other apprenticeship stories. Peter Griffin includes them however, in *Along with Youth: Hemingway, the Early Years.* Griffin judges "The Mercenaries" the best of Hemingway's efforts to write for the popular American magazines, noting that after

100

*Redbook* and the *Saturday Evening Post* rejected it, Hemingway never again submitted it for publication.[84]

The Spanish stories recall "The Mercenaries" because of its setting and theme, but especially because it also is a first-person story. The young Hemingway was trying for the first time to use his war experience in fiction, but he thought that the way to do it was to gear his material to the popular market. The story is set in the Café Cambrinus in Chicago. Like Chicote, Cambrinus runs "a special place." The knowing (and war of various sorts has trained the several cognoscenti of the story) gather to drink and to tell stories. Hemingway began, it is worth noting, with the crowded stage. The speech of the characters of different nationalities provides color and diversity, as we find at Chicote's. The narrator of "The Mercenaries" is overly fond of the epithet, a device Hemingway retained but learned to use more discriminatingly. What the characters eat and drink is already important. The narrator fits into this high, elect world—Cambrinus likes him. One-quarter Italian, Rinaldi had fought in World War I in Italy, but he seems not to have been much altered by the experience. He repeats instead the story of a duel, the telling of which is the major event of "The Mercenaries." But the story is too much "by the book," and the narrator appears something of a poseur, unsure about what his story means.

An attempt at creating a worldly young observer, the use of first person in "The Mercenaries" is mainly a convenience. The "I" of the Spanish stories, on the other hand, is not only experienced but he truly fits into the milieu of Chicote's and helps to shape it. The young Chicagoan Rinaldi does not affect events at the café but take his great satisfaction in mere admission. Hemingway teases us about the elusive personality of the narrator of his several Spanish stories, aware that the man behind Edwin Henry seemed to some his worst invented character. The best part of that character is his commitment to his art— and that is a great deal. The unified effect of the portrayal (moving from the somewhat cynical, even sinister figure of "The Denunciation" to the more compassionate listener and observer of soldiers going about the business of war, who nevertheless has hints of the bully) has accumulative force.[85] Henry has "authority"—though it is not always lovable.

# The Last Stories

In their foreward to *The Complete Stories of Ernest Hemingway: The Finca Vigía Edition,* Hemingway's sons—John, Patrick, and Gregory—declared that in the early years (the 1940s) at the Finca, his Cuban home, their father did not appear to write any fiction. Rather, their new stepmother Martha Gellhorn carried on the intensity of writing that their father had achieved in the period of the Spanish Civil War. But another war would help spur Hemingway to new writing projects, including new efforts with the short story.

By August 1956 he could write Charles Scribner, Jr., about his work on a new group of stories. He explained: "after I stopped working on the film [*The Spanish Earth*] I found it impossible to resume work on the African book without some disciplinary writing so I started writing short stories which is the hardest thing for me to do." He listed six (only one of which, "Get a Seeing-Eyed Dog," would be published during his lifetime), and he told Scribner that he had five more that he was going to write (*Letters* 868). His plans would not be fully realized, and he would not equal the burst of concentration that served him so well during the Spanish Civil War. Nevertheless, it is worth emphasizing his continuing attraction to the short story—and the difficult challenge he thought that genre. With *In Our Time* behind him, the novel emerged in the mid 1920s as the unfulfilled challenge to be met. In the last decade of his life, however, the short story seemed to him the more demanding form.[86]

Five of the stories that Hemingway cited in his letter to Scribner were stories about World War II. When in 1959 he turned his hand to a preface for a collection of his stories, a collection that would contain his own favorites as well as the favorites of student readers, he included one from this group. At least for now, it is the only one of the group available to the general reader, for the other World War II efforts did not become part of the Finca Vigía edition.[87] Hemingway's preface for the book he and Scribner had been talking about in 1959 (printed in part 2 of this book) cautions the reader to read "Black Ass at the Cross Roads" as fiction: "That means that the *I* is not me."

The Last Stories

The story cannot have been easy—nor probably pleasant—to write. As Hemingway told Scribner, his World War II stories are "a little shocking since they deal with irregular troops and combat and with people who actually kill other people" (*Letters* 868). The theme of the killing of other people was not new to Hemingway's writing. Inevitably, the story of this war would invite comparison with his treatment of killing in World War I. Of course, he had observed World War II from a very different perspective, and his methods of writing had also changed. The interchapters of *In Our Time* were appropriate to Hemingway's limited engagement in World War I, but also appropriate to the great wave of experimentation in poetry and writing current in the 1920s. Wisely, he refrained from trying to repeat those methods—or himself.

To illustrate the difference, "Black Ass at the Cross Roads" may appropriately be set next to chapter 3 of *In Our Time*. In Hemingway's brief paragraph that comprises the interchapter, understatement and a few precise details let the reader experience a soldier's sensations as he kills an enemy soldier at close range: "The first German I saw climbed up over the garden wall. We waited till he got one leg over and then potted him. He had so much equipment on and looked awfully surprised and fell down into the garden" (77). The unexpected "he looked awfully surprised" makes this interchapter a classic portrayal of startled innocence in battle.

Startled innocence does not describe the narrator of "Black Ass," though killing, and killing at close range, is again the subject. The narrator of this later story is the American commander of a small irregular company, placed strategically at a crossroads where his irregulars await retreating German soldiers (in disguise or otherwise) as the Allied invasion sweeps through France. Instead of the lean and spare method of the interchapter, here we find a fairly large cast of characters. Instead of the brief report of only a few minutes of action, we "watch" for several hours. Instead of a single outburst of killing four Germans (interchapter 3) we have a series of killings at the crossroads. We hear the narrator and his men talk, their tough dialogue useful for their handling of the awful business that engages them because such talk is one of the opiates available to soldiers. Hemingway had said as much in the retreat scene of *A Farewell to Arms*, but the intended obscenities were replaced with dashes to meet the publishing codes of the time. Publication in the Finca Vigía edition required no such muting of the soldiers' language.

The feelings of the soldiers are not of a piece—any more than the soldiers were of a single mind in their retreat from Caporetto or in their pondering the Crucifixion in "Today Is Friday." The first victim of the story is a French civilian, whom Red believes is a collaborator. Or so he says. Red does not seem to be emotionally involved in any of his killing. In truth, he enjoys killing other human beings. But such is not the case with Claude or the narrator. "'*Cette putain guerre,*' Claude said. 'This dirty whore of a war'" (588). Hemingway continued to view war with abhorrence, and the whorishness of it is made particularly explicit because of the narrator's role in the killings. He brings down a young German (one who looks about seventeen years old) who is fleeing toward Germany on a bicycle. Having been carried to the side of the road, the soldier "was trying to take it the way he'd always heard you should" (588). Whereas in the interchapter we get the sudden death, here we share a more lingering death—our victim by our side. The earlier story barely suggests the emotions of the killers, but this later story dares to admit them. The dying German never looks away from Claude, who tends him, and Claude bends over and kisses the soldier on the forehead. The narrator finds this act appropriate: "I should have kissed him myself if I was any good. It was just one of those things that you omit to do and that stay with you" (588). But, like Claude, the narrator has "the black ass." In the last line of the story, Claude and the narrator are dividing confiscated wine and sausage. The narrator knows exactly where to end his story: "We were splitting it even between us and neither of us liked our share" (589).

"Black ass" would torment Hemingway during the last decade of his life, even as it torments his narrator in this story. One way of dealing with depression is through the discipline of art. Although Hemingway would continue to look to the short story as an aid to combatting "black ass," he was having more difficulty completing his war stories—reversing the seeming ease of the Spanish stories. His writing efforts usually went to several novels in progress. These, too, suggest that war was no longer a subject most natural to his needs as a writer. But several of his efforts in the short story make powerful comment on other blacknesses of Hemingway's late years.

As we have seen, domestic life was an important theme in Hemingway's fiction from the start of his career. Not only in the tales of Nick Adams, but in other stories, Hemingway explored destructions and hungers and fulfillments within a family context. He was especially concerned with the relationship between fathers and sons. He explored that theme concurrently with the theme of war in *Islands in the Stream*, and the Finca Vigía edition includes two new stories that reflect the anguish Hemingway sometimes felt in his role as father.

The first of these, "I Guess Everything Reminds You of Something," was published concurrently with the Finca edition in the 10 November 1987 issue of *Family Circle* magazine. Its inclusion in this popular women's magazine must have surprised many readers who associated Hemingway more readily with the hunt and the world of violent action. Publication of his "An African Story" in *Sports Illustrated* as "An African Betrayal" (5 May 1986) would seem more predictable. But the precedents for the domestic "I Guess Everything Reminds You of Something" abound in Hemingway's short fiction.

Like "A Day's Wait," the story seems to be merely a transcription of events in the life of Ernest Hemingway and a son. Indeed, in *Papa: A Personal Memoir* (1976) Gregory Hemingway gives us an account of his father's instruction to him in the art of writing. The chapter "Lessons" recounts a summer of his boyhood in Havana when Gregory let Ernest believe that he wanted to be a writer, and Gregory probably thought that he did. But he showed bad judgment in copying a short story by Turgenev and offering it to his father as his own; Ernest was impressed. Gregory later submitted the story at school, where his teacher was equally impressed. Gregory was doubtless chagrined when it won a prize. Simultaneously, Gregory was showing great skills as a marksman, and since the activities of hunting and writing had often seemed similar to Ernest, he was even more willing to believe in Gregory's promise as a writer. Gregory was thankful that he was not around when his father discovered his deception.

But Hemingway apparently read a great deal into that deception, or so it would seem from the story he eventually wrote about it. The differences between Gregory's memoir account and Hemingway's fictional account are intriguing. From Gregory's side, we see how immense the event was in his life. He recalls his father's pleasure in the story he thought his son had written as being matched only by the pleasure he took in Gregory's success in tying for a pigeon-shooting championship. After the plagiarism, Gregory somehow lost his father, and his confession represents a partial assumption of responsibility for that loss. In no other chapter of his memoir does the title of his book ring more like a poignant cry for Papa's approval.

Hemingway's version softens the impact of the original violation. In it the boy does not write the story as a means to win his father's approval. Rather, he submits his plagiarized story at his school. Impressed with its fine craftsmanship, the teacher sends it to the boy's writer-father with the suggestion that the father help teach his son even more about writing. Stevie might now make a confession, but he easily slides into further deception. Hemingway skillfully portrays a father trying to be encouraging and helpful while talking to a son who feels increasingly awkward and uncomfortable. Gregory's chapter portrays Hemingway, too much under the influence of "the sauce," talking about literature and other writers, and not nearly as attentive to his son as the father is in Hemingway's story. Hemingway keeps his focus on the father, who remembers vividly the boy's promising skill as a hunter. The father's role as careful instructor to his son's development as a marksman is prominent in "I Guess Everything Reminds You of Something." In the father's vivid memory, we hear in Stevie's voice something ominous, something disturbing. At first it seems only a physical trait, "that low, hoarse voice that did not belong to a small boy" (598). But later his father is disturbed by an arrogance in the boy's approach to his shooting: "I don't understand how anyone ever misses a pigeon" (599). Stevie slides into an apology for his rudeness, and the narrator ends his description of the boy's summer visit with a paragraph of indirect discourse, which serves to underline the boy's quality of voice and disposition:

> He never showed his father the second story. It was not finished to his satisfaction at the end of vacation. He said he wanted to get it absolutely right before he showed it. As soon as he got it right he was going to send it to his father. He had had a very good vacation, he said, one of the best and he was glad he had such good reading too and he thanked his father for not pushing him too hard on the writing because after all a vacation is a vacation and this had been a fine one, maybe one of the very best, and they certainly had had some wonderful times they certainly had. (600)

Seven years later the father discovers the boy's deception, and the reader recalls the father's initial response to his reading of the story—knowing that it reminded him of something he had read a long time ago. The boy's line titles the story: "I guess everything reminds you of something" (597). The reader is reminded again of Stevie's hoarse voice and of Hemingway's frequent use of voice quality to suggest aspects of character and uncertainty about character.

From the father's perspective, the seeds of the boy's destruction were always in him, but he finds the event of the plagiarism a turning point in the boy's life. Readers of *Family Circle* encountered a painful concluding paragraph to the story, one that caught the essence of a broken family circle: "Now he knew that boy had never been any good. He had thought so often looking back on things. And it was sad to know that shooting did not mean a thing" (601). The lines seem harsh, but, having viewed the father's earlier care and concern, the reader must sense how painful the father's assessment is to himself— not a position he would readily have adopted.

The contrast to the ending of "A Day's Wait" could hardly be greater, and it is worth noting that Hemingway did not identify the writer-father as Nick Adams. His portrayals of Nick Adams usually show us a Nick overcoming darkness or at least attempting to do so. But the writer-father of "I Guess Everything Reminds You of Something" is the writer-protagonist of "Great News from the Mainland," with which it is closely linked. As he had juxtaposed "The End of Something" with "The Three-Day Blow" and "The Short Happy Life of Francis Macomber" with "The Snows of Kilimanjaro," Hemingway once again created companion stories.

"Great News from the Mainland" is a brief story of great irony and of great despair. Almost nothing happens during the narration because everything has already happened. Mr. Wheeler, an American writer living in Cuba, receives a telephone call from his son Stephen's psychiatrist on the mainland. Dr. Simpson is practiced at being cheerful, and he uses Mr. Wheeler's name repeatedly as he relates Stephen's "progress" under drug and shock therapy. When his father calls Stephen on Thursday, we hear the same "hoarse voice" and the same assuring voice that his father recalled when Stephen took his good-bye in "I Guess Everything." Like Mr. Wheeler, the reader is mindful of the tropical storms that have blown for days, causing damage that cannot be undone. Mr. Wheeler must accept hard facts, the end of great hopes—and that task is painful, as the reader recognizes in Mr. Wheeler's response to the houseboy who has asked how Stevie is: "'Fine,' I said. 'He says everything is fine'" (604). With these words the narrator ends his story, his realism at a hundred and eighty degrees from that of Nick Adams at the end of "The Three-Day Blow," which Hemingway evokes in his storm image. Nick believes that nothing is ever finished and nothing ever lost. "The wind blew it [the Marjorie business] out of his head. Still he could always go into town Saturday night. It was a good thing to have in reserve" (93). Hemingway's image of storm connects this story with the end of the "something" that is also at stake in the early Nick story. There Nick is trying to come to terms with his loss of Marjorie, but he is also pained by his psychological distance from his father. The distance between Mr. Wheeler and his son is much greater—literally and psychologically—and the finality of their separation is truly devastating.

It may be haunting that the writer of these two dark stories bears the name of Hemingway's first American traveler in "Homage to Switzerland"—though they are not the same character. Mr. Wheeler's is the least flattering portrait in "Homage to Switzerland" and one of the most unpleasant in Hemingway's short stories, for that Mr. Wheeler seems unable to make deep commitments. Incapable of love, he never takes chances. This second Mr. Wheeler has, of course, taken some chances, and his portrait is not reprehensible. He has taken the very serious chance of becoming a parent. The reasons that his relationship with Stevie has ended so badly are not fully fathomable. They may be, at bottom, like the forces of nature—beyond his control. Nevertheless, the name here may also on some deep level be partly Hemingway's judgment of himself in his tempestuous relationship with Gregory, a relationship that looms large in the story. We can understand how these two stories would not be stories that Hemingway would talk about in his letters, envisioning them as lead stories in a book. They were probably very difficult stories to write—stories written out of pain, as a way of getting rid of major parental disappointments, or at least as ways of living with those disappointments.

With the two Mr. Wheeler stories, Hemingway turned from the longer short story, a form that lent itself to the more journalistic emphasis and seeming casualness of the Spanish stories, and returned to the more compact short story. Perhaps the intensely personal basis of the Mr. Wheeler stories required a method closer to that cautious control of *In Our Time* and *Men Without Women*, those stories in which the real ending took place after the author had finished—to return to Malcolm Cowley's observation. Probably because the stories would have hurt Gregory, Hemingway did not attempt to publish them. Similarly, he had refrained from publishing "Summer People," which would have deeply hurt Katy Smith Dos Passos and her family. In his younger days, such concerns did not always hold him back—as Grace Hall Hemingway and Clarence Hemingway discovered. Whatever plans Hemingway may have had for these stories, we can easily imagine the therapeutic effect of the writing as he dealt with the "black ass" of his parental role.

Although Hemingway desired domestic and parental fulfillment, that desire sometimes warred with other instincts. If he sometimes breached his familial ties, he increasingly surrounded himself with numerous surrogate sons and daughters. The most famous examples are Adriana Ivancich (the prototype for Renata of *Across the River and Into the Trees*) and A. E. Hotchner, whose title *Papa Hemingway: A Memoir* makes clear the relationship. Through his surrogate offspring, Hemingway sought to make his fatherhood a means to happiness. Not surprisingly, the author of "A Day's Wait" could be very effective in a parent's role. Jack Hemingway's *Misadventures of a Fly Fisherman* (1986) as well as Gregory Hemingway's more critical *Papa: A Memoir* make clear that Hemingway had his successes in his relationships with his sons. Obviously, there were failures, too. Gregory emphasizes these.[88]

The parental role becomes a more insistent theme in Hemingway's late work, and its ambiguous nature is made more evident. But the theme was there from the start, especially in the short fiction. We have seen it in the stories about Nick Adams, but it is also present in numerous other short works. The desire for familial success is one of the strongest drives in Jack Brennan of "Fifty Grand"—one of Hemingway's most fulfilled protagonists. The relationship between Santiago and Manolin is one of the warm bonds in *The Old Man and the Sea*. In "Landscape with Figures" the parental instinct sneaks out in Edwin Henry, who calls Elizabeth "daughter," and his treatment of her is strongly parental.

One instance of Hemingway's nurturing disposition provided good results for his readers, as well as immediate pleasure to two children. In January 1950 he wrote two fables for a young nephew of Adriana Ivancich and for the daughter of Carlo Di Robillant, whose family had helped rekindle his admiration for pre-Fascist Italy. There was no reason not to share these stories with the public, and the March 1950 *Holiday* carried both "The Good Lion" and "The Faithful Bull."

These happy pieces contain just the right degree of fabulousness and brevity. But the best children's stories are usually written somewhat above their audience, and Hemingway's fables—delightful as they must have been to their first recipients—can mean many things to many people. They exemplify the Hemingway method of the short story. "I'm trying to do it so it will make it without you knowing it, and so the more you read it, the more there will be" (*MF* 138). Children will delight in the fabulous, and in the narrator's good humor, but the adult reader, especially the adult reader of Hemingway, will recognize quickly that the stories are multileveled.[89]

Companion stories, the fables present two sides of Hemingway, but somewhat paradoxically. The adult quickly sees that "The Good Lion" plays on the old notion of the literary lion, a role long familiar to Hemingway. This one has wings; so he is also like Pegasus. And he can soar above all of the other lions, who are quite jealous—none more so than the most wicked of them, who is a lioness. The female of the species could be the more deadly, an old pattern in Hemingway's work—as the reader of "The Doctor and the Doctor's Wife" will recall. In this lioness, readers can recognize Martha Gellhorn, Hemingway's writer-wife, from whom he was divorced in 1945 but whom he still thought of with great bitterness, though also with humor. One imagines that Gellhorn might also have been amused at the fable—recognizing her former husband's winning humor, a trait that originally attracted her to him. Certainly the fable seems written as much for Gellhorn as for the Italian children.

But the story also recalls Hemingway's African experiences, especially his literary use of his African safari. The wicked lioness echoes certain aspects of Margot Macomber. The good lion's transfiguration above the snarling lions (little better than hyenas) and his return to his father in Venice, a city in which there are many mansions—in short, a place like Kilimanjaro, an analogue of heaven—evoke "The Snows of Kilimanjaro." In a sense we get the scene of reunion to which Harry flies.

In recalling those religious overtones, Hemingway consciously plays on the rhythms of the King James Bible, powerfully with him in this period in which he was also writing *The Old Man and the Sea:*

> "My father lives in a city where he stands under the clock tower and looks down on a thousand pigeons, all of whom are his subjects. When they fly they make a noise like a rushing river. There are more palaces in my father's city than in all of Africa and there are four great bronze horses that face him and they all have one foot in the air because they fear him.
>
> "In my father's city men go on foot or in boats and no real horse would enter the city for fear of my father." (482–83)

Unlike the Harry of "Snows," this good lion goes to his father as "a dutiful son." Hemingway delighted in his bad boy image even as he maintained his belief in métier. With some amusement, then, he plays against the parable of the prodigal son, where the long-suffering father rushes to meet the son, falls on his neck, and kisses him. In "The Good Lion" the son kisses the father on both cheeks, then reports to him on life in Africa. Instead of the feast of the fatted calf of Luke's Gospel, the lion goes to Harry's bar, where he orders a "Hindu trader sandwich." The reunion of father and son (the "dutiful" son) is, however, a happy one, and it touches on Hemingway stories early and late. This "once upon a time" fable ends as it should, with the principal character living happily ever after—on "Kilimanjaro," as the last sentences so attractively suggest: "he knew that he was at home but that he had also traveled. He was very happy" (484).

Although most children would miss the allusions to the story of the Prodigal Son, many would be familiar with the story of Ferdinand that Hemingway points to in "The Faithful Bull." When Munro Leaf's classic *Ferdinand the Bull* appeared in 1936, the author of *Death in the Afternoon* (1932) must have been especially amused by it. The most striking difference between Hemingway's tale and Leaf's is the ending. Whereas Leaf's story ends with Ferdinand's contented retirement, Hemingway's fable ends with the bull's death. Tinged with sadness, calling even the youngest reader to reflection, Hemingway's second fable also contrasts with the more celebratory ending of his lion fable.

The humor of Hemingway's bull fable is gentler than that of the lion fable; it is mainly for the adult familiar with Hemingway's work. Hemingway the lion was also a bull; he was a nonthinker (he liked to pretend), and he caused damage in any number of chinashops. But the world of the bull and the bullfighter held many meanings for Hemingway, even sacred meanings. How could the author of *Death in the Afternoon* write a story about bullfighters and avoid the theme of death? And how could he avoid the theme of writing? As Hemingway imagines himself as the good lion, he also imagines himself as the faithful bull: "Fighting was his obligation and his duty and his joy" (485). And Hemingway's description of the bull makes clear that his bull is a writer:

> His horns were as solid as wood and they were as sharply pointed as the quill of a porcupine. They hurt him, at the base, when he fought and he did not care at all. His neck muscles lifted in a great lump that is called in Spanish the *morillo* and this *morillo* lifted like a hill when he was ready to fight. He was always ready to fight and his coat was black and shining and his eyes were clear. (485)

We hardly need the reference to "the quill" to let us know that Hemingway is writing about an artist using his talents intensely. Paradoxically, pain becomes pleasure, for his goal, like Harry's in "Snows," is the highest: "he would fight with deadly seriousness exactly as some people eat or read or go to church" (485).

Harry, we recall, got sidetracked from his goal. He got involved with the very rich, just as in *A Moveable Feast* Hemingway regrets being led astray by a "pilot fish" (usually seen as Dos Passos) from the rigorous discipline of his apprenticeship. Harry "sold vitality," he admits, and the faithful bull of Hemingway's parable is sent out to pasture for stud service. The amusing twist is that this bull falls in love with one cow and will pay attention only to her. The world being organized on economic principles, the bull's owner sends him into the arena, where he fights bravely and dies. "He fought wonderfully and everyone admired him and the man who killed him admired him the most" (486), Santiago-like, one might say. Irony and sadness radiate from this final line; this domestic fable touches tenderly on that ideal of faithfulness in love by which Hemingway judged himself.

The last short stories Hemingway presented for publication were also companion stories, written only months apart. "A Man of the World" and "Get a Seeing-Eyed Dog" appeared together as "Two Tales of Darkness" for the one-hundredth anniversary edition of the *Atlantic Monthly* (November 1957). Their order in the *Atlantic* reversed the order of their composition, and to good point. Carlos Baker faults the shapelessness and rambling quality of the war stories (including "Black Ass at the Cross Roads") that Hemingway had been trying to write in the summer of 1957, but judged "Get a Seeing-Eyed Dog" worse than all of them, labeling it "sentimental." And he thought that Hemingway had deceived himself in calling "A Man of the World" a "good story."[90] There is, however, more power in these stories than Baker found, and their inclusion as the only stories by Hemingway, save for "Big Two-Hearted River," in a recent American literature textbook suggests that at least its editors thought the late stories illustrated some valuable aspects of Hemingway's work.[91]

Set in Jessup, Wyoming, "A Man of the World" should remind us of Hemingway's appreciation of the American West, and especially of the ideals of that West that helped to shape his attitudes. Although Baker dismisses Blindy as "a malodorous bum," the title of Hemingway's story indicates that he is much more. He is like one of Sherwood Anderson's grotesques, his truth there if we look hard enough. The narrator finds it, and so does the bartender Frank of the Index Café, who belongs to the tradition of the skilled and sensitive bartender—at first tentatively there in Cambrinus of "The Mercenaries," but surely there in "A Clean, Well-Lighted Place" and in the legend of Chicote's.

The stranger in town learns from Frank the gruesome story of Blindy's fight with Willie Sawyer, in which Blindy lost both his eyesight and his masculinity. Repulsed, the narrator Tom refrains from repeating the tale. But the story does not dwell on the fight as much as it lets us see Blindy fulfilling an ideal of the Old West. The storms of the world may beat down on him (as they do), but Blindy proves himself "a man of the world," able to withstand what transpires. What has happened to him has happened, and he copes admirably. Not only is he "a man of the world," he is a man managing alone. Unlike Ad Francis of "The Battler," he needs no caretaker. His stoic fortitude and his saving humor place him in contrast to Willie Sawyer, who also suffered greatly in his fight with Blindy. But Willie "ain't got no sense of humor at all" (495). Shocking and on the surface grim, Hemingway's story is well-crafted and evocative, showing a way he would like to be, probably, and reaffirming an old stoic ideal—a way to combat "black ass."

Next to that story of the Old West ideal, Hemingway dared to place material that Baker found, and perhaps others find, sentimental. But the reader familiar with Hemingway's work will find many haunting echoes. Hemingway liked the quiet story. Short and taut, it returns us to the old drama of a man talking with a woman. Older than most of his fictional couples, this couple reminds us of that strong domestic strain in Hemingway's work. There is something poetically right about Hemingway's placement of this story, his last completed short story to be published in his lifetime.

Contemporary readers of "Get a Seeing-Eyed Dog" will not see the story in the same way that readers saw it when it was first published in the *Atlantic*. It is not just that contemporary readers know the end of Hemingway's life, for the story is clearly personal and deals rather directly with his life. (Carlos Baker reminds us that Hemingway was recalling his bout with erysipelas in 1949.) Rather, contemporary readers also have available to them other works that had occupied Hemingway during the last years of his life—especially *A Moveable Feast,* which this story anticipates, and may even be a preparation for. The domestic or familial had come to be Hemingway's most important theme in his last period.

If Hemingway made Hadley the heroine of *A Moveable Feast*, in "Get a Seeing-Eyed Dog" he pays tribute to Mary Welsh, whom we discern in the unnamed wife of the story. As the story begins, we listen as the newly blind writer and his wife play remembering games—anticipating the remembering scene of "A False Spring" in *A Moveable Feast*. There remembering is portrayed as happiness as Ernest and Hadley remember together. Here the game has a sense of urgency because the remembering is an exercise for recovery from some accident, apparently the accident that caused Philip's blindness. Accurate remembering is crucial to Philip's career as a writer; so he is trying to preserve his very identity.

The invitation of the story is not, however, to read it as autobiography but to see its relationship to many of Hemingway's already-published stories that he gently recalls. These many allusions pull the story away from the sentimental. Hemingway demands that the reader compare this particular writer-protagonist with other writer-protagonists who pervade his fiction.

First, there is "The Three-Day Blow." As Philip and his wife remember together, outside it is raining a big rain. Their remembering is different from the youthful remembering of Nick and Bill in the Michigan story. Philip is with a woman he loves. There may be some evasion in their talking, but most of it convincingly reveals their love and meaningful companionship, and they are fairly direct with each other—though Philip hides a very dark corner of his mind from his wife. The beech logs burning in the fireplace recall the burning beech of the Michigan story, a story wherein Nick is not yet ready to make a major commitment to a woman. Instead of the adolescent drinking of Bill and Nick, in the late story we get sustained attention to an adult ritual of drinking. The world is all before Nick, the Wagner apple still uneaten in the pocket of his macintosh. Three-day blows are survivable. But the reader senses mainly completed drama in the late story. Neither Philip nor his wife has the sense that better weather or better experiences lie ahead.

"Get a Seeing-Eyed Dog" also plays against "The Snows of Kilimanjaro"—another remembering story and one that builds on a contrast between present talking and the writer-protagonist's private thoughts. Whereas the talk of "Snows" shows a Harry adept at badgering his wife, the conversation between Philip and his wife reveals a couple who have shared a good deal more than drink, bed, and African safaris—activities both couples discuss. Whereas neither story gives the wife's name, the wife of the late story is addressed with a wifely "honey" as well as a "darling" (489). At story's end, she is graced with a "my blessed" (490) and finally with a *tu* and a metaphor of affection that provides a culmination to their discourse: "'Look, *tu*,' he said. 'We'll go down now and have lunch in our old fine place by the fire and I'll tell you what a wonderful kitten you are and what lucky kittens we are'" (491).

How different the tone of this speech is from that which characterizes the dialogue of the African story. The wife of the earlier story withholds drink, but the wife in Venice is happy to make the drinks. Whereas the dying Harry distresses his wife and his reader with his many insults, Philip here is wonderfully regardful of the wife with whom he has shared so many adventures.[92] Meditating on his blindness, he thinks, "I must figure out ways not to destroy her life and ruin her with it. She has been so good and she was not built to be good. I mean this sort of good. I mean good every day and dull good" (488).

Indeed, the essential difference between Harry's wife and Philip's wife is that one is dull, the other is not dull. Hemingway's title for his story is, in fact, appropriate for a couple of reasons. First, it emphasizes Philip's determination not to make his wife into a seeing-eye dog. It also reminds us of her ability to correct gently and of her own sensitivity to nuances of language, for she corrects Philip after he tells her that he does not want her to become just "a seeing-eyed dog": "I'm not and you know it. Anyway it's seeing-eye not seeing-eyed" (490). On other occasions, the story calls attention to the wife's ability to engage in word play. When she brings him the "Campari and Gordon's with ice," he praises her for not being a girl who would say "on the rocks." "No," she says, "I wouldn't ever say that. We've *been* on the rocks" (488). And they "remember" the time that they barred the phrase. In the present circumstances, the wife is asking Philip not say "you know." If we compare her to Bill or to Harry's wife, we see what a wonderfully adept companion she is. She has élan about matters other than language usage. When Philip says that he rather likes the dark, that he even finds it "in some ways an improvement," his wife tells him not to lie too much: "You don't have to be so bloody noble" (489). Because the husband's version of "seeing-eyed" dog prevails in the story's title, we may have a gentle, if ominous, suggestion about who will win the tug of wills that provides the basis for the story's action.

Tellingly, the wife is trembling in the story's final movement: she may be picking up on the more sinister aspects of Philip's thought.

How serious is he that "the dark" is an improvement? The idea of death is never very far from this story, again connecting it with "The Snows of Kilimanjaro." The rains that are beating down are the rains of death, and Philip would have very little difficulty imagining himself dead in it. When he tells his wife about "The Plan" (490), we catch the ominous note—the plan may carry an option for suicide: "I will have to try it another day, he thought. I must not be stupid about it. She feels so lovely and I love her so much and have done her so much damage and I must learn to take good care of her in every way I can. If I think of her and of her only, everything will be all right" (490). Thinking of her best interests would not necessarily rule out suicide. The real ending of "Out of Season," Hemingway had teased, occurs when Peduzzi commits suicide. In this "Tale of Darkness," if ever, the ending takes place on the page after the story has stopped.

Hemingway was using the metaphor of his earlier fear of blindness as a means for dealing with later darkness, the threatening "black ass." The probing of dark recesses in this fictional way is immensely moving. He does not surrender to that black ass entirely, and that is the reason that the contemporary reader may be reminded of "A False Spring" in *A Moveable Feast*. "Do you think it will ever be spring?" asks Philip. His wife replies, "It certainly doesn't act like it" (489). The line adds to the great darkness of the tale. It also reminds us of the threat to happiness of the married couple in *A Moveable Feast*.

The many similarities between the two pieces are extraordinary. There is the pleasure of talk and of memory, as I have observed, and the remembering is the woman's pleasure as well as the man's. About both couples there is an aura of their private pleasure and sufficiency. "People were always the limiters of happiness except for the very few that were as good as spring itself" (*MF* 49), Hemingway reports at the beginning of "A False Spring"; the wife of the late story sees one advantage in the rain: there will not be any tourists, and when they go down to dinner they can sit alone by the fire. Both couples talk about their luck in being where they are and reflect on the luck of their lives together. As Hadley wisely says, "Memory is hunger" (*MF* 57). Both works are hungerings for better days, especially days in which the challenge of writing provided abundant pleasure. Ernest writes in "A False Spring"; in "Get a Seeing-Eyed Dog" Philip is talking about the possibilities of writing using a tape recorder—something he would like to believe possible, perhaps; something to help convince his wife that he is going to be all right, more certainly. Sexuality and creativity are inseparable in both works. After their feast of remembering and a fine dinner at Michaud's, Ernest and Hadley return to their apartment where they make love "in the dark" (*MF* 57). As Hemingway knew, love is mankind's great protest against the darkness of life. In "Get a Seeing-Eyed Dog" instead of the sexual activity of the Paris memoir, we hear talk about "the wonderful things" they do in the dark (489). As "A False Spring" ends, Ernest looks at the lovely face of his wife in the moonlight on her pillow. In the late story, Philip talks about sleeping with his arms around a pillow while his wife is away. Both works are, poignantly, about the end of something—a very wonderful something.

About the darkness of Hemingway's last years, there can be no doubt. But it is consoling to find that the genre of the short story could still permit him to come to terms with his blackness from time to time. His war experience ceased to be his natural subject in his late years. Increasingly, he selected the domestic and the familial for his subjects—and nostalgia for better days. As a writer, he found the short unit again served his purpose best. If we consider the units of *A Moveable Feast* short stories (and Hemingway himself called them fiction), he indeed came close to fulfilling his desire as stated in his 1938 preface to *The Fifth Column and the First Forty-nine Stories*. Fearful that his memory was less keen, he effectively celebrated it and recaptured it in *A Moveable Feast*. His last published story, "Get a Seeing-Eyed Dog," is an invitation to the reader to remember other works. We should recall those works with gratitude. The motifs of that story play against some of the great stories of a master writer. Memory is hunger—and pleasure.

# Notes

1. John Peale Bishop, "Homage to Hemingway," in *The Collected Essays of John Peale Bishop*, ed. Edmund Wilson (New York: Charles Scribner's Sons, 1948), 45–46.

2. Ezra Pound, "A Retrospect," in *Literary Essays* (New York: New Directions, 1918, 1920, 1935), 3–14. This group of essays and notes first appeared under this title in *Pavannes and Divisions* (1918). "A Few Don'ts" was first printed in *Poetry* 1, no. 6 (March 1913).

3. Gertrude Stein, *The Autobiography of Alice B. Toklas*, in *Selected Writings of Gertrude Stein*, ed. Carl Van Vechten (New York: Vintage Books, Random House, 1962), 201.

4. For a probing of this influence, see Kenneth G. Johnston, "Hemingway and Cézanne: Patches of White," in *The Tip of the Iceberg: Hemingway and the Short Story* (Greenwood, Fla.: Penkevill Publishing Co., 1987), 11–25.

5. Cecelia Tichi, *Shifting Gears* (Chapel Hill and London: University of North Carolina Press, 1987), 216.

6. *Death in the Afternoon* (New York: Charles Scribner's Sons, 1932), 191. Subsequent references to this book appear parenthetically in the text as *DA*.

7. Tichi, *Shifting Gears*, 229.

8. Martha Gellhorn, "Guerre de Plume," *Paris Review* 23 (Spring 1981):301.

9. Virginia Woolf, "Mr. Bennett and Mrs. Brown," in *Collected Essays*, vol. 1 (London: Hogarth Press, 1966). Woolf read this paper at the Heretics at Cambridge on 18 May 1924.

10. James Jones, "Letter Home: Sons of Hemingway," *Esquire* 60 (December 1963):28–29. I quote the manuscript version (University of Texas) for the letter, rather than the *Esquire* version, which has *sewage* rather than *shit*. Apparently in 1963 *Esquire* was comfortable with *bullshit*, but not with *shit*. Jones wanted the human odor, however, not the general *sewage*. My basis for the manuscript version is *Frank MacShane: The Life of James Jones, American Writer* (Boston: Houghton Mifflin, 1985), 210.

11. Doris Betts, *Contemporary Authors*, New Revision Series, vol. 9, ed. Ann Evory and Linda Metzger (Detroit: Gale Research Co., 1983), 52.

12. The reader should bear in mind always that this work was left unfinished. The published version omits an entire plot thread; the published version is much shorter than the manuscript from which it was edited.

13. *The Garden of Eden* (New York: Charles Scribner's Sons, 1986), 181. Subsequent references to this novel appear parenthetically in the text as *GE*.

14. Earl Rovit and Gerry Brenner, *Ernest Hemingway*, rev. ed. (Boston: Twayne, 1986), 172.

15. "Fascism Is a Lie," in *Conversations with Ernest Hemingway*, ed. Matthew J. Bruccoli (Jackson and London: University Press of Mississippi, 1986), 193.

16. *Green Hills of Africa* (New York: Charles Scribner's Sons, 1935), 27. Subsequent references to this work appear parenthetically in the text as *GHOA*.

17. Joseph Conrad, preface to *The Nigger of the "Narcissus"* (Garden City, N.Y.: Doubleday, Page & Co., 1926), xiv. Conrad's preface and novel were first published in 1897.

18. Joan Didion, *The White Album* (New York: Simon & Schuster, 1979), 11.

19. Carlos Baker, *Ernest Hemingway: A Life Story* (New York: Charles Scribner's Sons, 1969), 504–6.

20. He might have felt some identification with Eliot on that score. *Hemingway* gets misspelled often enough in college courses (the number of *m*'s

perplexing to some), but the precedent was established by Edward O'Brien, who not only gave the struggling young writer important encouragement by accepting "My Old Man" for inclusion in *The Best Short Stories of 1923* but then dedicated the book to "ERNEST HEMENWAY." With one exception, his name was misspelled throughout the book. See Audre Hanneman, *Ernest Hemingway: A Comprehensive Bibliography* (Princeton, N.J.: Princeton University Press, 1967), 91.

21. T. S. Eliot, preface to *For Lancelot Andrewes: Essays on Style and Order* (London: Faber & Gwyer, 1928), ix. The bases for comparing these two Midwestern "expatriates" are numerous. Hemingway may have sensed these when he wrote "Mr. and Mrs. Elliott." Like Eliot, Hemingway had difficulties with marriage. The attitudes of both writers toward women have been a matter of debate; both have been categorized by some as homosexual. Both writers have also been charged with anti-Semitism.

22. Hemingway frustrated the left and radical wings of American politics, especially during the 1930s, because of his supposed political neutrality. For a sound discussion of Hemingway's politics, essentially in the conservative Midwestern tradition from which he sprang, see Stephen Cooper, *The Politics of Ernest Hemingway* (Ann Arbor, Mich.: UMI Research Press, 1987).

23. A. E. Hotchner, *Papa Hemingway: A Personal Memoir* (New York: Random House, 1955), 130.

24. *The Sun Also Rises* (New York: Charles Scribner's Sons, 1926), 97.

25. T. S. Eliot, "Tradition and the Individual Talent," in *Selected Essays of T. S. Eliot* (New York: Harcourt Brace & World, 1964), 5.

26. Ibid., 4.

27. For one example, see Arnold Samuelson's record of his months in 1934 with Hemingway, *With Hemingway: A Year in Key West and Cuba* (New York: Random House, 1984).

28. T. S. Eliot, "Tradition and the Individual Talent," 4.

29. Ibid., 6.

30. Ibid., 6–7.

31. Ibid., 8.

32. Kenneth S. Lynn, *Hemingway* (New York: Simon & Schuster, 1987), 102–8.

33. I have modified my reading of the story since I wrote *Hemingway's Nick Adams* (Baton Rouge: Louisiana State University Press, 1982). There I missed Nick's presence and his shock at the beach scene, from which scene he escaped into the woods. But Nick was not present at the doctor's exchange with his wife. I continue to believe in the doctor's complexity, even as I confirm the story's great complexity. It calls for fine discriminations—for understanding from Nick and from the reader. Nick's reading suggests more than escape.

34. Eliot, "Tradition and the Individual Talent," 10.

35. Ibid., 11.

36. The essay is published in part 2 of this book.

37. *The Complete Short Stories of Ernest Hemingway*, Finca Vigía Edition (New York: Charles Scribner's Sons, 1987), 291. Subsequent references to Hemingway's stories are to this edition unless otherwise noted and appear parenthetically in the text.

38. Hemingway's Spanish setting and his old man emphasize that crisis over faith and despair are constants in the human condition rather than some special province of the twentieth century. For a useful discussion of metaphysical darkness, see chapter 3, "Winner Take Nothing," of William Barrett's *Time of Need* (New York: Harper & Row, 1972), 64–95.

39. John V. Hagopian, "Tidying Up Hemingway's 'A Clean, Well-Lighted Place,'" *Studies in Short Fiction* 1 (1964), 140–46. For a useful summary of the history of conflicting interpretations, see David Lodge, "Hemingway's Clean, Well-lighted, Puzzling Place," in *The Novelist at the Crossroads and Other Essays on Fiction and Criticism* (Ithaca, N. Y.: Cornell University Press, 1971), 184–202.

40. Lodge reprints the unemended story. Although Scribner's emended the text for the 1967 edition of *The Short Stories of Ernest Hemingway*, some readers are still finding their way to the unemended text. It is the edition that X. J. Kennedy used in the fourth edition of the textbook, *An Introduction to Fiction* (Boston and Toronto: Little, Brown, 1987), 122–25.

41. Famous for its haunting dialogue and its statement of existential despair, the story has striking pictorial effects. Hemingway makes us "see."

42. Hemingway's father committed suicide in 1928. Although Hemingway could be very critical of his father for the action, he understood that there were circumstances when the deed was not despicable. He had, in fact, given the subject a great deal of thought long before Clarence Hemingway shot himself. But he doubtless had the action in his mind as he wrote "A Clean, Well-Lighted Place." The story shows profound sympathy for the old man's attempt. In *Death in the Afternoon* Hemingway declares that he is "much interested in suicides" (20).

43. Hemingway reminds his readers of *A Farewell to Arms* (New York: Charles Scribner's Sons, 1929). Just before Frederic Henry takes his nighttime leave of Catherine before returning to the front, he and Catherine observe a soldier and his girl in the shadow of one of the buttresses of the cathedral. Frederic wishes that the couple had some place to go. Although Catherine says that "they have the cathedral" (147), this couple is also threatened by the forces of night. Because the girl in "A Clean, Well-Lighted Place" has her hair uncovered, the reader also recalls the emphasis on Catherine Barkley's hair, useful as sensual detail but also for the image of protection. During scenes of love, Catherine surrounds Frederic with her hair, tentlike, much as the soldier attempts to shelter the girl with his cape.

44. Marcelline Hemingway Sanford, *At the Hemingways: A Family Portrait* (Boston: Little, Brown, 1962), 215–16.

45. See Jeffrey Meyers, *Hemingway: A Biography* (New York: Harper & Row, 1985), 144, and *The Nick Adams Stories* (New York: Charles Scribner's Sons, 1972), 90.

46. Peter Griffin, *Along with Youth: Hemingway, the Early Years* (New York and Oxford: Oxford University Press, 1985), 97.

47. Baker, *Ernest Hemingway: A Life Story*, 1, and Madelaine Hemingway Miller, *Ernie: Hemingway's Sister "Sunny" Remembers* (New York: Crown, 1975), 25.

48. Flora, *Hemingway's Nick Adams*, 19–21. The James family we associate with an earlier time, and that family drama has not been so dramatic as the Hemingway drama nor so wide in its appeal.

49. Malcolm Cowley, introduction to *The Sun Also Rises*, in *Three Novels of Ernest Hemingway* (New York: Charles Scribner's Sons, 1962), xxii.

50. Meyers, *Hemingway: A Biography*, 144.

51. Baker, *Ernest Hemingway*, 109.

52. Kenneth G. Johnston, "Out of Season," in *The Tip of the Iceberg: Hemingway and the Short Story*, 29–38.

53. As late as 1959, Hemingway takes pride in remembering that he wrote "The Killers," "Today Is Friday," and "Ten Indians" on a single day (see his "Art of the Short Story" in part 2)—an extraordinary day's output.

54. *Conversations with Ernest Hemingway*, 94.

55. His novels are another matter. Both *A Farewell to Arms* and *For Whom the Bell Tolls* are famous for their love stories, but both are equally famous for the dramatizations of the deaths that conclude the accounts.

56. Readers and critics have identified Nick in several first-person stories in which the "I" is unnamed. Situation, theme, and setting have made most readers confident about naming "The Light of the World" and "In Another Country" as Nick Adams stories. Phillip Young included "An Alpine Idyll" in *The Nick Adams Stories*. There are good reasons for doing so, as I discuss in *Hemingway's Nick Adams*, where I also argue that the unnamed narrator of "Wine of Wyoming" may well be Nick Adams. It seems clear that Hemingway did not find it necessary always to label Nick when he was writing about him, and the absence of his name in the first-person stories is often related to Nick's struggle to define, to hold on to personality. Nick's name is used only once in "Now I Lay Me," and then only his first name. Hemingway expected his reader to make connections, to respond to the unstated as well as to the stated.

57. *A Moveable Feast* (New York: Charles Scribner's Sons, 1964). Subsequent references to this work are cited parenthetically in the text as *MF*. Gerry Brenner cautions that there is no manuscript original for the preface to *A Moveable Feast*. Moreover, he reports that on several manuscript pages Hemingway

wrote unequivocably: "This book is fiction." See "Are We Going to Hemingway's *Feast*," in *Ernest Hemingway: Six Decades of Criticism*, ed. Linda W. Wagner (East Lansing: Michigan State University Press, 1987), 298. Brenner's essay first appeared in *American Literature* 54, no. 4 (December 1982):528–44.

58. *Conversations with Ernest Hemingway*, 61.

59. Meyers, *Hemingway: A Biography*, 144.

60. Stein, *The Autobiography of Alice B. Toklas*, 201.

61. Meyers, *Hemingway: A Biography*, 120.

62. Stegner, the Westerner, sides with Hemingway. Wallace Stegner, "Born a Square," in *The Sound of Mountain Water* (Garden City, N.Y.: Doubleday, 1969), 184.

63. Later, in "The Undefeated," Hemingway would again, and more powerfully, contrast the behavior of the unknowing crowd with the dignity of a fatally injured bullfighter who performs with courage.

64. Lynn, *Hemingway*, 408–11.

65. Baker, *Ernest Hemingway*, 227.

66. Virginia Woolf, "An Essay in Criticism," in *Granite and Rainbow: Essays* (New York: Harcourt Brace & World, 1958), 90. Reprinted from the *New York Herald Tribune Books*, 9 October 1927.

67. In memory of her father, Ernest Hall, in 1905 Mrs. Hemingway presented a copy of Hunt's "The Light of the World" to the Third Congregational Church of Oak Park. Ernest would see the reproduction weekly until he left Oak Park to begin his career. As Michael Reynolds speculates, his mother's honoring of the Halls must have rankled Ernest. For him, the painting exemplified her domineering piety. See Michael Reynolds, *The Young Hemingway* (Oxford and New York: Basil Blackwell, 1986), 104–5.

68. Baker, *Ernest Hemingway*, 241.

69. For a study of Hemingway's abiding interest in the pictorial arts, see Emily Watts, *Ernest Hemingway and the Arts* (Urbana: University of Illinois Press, 1971).

70. See Robert N. Essick and Morton D. Paley, *Robert Blair's "The Grave" Illustrated by William Blake: A Study and a Facsimile* (London: Scolar Press, 1982).

71. Jeffrey Meyers sees "The Snows of Kilimanjaro" as a conscious imitation (and transformation) of "The Death of Ivan Ilyich." Meyers, *Hemingway: A Biography*, 275–76.

72. Ibid., 268–71.

73. E. L. Doctorow, "Braver Than We Thought," in *Ernest Hemingway: Six Decades of Criticism*, 330. Reprinted from the *New York Times Book Review*, 18 May 1986.

74. Meyers, *Hemingway: A Biography*, 273.

75. Virgil Hutton, "The Short Happy Life of Macomber," *University Review* 30 (June 1964):253–63. Reprinted in *The Short Stories of Ernest Hemingway:*

*Critical Essays*, ed. Jackson J. Benson (Durham, N.C.: Duke University Press, 1975), 239–50.

76. Meyers, *Hemingway: A Biography*, 273.

77. Kenneth Lynn also cautions against an easy acceptance of Hemingway's pronouncement on Margot. See his analysis of the story in Lynn, *Hemingway*, 431–36.

78. A reproduction of *The Good Man on His Death-bed* may be seen in E. H. Gombrich, *The Story of Art* (New York: Phaidon, 1964), 203. A reproduction of the McGrady painting may be seen in Nancy Heller and Julia Williams, *The Regionalists* (New York: Watson-Guptil, 1976), 154.

79. Rovit and Brenner, *Ernest Hemingway*, rev. ed., 19.

80. *Ernest Hemingway: Selected Letters 1917–1961*, ed. Carlos Baker (New York: Charles Scribner's Sons, 1981), 479. Subsequent references to this collection are cited parenthetically in the text as *Letters*.

81. In other circumstances, the writer might be discovering from a couple like this the germ of stories like "Hills Like White Elephants," "The Sea Change," and other stories. In other words, the confession pointedly reminds us of Hemingway at work.

82. Baker, *Hemingway*, 338.

83. Cooper, *The Politics of Ernest Hemingway*, 91–92. Cooper expands on the comparison in "Politics over Art: Hemingway's 'Nobody Ever Dies,'" *Studies in Short Fiction* 25 (Spring 1988):17–20.

84. Griffin, *Along with Youth*, 104.

85. Each story, of course, has its individual force. John Steinbeck thought "The Butterfly and the Tank" one of the world's great short stories (Baker, *Hemingway*, 337).

86. Perhaps he deceived himself. He was also having difficulty with the novel form. At his death, *Islands in the Stream* was not finished, and *The Garden of Eden* had even less satisfactory shape. His novel about Nick, published as "The Last Good Country" in *The Nick Adams Stories*, was unfinished, as were two other beginnings of novels, one published as "A Train Trip" and "The Porter" in the Finca Vigía Edition and the other published there as "The Strange Country."

87. The remaining titled short stories are "A Room on the Garden Side" (14 pp. longhand), "The Monument" (14 pp. typescript), and "Indian Country and the White Army" (19 pp. typescript). There are three untitled war stories of 12 pages typescript, 17 pages typescript, 19 pages longhand and half a page typed, and a fragment in longhand, pages numbered 23–38. See Baker's note, *Letters*, 867.

88. The complex relationships between Hemingway and his sons—especially Patrick and Gregory—were the subject of Paul Hendrickson's lengthy feature "Papa's Boys: Hemingway's Older Sons, Scarred but Clinging to Tender Memories," which appeared in the *Washington Post*, 30 July 1987, "Style"

section, page 1 and following. The article provides new detail on these relationships and portrays Gregory as the son still having great difficulty coming to terms with his father.

89. Hemingway was returning to the fable form—this time getting it right, one might say. In 1922 his "A Divine Gesture" was published in the *Double Dealer* 3 (1922):267–68. That fable, however, does not contain the child's viewpoint nor the energy of the later fables. It does have God as a character, though less successfully than does "The Good Lion." "The Divine Gesture" is in the mode of post–World War I aestheticism. Hemingway counted it apprentice work. The fable was reprinted in a special pamphlet edition in 1974, "A Divine Gesture" (New York: Aloe Editions).

90. Baker, *Hemingway*, 538.

91. *The Harper American Literature*, vol. 2, ed. Donald McQuade (New York: Harper & Row, 1987).

92. The Philip of "Get a Seeing-Eyed Dog" contrasts with Philip Rawlings, the hard-boiled writer of *The Fifth Column*, who treats his women carelessly.

*Part 2*

# The Writer: Hemingway on the Short Story

# Preface to *The First Forty-nine**

The first four stories are the last ones I have written. The others follow in the order in which they were originally published.

The first one I wrote was "Up in Michigan," written in Paris in 1921. The last was "Old Man at the Bridge," cabled from Barcelona in April of 1938.

Beside *The Fifth Column,* I wrote "The Killers," "Today Is Friday," "Ten Indians," part of *The Sun Also Rises* and the first third of *To Have and Have Not* in Madrid. It was always a good place for working. So was Paris, and so were Key West, Florida, in the cool months; the ranch, near Cooke City, Montana; Kansas City; Chicago; Toronto, and Havana, Cuba.

Some other places were not so good but maybe we were not so good when we were in them.

There are many kinds of stories in this book. I hope that you will find some that you like. Reading them over, the ones I liked the best, outside of those that have achieved some notoriety so that school teachers include them in story collections that their pupils have to buy in story courses, and you are always faintly embarrassed to read them and wonder whether you really wrote them or did you maybe hear them somewhere, are "The Short Happy Life of Francis Macomber," "In Another Country," "Hills Like White Elephants," "A Way You'll Never Be," "The Snows of Kilimanjaro," "A Clean, Well-Lighted Place," and a story called "The Light of the World" which nobody else ever liked. There are some others too. Because if you did not like them you would not publish them.

In going where you have to go, and doing what you have to do, and seeing what you have to see, you dull and blunt the instrument you write with. But I would rather have it bent and dull and know I had to put it on the grindstone again and hammer it into shape and put a

*From *The Fifth Column and The First Forty-nine Stories* (New York: Charles Scribner's Sons, 1938), vi–vii. Reprinted by permission of Charles Scribner's Sons and Jonathan Cape.

whetstone to it, and know that I had something to write about, than to have it bright and shining and nothing to say, or smooth and well-oiled in the closet, but unused.

Now it is necessary to get to the grindstone again. I would like to live long enough to write three more novels and twenty-five more stories. I know some pretty good ones.

# The Art of the Short Story*

*When, in March 1959, Ernest Hemingway's publisher, Charles Scribner, Jr., suggested putting together a student's edition of the author's short stories, he listed the twelve stories most in demand for anthologies, but he thought the volume could include the writer's favorites as well. He also suggested that Hemingway write a preface for classroom use.*

*Hemingway liked the idea and composed this essay in Spain during May and June while following the bullfight competition he chronicles in* The Dangerous Summer. *This preface takes the form of an extemporaneous lecture to college students and shows Hemingway considering other writers, critics, his own work, and the art of the short story. Though Hemingway proposed changing the book to a collection for the general public, he never fully revised the preface for such an audience—as both his wife, Mary, and Scribner recommended. The idea of the book was eventually dropped. It should be noted that Hemingway never approved the preface for publication and almost certainly would have made changes in tone if not in substance before releasing it to a general audience.*

*The essay published here has been edited but is unchanged from the final draft except for the correction of obvious typographical errors and the standardization of punctuation pertaining to story titles. Significant variant material appearing in early drafts but later omitted by Hemingway may be found in the notes.*

Gertrude Stein who was sometimes very wise said to me on one of her wise days, "Remember, Hemingway, that remarks are not literature." The following remarks are not intended to be nor do they pretend to be literature. They are meant to be instructive, irritating and informative. No writer should be asked to write solemnly about what he has written. Truthfully, yes. Solemnly, no. Should we begin in the form of a lecture designed to counteract the many lectures you will have heard on the art of the short story?

*Previously unpublished. Printed by permission of Robert W. Lewis and the Ernest Hemingway Foundation, which retains all rights. (In spring 1981 the *Paris Review* published a version of this essay that was based on a different typescript.)

Many people have a compulsion to write. There is no law against it and doing it makes them happy while they do it and presumably relieves them. Given editors who will remove the worst of their emissions; supply them with spelling and syntax and help them shape their thoughts and their beliefs, some compulsory writers attain a temporary fame. But when merde—a word which teacher will explain—is cut out of a book, the odor of it always remains perceptible to anyone with sufficient olfactory sensibility.[1]

The compulsory writer would be advised not to attempt the short story. Should he make the attempt, he might well suffer the fate of the compulsive architect, which is as lonely an end as that of the compulsive bassoon player. Let us not waste our time considering the sad and lonely ends of these unfortunate creatures, gentlemen. Let us continue the exercise.

Are there any questions? Have you mastered the art of the short story? Have I been helpful? Or have I not made myself clear[?] I hope so.

Gentlemen I will be frank with you. The masters of the short story come to no good end. You query this? You cite me Maugham? Longevity, gentlemen, is not an end. It is a prolongation. I cannot say fie upon it, since I have never fie-ed on anything yet. Shuck it off, Jack. Don't fie on it.

Should we abandon rhetoric and realize at the same time that what is the most authentic hipster talk of today is the twenty-three skidoo of tomorrow? We should? What intelligent young people you are and what a privilege it is to be with you.[2] Do I hear a request for authentic ballroom bananas? I do? Gentlemen, we have them for you in bunches.

Actually, as writers put it when they do not know how to begin a sentence, there is very little to say about writing short stories unless you are a professional explainer. If you can do it, you don't have to explain it. If you can not do it, no explanation will ever help.

A few things I have found to be true. If you leave out important things or events that you know about, the story is strengthened. If you leave out or skip something because you do not know it, the story will be worthless. The test of any story is how very good the stuff is that you, not your editors, omit. A story in this book called "Big Two-Hearted River" is about a boy coming home beat to the wide from a war. Beat to the wide was an earlier and possibly more severe form of beat, since those who had it were unable to comment on this condition and could not suffer that it be mentioned in their presence. So the war, all mention of the war, anything about the war, is omitted. The river was the Fox river, by Seney, Michigan, not the Big Two-Hearted. The change of name was made purposely, not from ignorance nor carelessness but because Big Two-Hearted River is poetry, and because there were many Indians in the story, just as the war was in the story, and none of the Indians nor the war appeared. As you see, it is very simple and easy to explain.

In a story called "A Sea Change," everything is left out. I had seen the couple in the Bar Basque in St. Jean de Luz and I knew the story too too well, which is the squared root of well, and use any well you like except mine. So I left the story out. But it is all there. It is not visible but it is there.

It is very hard to talk about your work since it implies arrogance or pride. I have tried to get rid of arrogance and replace it with humility and I do all right at that sometimes, but without pride I would not wish to continue to live nor to write and I publish nothing of which I am not proud. You can take that any way you like, Jack. I might not take it myself. But maybe we're built different.

Another story is "Fifty Grand." This story originally started like this:

"How did you handle Benny so easy, Jack?" Soldier asked him.
"Benny's an awful smart boxer," Jack said. "All the time he's in there, he's thinking. All the time he's thinking, I was hitting him."

I told this story to Scott Fitzgerald in Paris before I wrote "Fifty Grand," trying to explain to him how a truly great boxer like Jack Britton functioned. I wrote the story opening it with the Britton conversation and when it was finished I was happy about it and I showed it to Scott. He said he liked the story very much and spoke about it in so fulsome a manner that I was embarrassed. Then he said, "There is only one thing wrong with it, Ernest, and I tell you this as your friend. You have to cut out that old chestnut about Britton and Leonard."

At that time my humility was in such ascendance that I thought he must have heard the remark before or that Britton must have said it to some one else. It was not until I had published the story, from which I had removed that lovely revelation of the metaphysics of boxing that Fitzgerald in the way his mind was functioning that year, had called such an historic statement an "old chestnut" because he had heard it once and only once from a friend, that I realized how dangerous that attractive virtue, humility, can be. So do not be too humble, gentlemen. Be humble after but not during the action. They will all con you, gentlemen. But sometimes it is not intentional. Sometimes they simply do not know. This is the saddest state of writers and the one you will most frequently encounter. If there are no questions, let us press on.

My loyal and devoted friend Fitzgerald, who was truly more interested in my own career at this point than in his own, sent me to Scribner's with the story. It had already been turned down by Ray Long of *Cosmopolitan Magazine* because it had no love interest. That was okay with me since I eliminated any love interest and there were, purposely, no women in it except for two broads. Enter two broads as in Shakespeare, and then they go out of the story. This is unlike what you will hear from your instructors, that if a broad comes into a story in the first paragraph, she must reappear later to justify her original presence. This is untrue, gentlemen. You may dispense with her, just as in life. It is also untrue that if a gun hangs on the wall when you open up the story, it must be fired by page fourteen. The chances are, gentlemen, that if it hangs upon the wall, it will not even shoot. If there are no questions, shall we press on? A question? Yes, the unfireable gun may be a symbol. That is true. But with a good enough writer, the chances are some jerk just hung it there to look at. Gentlemen, you can't be sure. Maybe he is queer for guns, or maybe an interior decorator put it there. Or both.

So with pressure by Max Perkins[3] on the editor, *Scribner's Magazine* agreed to publish the story and pay me two hundred and fifty dollars, if I would cut it to a length where it would not have to be continued into the back of the book. They call magazines books. There is significance in this but we will not go into it. They are not books, even if they put them in stiff covers. You have to watch this, gentlemen. Anyway, I explained without heat nor hope, seeing the built-in stupidity of the editor of the magazine and his intransigence, that I had already cut the story myself and that the only way it could be shortened by five hundred words and make sense was to amputate the first five hundred. I had often done that myself with stories and it improved them. It would not have improved this story but I thought that was their ass not mine. I would put it back together in a book. They read differently in a book anyway. You will learn about this.

No, gentlemen, they would not cut the first five hundred words.

They gave it instead to a very intelligent young assistant editor who assured me he could cut it with no difficulty. That was just what he did on his first attempt, and any place he took words out, the story no longer made sense. It had been cut for keeps when I wrote it, and afterwards at Scott's request I'd even cut out the metaphysics which, ordinarily, I leave in. So they quit on it finally and eventually, I understand, Edward Weeks got Ellery Sedgwick to publish it in the *Atlantic Monthly*. Then everyone wanted me to write fight stories and I did not write any more fight stories because I tried to write only one story of anything, if I got what I was after, because Life is very short if you like it and I knew that even then. There are other things to write about and other people who write very good fight stories. I recommend to you "The Professional" by W. C. Heinz.

Yes, the confidently cutting young editor became a big man on *Reader's Digest*. Or didn't he? I'll have to check that. So you see, gentlemen, you never know and what you win in Boston you lose in Chicago. That's symbolism, gentlemen, and you can run a saliva test on it. That is how we now detect symbolism in our group and so far it gives fairly satisfactory results. Not complete, mind you. But we are beginning to see our way through. Incident[al]ly, within a short time *Scribner's Magazine* was running a contest for long short stories that broke back into the back of the book, and paying many times two hundred and fifty dollars to the winners.

Now since I have answered your perceptive questions, let us take up another story.

This story is called "The Light of the World." I could have called it "Behold I Stand at the Door and Knock" or some other stained-glass window title, but I did not think of it and actually "The Light of the World" is better. It is about many things and you would be ill advised to think it is a simple tale. It is really, no matter what you hear, a love letter to a whore named Alice who at the time of the story would have dressed out at around two hundred and ten pounds. Maybe more. And the point of it is that nobody, and that goes for you, Jack, knows how we were then from how we are now. This is worse on women than on us, until you look into the mirror yourself some day instead of looking at women all the time, and in writing the story I was trying to do something about it. But there are very few basic things you can do anything about. So I do what the French call *constater*. Look that up. That is what you have to learn to do, and you ought to learn French anyway if you are going to understand short stories, and there is nothing rougher than to do it all the way. Constater I mean. Not learn French. It is hardest to do about women and you must not worry when they say there are no such women as those you wrote about. That only means your women aren't like their women. You ever see any of their women, Jack? I have a couple of times and you would be appalled and I know you don't appall easy.

What I learned constructive about women, not just ethics like never blame them if they pox you because somebody poxed them and lots of times they don't even know they have it—that's in the first reader for squares—is, no matter *how* they get, always think of them the way they were on the best day they ever had in their lives. That's about all you can do about it and that is what I was trying for in the story.

Now there is another story called "The Short Happy Life of Francis Macomber." Jack, I get a bang even yet from just writing the titles. That's why you write, no matter what they tell you. I'm glad to be with somebody I know now and those students have gone.[4] They haven't? Okay. Glad to have them with us. It is in youth that our hope is. That's the stuff to feed the troops. Students, at ease.

This is a simple story in a way, because the woman, who I knew very well in real life but then invented out of, to make the woman for this story, is a bitch for the full course and doesn't change. You'll probably never meet the type because you haven't got the money. I haven't either but I get around. Now this woman doesn't change. She has been better, but she will never be any better anymore. I invented her complete with handles from the worst bitch I knew (then) and when I first knew her she'd been lovely. Not my dish, not my pigeon, not my cup of tea, but lovely for what she was and I was her all of the above which is whatever you make of it. This is as close as I can put it and keep it clean. This information is what you call the background of a story. You throw it all away and invent from what you know. I should have said that sooner. That's all there is to writing. That, a perfect ear (call it selective absolute pitch),[5] the devotion to your work and respect for it that a priest of God has for his, and then have the guts of a burglar, no conscience except to writing, and you're in, gentlemen. It's easy. Anybody can write if he is cut out for it and applies himself. Never give it a thought. Just have those few requisites.

I mean the way you have to write now to handle the way now is now. There was a time when it was nicer, much nicer and all that has been well written by nicer people. They are all dead and so are their times, but they handled them very well. Those times are over and writing like that won't help you now.

But to return to this story. The woman called Margot Macomber is no good to anybody now except for trouble. You can bang her but that's about all. The man is a nice jerk. I knew him very well in real life, so invented him too from everything I know. So he is just how he really was, only he is invented. The White Hunter is my best friend and he does not care what I write as long as it is readable, so I don't invent him at all. I just disguise him for family and business reasons, and to keep him out of trouble with the Game Department. He is the furthest thing from a square since they invented the circle, so I just have to take care of him with an adequate disguise and he is as proud as though we both wrote it, which actually you always do in anything if you go back far enough. So it is a secret between us.

That's all there is to that story except maybe the lion when he is hit and I am thinking inside of him really; not faked. I can think inside of a lion; really. It's hard to believe and it is perfectly okay with me if you don't believe it. Perfectly. Plenty of people have used it since, though, and one boy used it quite well, making only one mistake. Making any mistake kills you.

This mistake killed him and quite soon everything he wrote was a mistake. You have to watch yourself, Jack, every minute, and the more talented you are the more you have to watch these mistakes because you will be in faster company. A writer who is not going all the way up can make all the mistakes he wants. None of it matters. He doesn't matter. The people who like him don't matter either. They could drop dead. It wouldn't make any difference. It's too bad.

As soon as you read one page by anyone you can tell whether it matters or not. This is sad and you hate to do it. I don't want to be the one that tells them. So don't make any mistakes. You see how easy it is? Just go right in there and be a writer.

That about handles that story. Any questions? No, I don't know whether she shot him on purpose any more than you do. I could find out if I asked myself because I invented it and I could go right on inventing. But you have to know where to stop. That is what makes a short story. Makes it short at least. The only hint I could give you is that it is my belief that the incidence of husbands shot accidentally by wives who are bitches and really work at it is very low. Should we continue?

If you are interested in how you get the idea for a story, this is how it was with "The Snows of Kilimanjaro." They have you ticketed and always try to make it that you are someone who can only write about theirself. I am using in this lecture the spoken language, which varies. It is one of the ways to write, so you might as well follow it and maybe you will learn something. Anyone who can write can write spoken, pedantic, inexorably dull, or pure English prose, just as slot machines can be set for straight, percentage, give-away or stealing. No one who can write spoken ever starves except at the start. The others you can eat irregularly on. But any good writer can do them all. This is spoken, approved for over fourteen I hope. Thank you.

Anyway we came home from Africa, which is a place you stay until the money runs out or you get smacked, one year and at quarantine I said to the ship news reporters when somebody asked me what my projects were that I was going to work and when I had some more money go back to Africa. The different wars killed off that project and it took nineteen years to get back. Well it was in the papers and a really nice and really fine and really rich woman invited me to tea and we had a few drinks as well and she had read in the papers about this project, and why should I have to wait to go back for any lack of money? She and my wife and I could go to Africa any time and money was only something to be used intelligently for the best enjoyment of good people and so forth. It was a sincere and fine and good offer and I liked her very much and I turned down the offer.

So I get down to Key West and I start to think what would happen to a character like me whose defects I know, if I had accepted that offer. So I start to invent and I make myself a guy who would do what I invent. I know about the dying part because I had been through all that. Not just once. I got it early, in the middle and later. So I invent how someone I know who cannot sue me—that is me—would turn out, and put into one short story things you would use in, say, four novels if you were careful and not a spender.[6] I throw everything I had been saving into the story and spend it all. I really throw it away, if you know what I mean. I am not gambling with it. Or maybe I am. Who knows? Real gamblers don't gamble. At least you think they don't gamble. They gamble, Jack, don't worry.[7] So I make up the man and the woman as well as I can and I put all the true stuff in and with all the load, the most load any short story ever carried, it still takes off and it flies. This makes me very happy. So I thought that and the Macomber story are as good short stories as I can write for a while, so I lose interest and take up other forms of writing.

Any questions? The leopard? He is part of the metaphysics. I did not hire out to explain that nor a lot of other things. I know, but I am under no obligation to tell you. Put it down to *omertà*. Look that word up.[8] I dislike explainers, apologists, stoolies, pimps. No writer should be any one of those for his own work. This is just a little background, Jack, that won't do either of us any harm. You see the point, don't you? If not it is too bad.

That doesn't mean you shouldn't explain for, apologize for or pimp or tout for some other writer. I have done it and the best luck I had was doing it for Faulkner. When they didn't know him in Europe, I told them all how he was the best we had and so forth and I over-humbled with him plenty and built him up about as high as he could go because he never had a break then and he was good then. So now whenever he has a few shots, he'll tell students what's wrong with me or tell Japanese or anybody they send him to to build up our local product.[9] I get tired of this but I figure what the hell he's had a few shots and maybe he even believes it. So you asked me just now what I think about him, as everybody does and I always stall, so I say you know how good he is. Right. You ought to. What is wrong is he cons himself sometimes pretty bad. That may just be the sauce. But for quite a while when he hits the sauce toward the end of a book, it shows bad. He gets tired and he goes on and on, and that sauce writing is really hard on who has to read it. I mean if they care about writing. I thought maybe it would help if I read it using the sauce myself, but it wasn't any help. Maybe it would have helped if I was fourteen. But I was only fourteen one year and then I would have been too busy. So that's what I think about Faulkner. You ask that I sum it up from the standpoint of a professional. Very good writer. Excellent writer. Has been a superior writer many times. A great writer if we used the word great. Cons himself now. Too much sauce. But he wrote a really fine story called "The Bear" and I would be glad to put it in this book for your pleasure and delight, if I had written it. But you can't write them all, Jack. It's unfeasible.[10]

It would be simpler and more fun to talk about other writers and what is good and what is wrong with them, as I was when you asked me about Faulkner. He's easy to handle because he talks so much for a supposed silent man. Never talk, Jack, if you are a writer, unless you have the guy write it down and have you go over it. Otherwise they get it wrong. That's what you think until they play a tape back at you. Then you know how silly it sounds. You're a writer aren't you? Okay, shut up and write. What was that question?

Did I really write three stories in one day in Madrid, the way it said in that interview in the *Paris Review* and *Horizon*? Yes sir. I was hotter than a—let's skip it, gentlemen. I was laden with uninhibited energy. Or should we say this energy was canalized into my work. Such states are compounded by the brisk air of the Guadarramas (Jack, was it cold) the highly seasoned Bacalao Viscayina (dried cod fish, Jack) a certain vague loneliness (I was in love and the girl was in Bologna and I couldn't sleep anyway, so why not write.) So I wrote.[11]

The stories you mention I wrote in one day in Madrid on May 16 when it snowed out the San Isidro bullfights. First I wrote "The Killers" which I'd tried to write before and failed. Then after lunch I got in bed to keep warm and wrote "Today Is Friday." I had so much juice I thought maybe I was going crazy and I had about six other stories to write. So I got dressed and walked to Fornos, the old bull fighter's cafe, and drank coffee and then came back and wrote "Ten Indians." This made me very sad and I drank some brandy and went to sleep. I'd forgotten to eat and one of the waiters brought me up some Bacalao and a small steak and fried potatoes and a bottle of Valdepeñas.

The woman who ran the Pension was always worried that I did not eat enough and she had sent the waiter. I remember sitting up in bed and eating, and drinking the Valdepeñas. The waiter said he would bring up another bottle. He said the Señora wanted to know if I was going to write all night. I said no, I thought I would lay off for a while. Why don't you try to write just one more, the waiter asked. I'm only supposed to write one, I said. Nonsense, he said. You could write six. I'll try tomorrow, I said. Try it tonight, he said. What do you think the old woman sent the food up for?

I'm tired, I told him. Nonsense, he said (the word was not nonsense). You tired after three miserable little stories. Translate me one.

Leave me alone, I said. How am I going to write it if you don't leave me alone. So I sat up in bed and drank the Valdepeñas and thought what a hell of a writer I was if the first story was as good as I'd hoped.

I have used the same words in answering that the excellent Plimpton elicited from me in order to avoid error or repetition. If there are no more questions, should we continue?

It is very bad for writers to be hit on the head too much. Sometimes you lose months when you should have and perhaps would have worked well but sometimes a long time after the memory of the sensory distortions of these woundings will produce a story which, while not justifying the temporary cerebral damage, will palliate it. "A Way You'll Never Be" was written at Key West, Florida, some fifteen years after the damage it depicts, both to a man, a village and a countryside, had occurred. No questions? I understand. I understand completely. However, do not be alarmed. We are not going to call for a moment of silence. Nor for the man in the white suit. Nor for the net. Now gentlemen, and I notice a sprinkling of ladies who have drifted in attracted I hope by the sprinkling of applause. Thank you. Just *what* stories do you yourselves care for? I must not impose on you exclusively those that find favor with their author. Do *you* too care for any of them?

You like "The Killers"? So good of you. And why? Because it had Burt Lancaster and Ava Gardner in it? Excellent. Now we are getting somewhere. It is always a pleasure to remember Miss Gardner.[12] No, I never met Mr. Lancaster. I can't tell you what he is really like but everyone says he is terrific. He was the hottest muzzle in Hollywood at that time.

The background of that story is that I had a lawyer who had cancer and he wanted cash rather than any long term stuff. You can see his point I hope. So when he was offered a share in the picture for me and less cash, he took the more cash. It turned out badly for us both. He died eventually and I retained only an academic interest in the picture. But the company lets me run it off free when I want to see Miss Gardner and hear the shooting. There is one place where there is a lot of shooting.

It is a good picture and the only good picture ever made of a story I wrote. One of the reasons for that is that John Huston wrote the script. Yes I know him. Is everything true about him that they say? No. But the best things are. Isn't that interesting. I guess so in a way.

You mean background about the story not the picture? That's not very sporting, young lady. Didn't you see the class was enjoying itself finally? Besides it has a sordid background. I hesitate to bring it in, on account of there is no statute of limitations on what it deals with. Gene Tunney, who is a man of wide culture, once asked me, "Ernest, wasn't that Andre Andreson in 'The Killers'?" I told him it was and that the town was Summit, Illinois, not Summit, N. J. We left it at that. I thought about that story a long long time before I invented it, and I had to be as far away as Madrid before I invented it properly. That story probably had more left out of it than anything I ever wrote. More even than when I left the war out of "Big Two-Hearted River." I left out all Chicago, which is hard to do in 2951 words.

Another time I was leaving out good was in "A Clean, Well-Lighted Place." There I really had luck. I left out everything. That is about as far as you can go, so I stood on that one and haven't drawn to that since.

I trust you follow me, gentlemen. As I said at the start, there is nothing to writing short stories once you get the knack of it.

A story I can beat, and I promise you I will, is "The Undefeated." But I leave it in to show you the difference between when you leave it all in and when you take it out. The stories where you leave it all in do not re-read like the ones where you leave it out. They understand easier, but when you have read them once or twice you can't re-read them. I could give you examples in everybody who writes, but writers have enough enemies without doing it to each other. All really good writers know exactly what is wrong in all other good writers. There are no perfect writers unless they write just a very little bit and then stand on it. But writers have no business fingering another writer to outsiders while he is alive. After a writer is dead and doesn't have to work any more, anything goes. A son of a bitch alive is a son of a bitch dead. I am not talking about rows between writers. They are okay and can be comic. If someone puts a thumb in your eye, you don't protest. You thumb him back. He fouls you, you foul him back. That teaches people to keep it clean.

What I mean is, you shouldn't give it to another writer, I mean really give it to him. I know you shouldn't do it because I did it once to Sherwood Anderson. I did it because I was righteous, which is the worst thing you can be, and I thought he was going to pot the way he was writing and that I could kid him out of it by showing him how awful it was. He had written a book called *Dark Laughter*. So I wrote *The Torrents of Spring*. It was cruel to do, and it didn't do any good, and he just wrote worse and worse. What the hell business of mine was it if he wanted to write badly? None. He had written good and then he lost [it].

But then I was righteous and more loyal to writing than to my friend. I would have shot anybody then, not kill them, maybe just shoot them a little, if I thought it would straighten them up and make them write right. Now I know that there is nothing you can do about any writer ever. The seeds of their destruction are in them from the start, and the thing to do about writers is get along with them if you see them, and try not to see them. All except a very few, and all of them except a couple are dead. Like I said, once they're dead anything goes as long as it's true.

I'm sorry I threw at Anderson. It was cruel and I was a son of a bitch to do it. The only thing I can say is that I was as cruel to myself then. But that is no excuse. He was a friend of mine, but that was no excuse for doing it to him.[13] Any questions? Ask me that some other time.

This brings us to another story, "My Old Man." The background of this was all the time we spent at the races at San Siro when I used to be in hospital in Milan in 1918, and the time put in at the tracks in Paris when we really worked at it. Handicapping I mean. Some people say that this story is derived from a story about harness racing by Sherwood Anderson called "I'm a Fool." I do not believe this. My theory is that it is derived from a jockey I knew very well and a number of horses I knew, one of which I was in love with. I invented the boy in my story and I think the boy in Sherwood's story was himself. If you read both stories you can form your own opinion. Whatever it is, it is all right with me. The best things Sherwood wrote are in two books, *Winesburg, Ohio* and *The Triumph of the Egg*. You should read them both. Before you know too much about things, they are better. The best thing about Sherwood was he was the kind of guy at the start his name made you think of Sherwood Forest, while in Bob Sherwood the name only made you think of a playwright until of course he did so many other things.[14]

There are a few stories in this book you probably have not read before and there are two fables. They were both written for the children of Venetian friends. I try to keep my fables short and fabulous. They are fun to write but you should not overdo it.

The Cuban story was written when Fidel Castro was around fourteen years old. Not that it matters.

There is one story called "The Cross Roads." It is fiction. That means the *I* is not me. You make it up from what you know about. Knowing too much about such stuff is both bad and good for a writer. You get a little of both, Jack. In the end it is supposed to all even up. But somebody's always got a percentage.

There are eleven other stories written that I have not published.[15] It is wise gentlemen to keep a reserve; especially the way things have been going. I hope you agree.

Any other stories you find in this book are in because I liked them.

If you like them too I will be pleased. Thank you very much. It has been nice to be with you.[16]

# Notes

The Hemingway Collection at the John F. Kennedy Library holds the original holograph manuscript signed and dated "13/6/59" (item 251a); the manuscript of the addendum written for other possible story selections for the book (item 251b); a typescript including the addendum (item 251c); and two copies of the same carbon typescript dated "June, 1959," one showing no editing marks (item 251), the other (item 251d)—a copy sent to Charles Scribner, Jr., and preceded by a list of his recommended changes—containing several additions in Hemingway's hand, as well as the earlier addendum to the preface.

Since item 251d contains the earlier addendum plus several entirely new additions, it would seem to be the final draft. Therefore, I have worked from it in preparing the essay. Thus, the essay printed here differs from that published in the *Paris Review*, 23 (Spring 1981):85–102, which follows the other final carbon typescript (item 251).

1. In 251d this sentence begins "But when shit or, merde. . . ." The words *shit or*, which had been crossed out in an earlier draft (251c), were again crossed out in 251d.

2. In 251d the word *young* appears to be crossed out, probably by Charles Scribner, Jr. I retain it here since Hemingway's essay was never fully amended for a general audience.

3. In 251a Hemingway has crossed out the clause following *Max Perkins*—"who when he died I did not give a shit about anything for a year."

4. In 251c the word *fucking* modifies students. In 251d, the modifier is changed to *feecking*, and is crossed out.

5. Here I have reverted to the punctuation of 251c and added a comma for clarity since Hemingway's use of dashes in 251 ("That, a perfect ear—call it selective—absolute pitch,") and 251d ("That, a perfect ear, call it selective—absolute pitch,") confuse the sense of the phrase.

6. In 251a the line reads "a careful guy and not a spender." However, the word *guy* is crossed out. Subsequent versions wrongly retain the *a* so as to read "a careful and not a spender." I have omitted this unnecessary *a*.

7. *Jack* originally read *jerks* in 251c.

8. Hemingway put a question mark in the margin of the typed manuscript (251c), apparently unsure of the accent mark, for the Italian *omertà*, which means code of silence or knowing how to be silent. He had the accent acute, but it is grave as corrected here. It is a splendid word for his argument, as he emphasizes.

9. The manuscript reveals that at one time Hemingway had a comma

between the two *to*s: "send him to, to build up our local product." He then deleted the comma. A more traditional punctuater might have rendered the sentence: "So now whenever he has a few shots, he'll tell students what's wrong with me, or tell Japanese, or anybody they send him to to build up our local product." But his ear was right; the comma between the *to*s harms the sentence.

10. An addendum to 251a labeled as manuscript page 31 and resembling a false start reads as follows:

> There are so many other good writers I would like to include them and their stories in this book. Maybe we can do that sometime. This is too much like a reading from your own works, a thing I have never done. Practically everybody does what they say they will never do. Nothing can happen to you except the bomb that has not happened to others. As you know the atom bomb is nothing if you take a good long breath and recite an act of contrition. Squares welcome it. They have their act of contrition sewed into their underwear. All they have to do is touch it. It is easy gentlemen. Let us accept the future as we have the past and say schuck it off Jack until it happens.

11. The following four paragraphs are taken directly from George Plimpton's interview with Hemingway that appeared in the *Paris Review*, vol. 18 (Spring 1958):79–80. In previous drafts of the essay, these paragraphs appear in quotation marks. In 251d, the quotation marks are dropped either by Hemingway or by Charles Scribner, Jr. Since such punctuation seems unnecessary and only likely to confuse the reader, the 251d amendment is adhered to here.

12. 251d reads ". . . Miss Gardner as she was then." The modifying phrase has been crossed out.

13. 251a reads "He was a friend of mine. I was no friend of mine but that was no excuse. . . ."

14. The next three paragraphs were additions to the preface headed "Add to Preface—insert if decide to use the other stories—E. H." in 251b, 251c, and 251d. It was to be used if Hemingway and Scribner's decided to issue the collection for a general audience. In 251c they appear, rather arbitrarily, after the essay's introductory paragraph and are followed by the lines from manuscript 251b:

> Thus merrily we came into the light and did see a city perched high above the plain—
> Denver yclept and known for houses of ill fame
> Listen, Jack, I'll tell you a funny thing. Who hasn't been crazy hasn't been nowhere.

15. This paragraph was added in Hemingway's hand to the above addition to the preface, 251d. It seems to follow naturally in this position. How-

ever, the word *cut* is written in the margin, probably by Charles Scribner, Jr.
  16. A few odd notes appear at the end of 251a:

> Gentlemen at 14 to 21 I take it that you are all grown up to and past man's
> estate[.] My own sons, the youngest and truly more ignorant one, is more
> grown up than any man can be and function and I find it admirable[.]
>   Writing spoken, Dante started it of course. (Look him up)

*Part 3*

# THE CRITICS

# Ernest Hemingway's
# Unhurried Sensations
*Tony Tanner**

One of the richest chapters in *Death in the Afternoon* is the last, in which Hemingway describes all those things he has not managed to get into the book but which he thinks deserve a place: and of course in the very enumeration of the missing material he is in fact inserting it. This whole chapter seems to me to provide a most interesting point of departure for a discussion of Hemingway's whole attitude towards experience, but before pursuing that discussion I must quote at some length from the chapter itself. This will give us a preliminary clue to the structure of reality as perceived by the Hemingway eye.

> If I could have made this enough of a book it would have had everything in it. The Prado, looking like some big American college building with sprinklers watering the grass early in the bright Madrid summer morning; the bare white mud hills looking across toward Carabanchel; days on the train in August with the blinds pulled down on the side against the sun and the wind blowing them; chaff blown against the car in the wind from the hard earthen threshing floors; the odour of grain and the stone windmills. . . .
>
> It should have the smell of burnt powder and the smoke and the flash and the noise of the traca going off through the green leaves of the trees, and it should have the taste of horchata, ice-cold horchata, and the new-washed streets in the sun, and the melons and beads of cool on the outside of the pitchers of beer; the storks on the houses in Barco de Avila and wheeling in the sky, and the red-mud colour of the ring; and at night dancing to the pipes, and the drum with lights through the green leaves and the portrait of Garibaldi framed in leaves. . . .
>
> Let those who want to save the world *if you can get to see it clear* and as a whole. *Then any part you make will represent the whole* if it's made truly. The thing to do is work and learn to make it. No. It is

*From *The Reign of Wonder: Naivety and Reality in American Literature* (Cambridge: Cambridge University Press, 1965), 228–48. Reprinted by permission of the publisher.

147

not enough of a book, but still there were a few things to be said. There were a few practical things to be said.[1][my italics]

The reality of the world can best be attested to by certain experienced sensations—smells, feels, above all sights—not classified or related or theorized about, but simply put one alongside the other; separate yet cohabitating, their original sharp clarity undiminished and unblurred. The syntax is essentially paratactic because that is how the vision operates. And Hemingway has got all those impressions into his book, got them in in a manner which looks rather like Whitman's loose lines contracted into imagist incisiveness, and yet got them in in a manner which seems to him not to be the proper mode of inclusion. It is as though he feels he has not had any warrant for giving us those sensory particulars although they mean so much to him. They represent a veritable treasure-trove of unused particulars, an unspendable horde which he yet feels moved to display. There is a similar moment in "The Snows of Kilimanjaro" where the dying writer thinks over those things which he had not written about and which somehow could not be committed to paper. I give only a very short sample: "you could not dictate the Place Contrescarpe where the flower sellers dyed their flowers in the street and the dye ran over the paving where the autobus started and the old men and the women, always drunk on wine and bad marc; and the children with their noses running in the cold; the smell of dirty sweat and poverty and drunkenness at the Café des Amateurs and the whores at the Bal Musette they lived above."[2] There is a great deal more, all of it taken up with set scenes, perceived fragments, place names, and occasionally very abrupt incidents. This is Hemingway's wealth: meticulously retained sensations of the scattered munificence of the world. Hemingway has Clemens's gift of vivid recollection: he too can "call it all back and make it as real as it ever was, and as blessed"; and, in these passages at least, he, like Clemens, can do little more with it than "call it all back." Once again the problem of form arises. How is the writer to organize, distribute and employ the harvest of valued particulars which the wondering eye has garnered for him? The two pieces quoted manage, by skilful and quite legitimate legerdemain, to bring the details before us with no form but the flow of rapt reminiscence. This interesting phenomenon permits us to speculate on Hemingway's criteria for inclusion: which details did get properly into his work, and why? Or put in another way: what is the function of the registered particular in Hemingway's fiction? Is it just one of a random inventory—as the publishers who rejected the short prose pieces which composed the first *in our time* doubtless thought—or does it have real artistic work to do? To what end does the Hemingway eye work? It will be worth bearing in mind those italicized words: see things clearly and the part, the particular, will represent the whole. Remember Emerson's words: "the truth-speaker may dismiss all solicitude as to the proportion and congruency of the aggregate of his thoughts, so long as he is a faithful reporter of particular impressions." Hemingway is repeating, as an artistic principle, what Emerson prescribed as a philosophic strategy: be faithful to the particular and the over-all pattern and meaning will emerge of their own accord. What we must examine is the use Hemingway made of the clear particulars which his naive wondering eye afforded him. Let us take two examples from his short stories, examples of the scrupulous itemization of sensory details, and try to suggest why they are where they are, just those details in just that order:

> They were seated in the boat, Nick in the stern, his father rowing. The sun was coming up over the hills. A bass jumped, making a circle in the water. Nick trailed his hand in the water. It felt warm in the sharp chill of the morning.[3]
>
> ("Indian Camp")

> There was no breeze came through the open window. The American lady pulled the window-blind down and there was no more sea, even occasionally. On the other side there was glass, then the corridor, then an open window, and outside the window were dusty trees and an oiled road and flat fields of grapes, with grey-stone hills behind them.[4]
>
> ("A Canary for One")

The first passage occurs just after the child has been brought into contact with death for the first time: thus the delight in physical movement, the rising sun, the leaping fish, the touch of water and the feel of morning air are absolutely relevant to the boy's state of mind at that particular moment. It is a moment of intense awareness of the livingness of live things and the delights of the senses. The second passage describes the railway carriage which contains a couple on the point of break-up and an insensitive hard talkative American woman who makes the journey peculiarly agonizing. We learn the facts only at the end; but such passages as this bring home to us the claustrophobic, oppressive feeling in the compartment. The elimination of sea and breeze, the eye listlessly, desperately seeking some outlet through two windows and noting, with that curious lucidity which can come at moments of stifling tension, the details of the outer landscape: being given so much we are given as it were the environmental truth of the situation, as opposed to the psychological truth of it. Not the inward facts, but how the inward facts determine the registering of the outward scene.

One could easily list the particular moments that Hemingway chooses to focus on in his short stories and nearly always they will be found to be moments of crisis, tension and passion. This is not to say that they are epiphanies in Joyce's sense, but rather that they deal with moments of pain, shock, strain, test, moments of emotional heightening of some kind. It may be an ageing courageous bull fighter facing and succumbing to his last bull, it may be a man listening to his wife say that she is leaving him to go off with a woman: the subject matter varies widely, the emotional pitch of the characters is almost uniformly high. And it is at such moments that the details of the encompassing world seem saturated with relevance in an unusually intense way. They do not become symbolic, it is a weakness in the later Hemingway that he pushes them too far in that direction: they can be full of mute menace (as rain, for instance, always is in his stories): but usually they function as the recipients of the characters' intense attention. The character's emotion and the surrounding concrete details inter-permeate. In *A Farewell to Arms* there are at least three detailed accounts of meals, detailed to an extent which would be boring if they were simply meals taken by habit for sustenance. But they occur—immediately before the hero is bombed; while he and Catherine are enjoying a snatched few moments of ecstasy away from the war; and while he is waiting to hear the result of her fatal delivery. In the first case the vividness is retrospective: the moment frozen and etched in the memory before the shattering upheaval. In the other two cases the mundane minutiae are included because the intensity of the hero's emotions has so sharpened his sensory faculties that details are elevated from the mundane to the significant. It is as though anything he touches or smells or sees becomes a temporary reflector, even container, of his emotion. The scrupulous registration of details will give the most accurate morphology of the feeling. Only sensory evidence is veridical, and then only when the accounting senses have been pressed into a state of raw hyper-lucidity. . . .

To find any truth a man must be alone, alone with his senses and the seen world. Hence the specific renunciation of social engagement in *Green Hills of Africa*. "If you serve time for society, democracy, and the other things quite young, and declining any further enlistment make yourself responsible only to yourself, you exchange the pleasant, comforting stench of comrades for *something you can never feel in any other way than by yourself*"⁵[my italics]. This, among other reasons, is why the old fisherman has to be utterly alone when he takes on the big fish.

> My choice was to go there to find him beyond all people. Beyond all people in the world. . . . Aloud he said, "I wish I had the boy."
> But you haven't the boy, he thought. You have only yourself. . . .⁶

Only what the isolated self can do on its own is valuable, only what the isolated ego can perceive for itself is true. To have any significant experience the Hemingway hero must, in one sense or another, for one reason or another (a wound for instance), be "beyond all people." Any peace he makes with the world will be personal rather than social, not communal but "separate."⁷ Having discussed the relationship between the hero and the world in Hemingway's work I want now to suggest how this had a direct shaping influence on the prose style of his work. For since syntax is simply vision in action, the preferred manner of arranging perceptions, we can expect to find the ethics of the eye reflected in the order of the words. And one of the most notable aspects of Hemingway's prose is the way it avoids summary and insists on recording sequences in detail. A good example is this passage from *The Sun Also Rises:*

> After a while we came out of the mountains, and there were trees along both sides of the road, and a stream and ripe fields of grain, and the road went on, very white and straight ahead, and then lifted to a little rise, and off on the left was a hill with an old castle, with buildings close around it and a field of grain going right up to the walls and shifting in the wind. I was up in front with the driver and I turned around. Robert Cohn was asleep, but Bill looked and nodded his head.⁸

Jake notes everything carefully, reverently, meticulously as the bus travels through the beautiful countryside: each glimpse is caught in its transient perfection. Cohn, typically, lacks the Hemingway eye and reveals his insensitivity by sleeping. But Bill understands; no words need to be exchanged between people who know how to look at the natural world. And the prose makes permanent the attentive wonder of the senses: it mimes out the whole process, impression by impression. How far Hemingway will take this can be demonstrated by such examples as the following: "The red door of the ring went shut, the crowd on the outside balconies of the bull-ring were pressing through to the inside, there was a shout, then another shout."[9] Not "there were some shouts": that would be summary, a collapsing together of separate moments. The pause in reality must reappear in the prose. It was part of the truth of things. This pursuit of the exact progress of the senses is everywhere in evidence in Hemingway, even in his earliest work, as for example in the story "The Three-Day Blow." "They stood together, looking out across the country, down over the orchard, beyond the road, across the lower fields and the woods of the point to the lake."[10] Out, down, beyond, across—as the eye shifts its direction and focus, the prose follows it. As a result the prose very often has recourse to the words "then" and "and," and participles: these become important structural factors. They serve to thrust the reader much closer to the actual moment.

Here we should quote again from Robert Jordan: "but if there is only now, why then now is the thing to praise and I am very happy with it."[11] Hemingway's practice of unravelling the instant, of hugging the details of a sequence with his whole attention, is not merely the developed habit of a graphic news reporter, no matter how much Hemingway owes to his early journalism. It is a reflection of his faith in the ultimate veracity of the attuned and operating senses and the unsurpassable value of the registered "now." As Jordan realizes: "*Now*, it has a funny sound to be a whole world and your life."[12] A moment is "a whole world": this is why Hemingway explores its geography with such delicate care. Perhaps we can understand why Hemingway's prose always works to extract and arrest the significant fragments from the endless continuum of sense impressions which constitutes experience. His unflagging efforts to discover and hold "the real thing, the sequence of motion and fact which made the emotion"[13] constitute a creed and not a gimmick. Hemingway's style has been called "matter-of-fact" as though its laconic understatement was its main achievement: but we could more accurately rephrase that and say his style was after the facts of matter, those items of the material world which prompted and provoked the attention of his characters. In this he could be compared with Thoreau who, we recall, also made it his aim to "front only the essential facts," to ascertain "the case that is." And it is surely significant that in Hemingway's later work the facts tended to become fabulous, to expand into myth—just as Thoreau asserted they would do if seen properly. . . .

## Notes

1. *Death in the Afternoon* (Cape, London, 1932), pp. 254, 255, 258, 259, 261.
2. *The First Forty-nine Stories* (Collier, New York, 1938), p. 167.
3. Ibid. p. 193.
4. Ibid. p. 435.
5. *Green Hills of Africa*, p. 148.
6. *The Old Man and the Sea*, pp. 55–7.
7. *The Sun Also Rises*, p. 204.
8. Ibid. p. 204.
9. Ibid. p. 204.
10. *The First Forty-nine Stories*, p. 213.
11. *For Whom the Bell Tolls*, p. 166.
12. Ibid. p. 166.
13. *Death in the Afternoon*, p. 10.

# "In Another Country"
### *Earl Rovit and Gerry Brenner**

. . . "In Another Country," surely one of Hemingway's masterpieces in the short story form, also takes a professional into a challenge situation for which he has not been prepared, but with very different results from the satiric "Fifty Grand." The Major of the story is Hemingway's most attractive tutor figure, and he is also the most intelligent and sensitive. A professional soldier, and before the war a champion fencer, he is undergoing mechanical therapy for a wound which has left his fencing hand shrunken to baby size. Disabling

*From *Ernest Hemingway, Revised Edition* (Boston: Twayne Publishers, 1986), 45–48. Reprinted by permission of Twayne Publishers, a division of G. K. Hall & Co.

wounds and death are foreseeable eventualities for professional soldiers, and the Major accepts his lot with equanimity. Out of a sense of duty he reports to the hospital every afternoon to be treated by the therapeutic machines (designed to rehabilitate industrial accidents), even though he does not believe in their efficacy. When he engages the tyro (the first-person narrator) in conversation, he insists with characteristic professionalism that the boy speak Italian grammatically. As Hemingway presents him, the Major is a figure of considerable dignity and somewhat stuffy rectitude who "did not believe in bravery," presumably because, like Santiago, he chooses precision and exactness over the uncontrollable results of impulse action.

But one afternoon he comes to the hospital in an irritable mood and provokes the tyro into a rude argument over marriage, declaiming angrily that a man must not marry. "If he is to lose everything, he should not place himself in a position to lose that. He should not place himself in a position to lose. He should find things he cannot lose." He makes a telephone call and returns to the room where the tyro is sitting.

> He was wearing his cape and had his cap on, and he came directly toward my machine and put his arm on my shoulder.
> "I am so sorry," he said, and patted me on the shoulder with his good hand. "I would not be rude. My wife has just died. You must forgive me."
> "Oh—" I said, feeling sick for him. "I am *so* sorry."
> He stood there biting his lower lip. "It is very difficult," he said. "I cannot resign myself."
> He looked straight past me and out through the window. Then he began to cry. "I am utterly unable to resign myself," he said and choked. And then crying, his head up looking at nothing, carrying himself straight and soldierly, with tears on both his cheeks and biting his lips, he walked past the machines and out the door.

One final paragraph concludes the story, in which we are told that the Major returns for his regular treatments three days later with mourning crepe on his uniform sleeve. The doctors had placed photographs of wounds before and after treatment in front of his machine. "The photographs did not make much difference to the major because he only looked out of the window."

This is the one certain case in Hemingway's work where the tutor rises far beyond the artificial boundaries that restrict his need to make decisions. As we have seen, the code of professionalism with its severe conditioning in special pragmatic skills and attitudes is designed to minimize the multiplicity of possibilities existing in any challenge situation. Or, to express it more simply, the professional attitude creates an arbitrary chart of the future—like a contour map of preselected terrain—in which only a few items are considered significant and the rest are ignored. The rationale for the adoption of such a code is suggested in the Major's passionate cry: "[Man] should not place himself in a position to lose. He should find things he cannot lose." He will eventually lose everything when he loses himself, but along the way he will be able to control his losses and also the sequence of "holding attacks" through which he wages his battles.

If such a life code were adhered to strictly, a man would have to be either "the dumb ox" (the "simpler man") of so much Hemingway criticism or an unbelievable monster of machined egotism living, as it were, in an almost impregnable pillbox with no exits or entrances. The Major of this story is neither; his adoption of a code of life does not preclude his exposure to the risks of the incalculable in spite of his angry cry of outrage. Because he is human, he has loved; and, to continue the military metaphor, he has wittingly exposed his flanks to undefendable attack. His commitment to love and his shock at his wife's death have placed him "in another country" than the one he has prepared to defend. That other country is nothing less than the human condition itself, for the human will is always vulnerable to ruthless destruction. And Hemingway's ultimate test of human performance is the degree of stripped courage and dignity that man can discover in himself in his moments of absolute despair. It would have been quite simple for the Major to have died well; his challenge is far greater than his own death (a challenge that Hemingway has typically considered a relatively easy one to face). The Major, in losing his wife, suffers a death of himself accompanied by the absurdity of his own continued life. It is meaningless—*nada*—that confronts the Major in full assault.

And like Jesus in "Today Is Friday," the Major is "good in there." He is badly broken, but not destroyed. He refuses to resign himself to the chaos of unmeaning, but he refuses also to deny the actuality of his fearsome defeat. He holds tight to the superficial conventions of his training—the empty forms of innate courtesy and soldierly duty—and sits within them to begin the laborious process of making the broken places within himself strong again. His response can be characterized as neither acceptance nor denial; he is neither victim nor rebel. The least and the best that can be said of him is that he survives with dignity, and it is possible that he may be considered Hemingway's most eloquent portrait of ideal heroism—unquixotic, unathletic, profoundly humanistic.

The characteristic of dignity, so important to Hemingway as to have furnished him with one of the major themes in his fiction, is relevant to our discussion at this point. The peculiar problems of twentieth-century life have made the depictions of human dignity almost anomalous in modern literature. Our characteristic heroes have been antiheroes or nonheroes, aggressive doomed men in revolt or essentially pathetic dupes at the mercy of nonmalicious and implacable victimization. Dignity in either situation is difficult to ascribe to such heroes who tend by choice to divest themselves of the traditional values of rational intelligence and moral integrity on which dignity has always rested. The great majority of modern heroes in literature are purposely grotesque—picaresque saints, rebels, victims, and underground men of all shapes and colors. Their individual value as artistic achievements and embodiments of viable life attitudes is undeniable, but dignity is a quality largely beyond their grasp. Hemingway's attempt to retain the ideal of dignity without falsifying the ignobility of the modern human condition (that impulse in his work that leads many commentators to associate his beliefs with those of classical Stoicism) is one of his signal triumphs as a modern writer. And it is generally through his characterizations of the tutor figure that this quality of dignity is manifested. . . .

# Opportunity: Imagination Ex Machina II

*Cecelia Tichi**

[*The artist's task is*] *a task in the same sense as the making of an efficient engine.*

—T. S. Eliot, *Literary Essays*, 1924

John Dos Passos invigorated the novel with engineering design, but his contemporary, Ernest Hemingway (1898–1961), brought engineering values into prose style. Dos Passos used structures and machines as the organizational model for the modern novel, but Hemingway enacted the values of engineering in his tight, functional prose. His was the efficient modern style for which Ezra Pound had argued. In the era of the antiwaste Efficiency Movement Hemingway's terse, economical lines brought engineering values into the very sentence itself. He reduced the sentence to its essential, functional components. The famous Hemingway style was essentially the achievement, in novels and stories, of the engineers' aesthetic of functionalism and formal efficiency.

Hemingway's engineering aesthetic, it must be noted, did not come unheralded to American readers. A 1911 best-selling novel explicitly encoded engineering values in a prose style warmly welcomed by the American reading public. We have no evidence that Hemingway read Edith Wharton's *Ethan Frome* (1911), but the style of Wharton's novel of thwarted passion in up-country New Hampshire announced the engineering aesthetic Hemingway would display in his own fiction of the 1920s. The reception of *Ethan Frome* anticipated the broad-based popularity of Hemingway's style from the 1920s onward. It is therefore useful to take notice of Wharton's one effort to master the prose style she felt characteristic of the engineering mind.

For Wharton, *Ethan Frome* was an anomalous work, a single deliberate experiment in technique intended to capture what Wharton termed the "granite outcroppings" of rural New England. The book

*From *Shifting Gears: Technology, Literature, Culture in Modernist America* by Cecelia Tichi (Chapel Hill: University of North Carolina Press, 1987), 216–29. Reprinted by permission.

157

has an odd history. Begun as a copybook exercise in French composition, it was abandoned until Wharton caught sight of a mountain that reminded her of "Ethan" one summer at her home in Lenox, Massachusetts. She recounts writing the novel the following winter in Paris. It dealt, in her terms, "with the lives led in those half-deserted villages before the coming of motor and telephone" (*Backward Glance* 296).

In a retrospective preface like those of Henry James, Wharton described the problems of the "construction" (her own term) of the novel. Its hard-edged regionalism demanded, she felt, a stark and summary treatment, much like that which the modernist American painter, Charles Sheeler, would give the angular barns of rural America in the 1920s. Wharton needed to avoid what she called "added ornament, or a trick of drapery or scenery" (vii). Her style and structure must match her subject, both being hard-edged. If the modernist writers preferred to evoke that hard-edged quality with images of metals, especially steel, Wharton was just as insistent upon it with her figure of granite. She felt it would not be appropriate to treat "rudimentary" characters in the voice evocative of cosmopolitan elegance. She must reject the kind of narrator who would utter the characteristically ornate Wharton sentences, those that had brought her into stylistic comparison with Henry James. The "granite outcroppings" in *Ethan Frome* demanded a narrator who would not, in fact, speak the typical Edith Wharton sentence of the sort exemplified in Wharton's *Madame de Treymes* (1907). That novella had opened with an American businessman, John Durham, standing in a Paris hotel doorway overlooking the Tuileries gardens: "His European visits were infrequent enough to have kept unimpaired the freshness of his eye, and he was always struck anew by the vast and consummately ordered spectacle of Paris: by its look of having been boldly and deliberately planned as a background for the enjoyment of life, instead of being forced into grudging concessions to the festive instincts, or barricading itself against them in unenlightened ugliness, like his own lamentable New York" (165). At once a reader sees the Latinate phrasing, the liberal use of adjectival and adverbial structures, the string of qualifying phrases that contrast Paris with New York, the very fact of a mind characterized by the long, ornate, intricate sentence.

Wharton needed a very different narrative voice for *Ethan Frome*. She felt the novel demanded an educated narrator who spoke directly in plain, declarative statements. The subject matter, those "granite outcroppings," required a plain-spoken sophisticate who could communicate subtlety and nuance without the syntactical labyrinths of compound-complex sentences.

Wharton found a solution. For her narrator she chose an engineer. In the course of the novel he must piece together the story of Ethan Frome's tragedy and report his findings to those of "complicated minds," meaning the readers. Wharton virtually takes a page from the engineers' own guidelines for composition. As a onetime dean of a college of engineering wrote in 1939, looking back upon his half-century in engineering, "Those who attempt high-flown descriptions and impressions in writing reports make a mistake. The man who is thoroughly acquainted with his subject has no trouble in finding just the words to express his meaning, and when his meaning is expressed, he quits. There should be no padding, just sufficient detail to tell a story and no more. . . . [T]hat's all there is to a report. The simpler, the better."[1]

As if designing her narrator's voice to these specifications, Wharton has her engineer-narrator in *Ethan Frome* identify himself in this statement at the opening of the novel: "I had been sent up by my employers on a job connected with the big power-house at Corbury Junction, and a long-drawn carpenters' strike had so delayed the work that I found myself anchored at Starkfield—the nearest habitable spot—for the better part of the winter. I chafed at first, and then, under the hypnotising effect of routine, gradually began to find satisfaction in the life" (8). The engineer's statement is directly declarative. It avoids participial phrases and is sparing of adjectives and adverbs. His style, that of a sensitive, educated, and expressive person, is nonetheless as spare as the businessman's in *Madame de Treymes* is ornate.

By this style Wharton gained concision, an economy of phrasing that never compromises—in fact, intensifies—the emotional impact of the discourse. Her narrator's occupation suggested, in its values, the traits she thought necessary for the narrator of her novel. To achieve her stylistic objectives, however, Wharton needed more than an occupational label; she had to imagine herself in the mind of an engineer. In this Wharton evidently had help from her close friend, the lawyer-diplomat Walter Berry, who scrutinized each day's work on the manuscript of *Ethan Frome* in her Paris apartment in successive evenings. Wharton's memoir, *A Backward Glance* (1934), recalls Berry encouraging her always to follow her instincts but adds that this friend prized, above all, "clarity and austerity." Upon the completion of a manuscript draft, Wharton recalled, Berry joined her in "'adjective hunts' from which

[they] often brought back such heavy bags." With each book her friend "exacted a higher standard in economy of expression, in purity of language." We must surmise that Wharton's design for *Ethan Frome* gave Berry an unparalleled opportunity to press for the "economy of expression" characteristic of the novel. On that text his tastes converged with her technical-aesthetic objectives (116, 209, 296).

This editorial and imaginative rigor gave Wharton a double advantage of the vernacular and the sophisticated. For example, in the story Ethan's whining, hypochondriac wife, Zeena, complains of the young cousin who has come to help out in the household: "She don't look much on housework" (33). The narrator designates the same quality in the modern term "the girl's inefficiency," the very phrase one of efficiency itself (35). Wharton's engineering style also proved the power of understatement, as readers learned from the unfolding story of Ethan Frome, himself a frustrated engineer. Caught in a wretched marriage on a marginal farm, Ethan falls in love with the cousin-housekeeper with whom he tries to commit suicide when faced with the impossibility of running away with her or continuing as they are. Ironically, the failed suicide attempt ends with Ethan lamed, his lover paralyzed and demented, and the shrewish wife permanently in charge. The power of the novel comes from its stylistic restraint, its ability to convey extremes of emotion and action in an understated style. Wharton said that with the writing of *Ethan Frome* she "suddenly felt the artisan's full control of his implements" (*Backward Glance* 209). A full decade before Ernest Hemingway published the first of his major works, Edith Wharton had discovered the power of the machine-age plain style.

When *Ethan Frome* appeared, Hemingway was just entering his teens, writing for the newspaper and literary magazine of his suburban Oak Park, Illinois, high school that emphasized the classics, not contemporary writings like those of Mrs. Wharton. The son of a doctor and a musician and the second of six children, Hemingway was raised as an upper-middle-class white Anglo-Saxon Protestant. (His first pair of long pants were worn to a reception his parents gave in their Oak Park home for the Sons and Daughters of the American Revolution.[2])

Hemingway's route to the postwar avant-garde Parisian literary scene began with work on the *Kansas City Star* in 1917 as a cub reporter. His service as a World War I Red Cross ambulance driver took him to Europe, where he was wounded and to which he returned after additional journalistic experience in Chicago and on the *Toronto Star.* Encouraged by Sherwood Anderson, he spent the early 1920s in Paris, where he was befriended and helped by Gertrude Stein and Ezra Pound.

Although he grew up in the era which celebrated engineering feats, Hemingway's efficient style, unlike Wharton's, was not developed in self-conscious empathy with the mentality of the engineer. He did occasionally reveal the machine-age sensibility common to the time. In 1922 he submitted a poem to Harriet Monroe's *Poetry*, comparing his typewriter to a machine gun which "chatters in mechanical staccato, / Ugly short infantry of the mind."[3] At least once he spoke of himself in machine imagery, remarking that the mind and body need exercise "as a motor needs oil and grease."[4] Overtly mechanistic figures, however, are rare in his writing; organic terms predominate, for instance in his comparison of F. Scott Fitzgerald's talent to "the pattern made by the dust on a butterfly's wings." Readers alert to Hemingway's technological outlook may only see hints of it in his reference to the "construction" of those wings (*EHW* 106).

Major evidence of Hemingway's engineering values lies elsewhere. He did not enter imaginative literature by pretending to write engineering reports, but Hemingway's preparation in journalism was analogous in one important way to the rigor of technical writing. The former dean who advised young engineers to seek simplicity, to include salient but minimal detail, and to avoid padding sought to reassure them that they need not be reporters or "literary" writers.[5] Yet the style sheet Hemingway was given as a young reporter on the *Kansas City Star* at the height of the Efficiency Movement similarly directed news reporters to "use short sentences," "short first paragraphs," smooth and vigorous English. "Avoid the use of adjectives," said one stylebook rule, "especially such extravagant ones as *splendid, gorgeous, grand, magnificent*."[6]

Hemingway benefited from these strictures at a timely moment, for during the years of the Efficiency Movement the *Star*, a leading American paper, was in the vanguard of change in issuing such guidelines. Its editors and reporters helped American newspaper journalism emerge from a period of "heavy, turgid prose," which the novelist Robert Herrick complained about in 1904 when he described a news account of a fire: "the newspaper account wandered on, column after column, repeating itself again and again, confused, endlessly prolix, [a] waste of irrelevancy."[7] *Star* reporters of the 1910s, Hemingway included, were forced to free themselves of those offenses. "On the *Star*," Hemingway wrote, "you were forced to learn to write a simple declarative sentence" (*EHW* 38).

161

In the early 1920s, when he wrote entertaining feature articles for the less rigorous *Toronto Star* and *Star Weekly,* Hemingway sustained the concise, direct style of his Kansas City apprenticeship. The economics of telegraphy helped him do so when he became a foreign correspondent. In an era of telegraphic dispatches the journalist, like the engineer, underwent the discipline of severely economical expression. Here by cable, for instance, Hemingway describes the opening of the Conferenza Internazionale Economica di Genova in a report dispatched to the *Toronto Daily Star* from Genoa on April 24, 1922: "Delegates began to come into the hall in groups. They cannot find their seats at the table, and stand talking. The rows of camp chairs that are to hold the invited guests begin to be filled with the top-hatted, white-mustached senators and women in Paris hats and wonderful, wealth-reeking fur coats. The fur coats are the most beautiful things in the hall."[8] The rudiments of Hemingway's efficient style are in place here. Words are pared to a minimum. The declarative sentence dominates, free of subordination and of surrounding complex or compound-complex sentences. The adjectives are common ones, made powerful in the context by juxtaposing camp chairs to the top hats and fur coats. The critical tone surfaces in the figure of the "wealth-reeking" furs, but the passage, in fact the entire dispatch, avoids explicit editorializing. Like the other newspaper pieces collected in the volume *By-line: Ernest Hemingway,* it is tight, compact, concise. If the passage lacks the experiential intensity of Hemingway's fiction, it is important to recognize that the young writer retained the stylistic traits of such telegraph-wire journalism after he left newspaper work to write fiction full time.

A 1940 Hemingway letter to Charles Scribner contains a revealing statement on the relation between his efficient style and journalism. "Don't worry about the words," he told Scribner, "I've been doing that since 1921. I always count them when I knock off. . . . Guess I got in the habit writing dispatches. Used to send them from some places where they cost a dollar and a quarter a word and you had to make them awful interesting at that price or get fired" (*EHW* 57).

Hemingway joked, in this Mark Twain fashion, about achieving an economical yet engaging style from the rationed words of a telegraphed dispatch. It is, however, an achievement whose power he valued and one that ought not be taken for granted, as if the newspaper journalist would inevitably adapt his concise style to fiction. Nothing was further from the truth, and we can gain a renewed appreciation for Hemingway's innovation in stylistic efficiency by glimpsing a now-forgotten novel of 1921 that concerns the relation between art, journalism, and telegraphic dispatches.

Samuel Adams's *Success* (1921) recounts the rise of a young journalist, Banneker, who eventually writes successful "mood pieces" for New York City newspapers. The opening scenes of the novel especially pertain to traditional literary attitudes against which Hemingway rebelled. In a remote western railroad hamlet we meet the aspirant writer, the rustic young Banneker, a telegraph operator whose principal connection with civilization is the mail-order catalog. The nearby wreck of a passenger train becomes "his first inner view of tragedy," and immediately he begins to telegraph reports on the accident. His telegram, says the novel, "was a little masterpiece of concise information. Not a word in it that was not dry, exact, meaningful" (*Success* 18).

Meaningful, yes, but not imaginative. According to the author of *Success*, the "dry, exact, meaningful" dispatch could not in any way be imaginatively expressive. Young Banneker's state of mind, to be sure, is imaginatively excited. "His brain was seething with impressions, luminous with pictures, aflash with odds and ends of significant things heard and seen and felt" (18). As described, this state is much like that on which Hemingway based his own advice to an aspirant writer. "Remember," Hemingway advised, "what the noises were and what was said. Find out what gave you the emotion; what the action was that gave you the excitement" (*EHW* 30). These intensely felt recollections are the authentic origins of imaginative expression, says Hemingway, apparently in full accord with the traditional views of the author of *Success*.

The two part company, however, on the question of legitimate channels for the aesthetic expression of experience. *Success*, voicing the traditional viewpoint, assumes that the young telegrapher must fulfill his imaginative drives in a form permitting unlimited verbal expansiveness, which is to say a form antithetical to the telegraph. His official dispatches sent, Banneker sets to work on "some sheets of a special paper." "He wrote and wrote and wrote," says the novel, "absorbedly, painstakingly, happily. . . . [T]he soul of the man was concerned with committing its impressions . . . to the secrecy of white paper" (18–21).

This portrait of the young writer at work indicates an aesthetics of writing opposite to Hemingway's. Of course Hemingway, too, repeatedly said that writing made him happy and, like any writer, he worked in painstaking absorption. *Success*, however, works to validate the writer's imagination in his profusion of words, his voluminous outpouring of the soul. Banneker's journal, not the telegraph, provides his real "outlet of expression." The concision of his telegraphy is irrelevant to his imagination as a writer. Worse, it constrains him, distracts him from his genuinely imaginative state of mind.

*Success* really presents the traditional view of literary action. Its post-train wreck scenario says that the imagination of the true writer finds expression in verbal profusion. The more intense the experience (for example, a deadly train wreck), the more the words necessary to its expression. The writer may earn his living telegraphing dispatches (whether for the railroad or, by extension, for a news organization). His telegraphic concision may be exact and meaningful, but it is not really imaginative and has no place in genuine literature.

In hindsight it is easy to see how wrong the author of *Success* was in thinking that telegraphic concision precludes the expression of powerful emotion. *Success* argues that the verbal economy imposed by telegraphy is a kind of discipline that is hostile to imaginative expression. The novel follows its author's dictates; it is long (553 pages), thick with description and dialogue. By current standards it is prolix, melodramatic, and sentimental—qualities that are apparent now precisely because Hemingway helped to pose a successful challenge to them.

Telegraphic technology and its economics gave Hemingway the basis on which to invent a style of writing in which emotional power would be conveyed virtually in an inverse relation to the number of words used. Here is one of the concentrated true sentences Hemingway wrote in Paris in 1922: "I have watched two Senegalese soldiers in the dim light of the snake house of the Jardin des Plantes teasing the King Cobra who swayed and tightened in tense erect rage as one of the little brown men crouched and feinted at him with his red fez." It is not by chance that he copied the group of six such "carefully pruned statements"—declarative, straightforward, and forceful as a right to the jaw"—in long hand on telegraph blanks "as if they had been despatches to the *Star.*"[9] The power of this concentrated style was immediately apparent to some of Hemingway's contemporaries. Upon publication of *Three Stories and Ten Poems* (1923) and *In Our Time* (1924), Ford Madox Ford's secretary, Marjorie Reid, described Hemingway's rendering of "moments when life is condensed and clean-cut and significant" and doing so in "minute narratives that eliminate every useless word."[10] Virtually all the critical commentary on Hemingway has elaborated upon these insights. The journalist's verbal economy, Hemingway learned, could comprehend and evoke a full range of human experience.

Hemingway's fidelity to the concision he learned in journalism goes far to explain why he was so receptive to Ezra Pound's teachings on efficient writing in Paris in the early 1920s. Pound, as we saw, compared the position of the literary person with that of the powerful engineer, praising efficiency in machine design, in social credit economics, in writing itself. All this put Hemingway in the perfect ideological position vis-à-vis himself and Pound. The writer-editor was in the ideal position to ratify Hemingway's journalistic ethos and to help him perfect it by urging an appreciative Hemingway to distrust adjectives.[11] Pound, by way of Imagism and Vorticism, taught that severe concision was the basis for contemporary writers' formulations of power, energy, action, and intensity. Hemingway's barter, with Pound, of boxing lesson for lessons in writing was a swap in methods of power. Hemingway's reference to prose "so tight and so hard" resonates male sexual intensity and thus reinforces his knowledge that the efficient style is that of power (*EHW* 79).

What precisely was the aesthetics of the efficient style? What was the underlying theory of its power? And what was its connection with engineering values? First, Hemingway's efficient style is axiomatic with his obsession with how things work, especially at their most efficient—or as he termed it, properly.[12] Hemingway, like the American painter Thomas Eakins, shows a covert preoccupation with technics. In the late nineteenth century Eakins revealed his technological interest in paintings of surgical procedures, of musical instruments, of oarsmen. He showed an attraction to mechanical precision both in his subjects, for instance the Schuylkill River oarsmen of *The Pair-Oared Shell* and the engineering-type drawings he prepared as preliminary studies for the work. In the 1920s Hemingway expressed his similar interest in mechanism in his portrayals of bullfights and outdoor sports.

Like Eakins, Hemingway gravitated to subjects susceptible to analysis of their interworkings, and like the Philadelphia artist, he treated those subjects with precision of line, which he achieved with severe verbal economy. Hemingway's treatment, in short, was congruent with his appreciation of efficient structural or mechanistic entities, including those he discerned in the out-of-doors. In "The End of Something" in *In Our Time*, for instance, we see Nick Adams and his girlfriend, Marjorie, setting their fishing lines in a Michigan lake:

> She came in with the boat and ran the second line out the same way.
> Each time Nick set a heavy slab of driftwood across the butt of the
> rod to hold it solid and propped it up at an angle with a small slab.
> He reeled in the slack line so the line ran taut to where the bait
> rested on the sandy floor of the channel and set the click on the reel.
> When a trout, feeding on the bottom, took the bait it would run
> with it, taking line out of the reel in a rush and making the reel sing
> with the click on. (33)

The visual composition here is minimalist, formed of two angled lines, those of the rod and taut filament, coupled with the essential (as Ezra Pound would say, luminous) details of the driftwood and sandy channel floor. Thematically, Marjorie's fishing know-how allies her temperamentally with Nick and makes his imminent breakup with her all the more poignant. But the passage shows us something else. Characteristic of Hemingway's economical prose, it also exemplifies his need to show the reader exactly how the action, in this case fishing, is to be undertaken, what sequence of procedures is necessary. Slabs of wood stabilize the rods, whose reels, mechanisms themselves, are adjusted for optimal use. The entire apparatus is deployed for maximal efficiency and described accordingly, as if in a summary report.

Hemingway continues this method in "Big Two-Hearted River," the concluding story of *In Our Time* in which Nick Adams, now a writer and war veteran, returns to the Michigan forest to regain his psychological equilibrium by camping and fishing in solitude. Making camp, cooking, and fishing have a personal ritual value for Nick, as all readers have recognized, but these sequences can also be read virtually as a handbook on the efficient techniques of outdoor life. Here, for instance, are the step-by-step components of tenting. They show Nick's intense consciousness in the moment but provide as well an aesthetics of the technical interworkings of procedures and materials. Each component part of the action is revealed. First we see Nick find a level spot between two trees, chop out protruding roots with an ax, smooth the soil, then spread three blankets in certain precise ways, after which he pitches the tent:

> With the ax he slit off a bright slab of pine from one of the stumps
> and split it into pegs for the tent. He wanted them long and solid to
> hold in the ground. . . . Nick tied the rope that served the tent for
> a ridge-pole to the trunk of one of the pine trees and pulled the tent

up off the ground with the other end of the rope and tied it to the other pine. The tent hung on the rope like a canvas blanket on a clothesline. Nick poked a hole he had cut up under the back peak of the canvas and then made it a tent by pegging out the sides. He pegged the sides taut and drove the pegs deep, hitting them down into the ground with the flat of the ax until the rope loops were buried and the canvas was drum tight. (138–39)

The passage concludes with a perfect tent and works aesthetically on several levels. Visually, readers once again see the achievement of an angular composition comprised solely of straight lines. The "drum tight" canvas shows Nick's own satisfaction in the lines and flat planes, and Hemingway's declarative sentences become themselves the discursive equivalents of those visual lines. But the description is grounded in the step-by-step mechanics of tent-making. These and similar passages make "Big Two-Hearted River" a camper's guidebook. Hemingway finds and conveys an aesthetics in the mechanics themselves. How the thing itself—tent, fire, fishing—works when done efficiently is of intrinsic interest and value to him. Each component part is discrete and valued.

Other familiar scenes from Hemingway's fiction work similarly to present the technics of operations. The packing of trout in ferns in *The Sun Also Rises* is a good example. In the novel the protagonist, Jake Barnes, and his close friend, Bill Gorton, go off for a day of trout fishing in the Spanish countryside near Burguette. Jake quickly catches six trout, lays them out to admire them, cleans and washes them, and then packs them in a deliberate, step-by-step process that many readers have identified as a secular ritual of personal restoration. Jake recounts that he "picked some ferns and packed them all in the bag, three trout on a layer of ferns, then another layer of ferns, then three more trout, and then covered them with ferns. They looked nice in the ferns, and now the bag was bulky" (119–20). Once again Hemingway emphasizes the intrinsic importance of the precise operational steps. In fact he divides his characters according to their ability to understand or to fail to understand the spiritual importance of these technical procedures, properly executed.

Hemingway's fascination with the bullfights is an extension of this aesthetic of function. All readers have recognized the ritual importance Hemingway attached to bullfighting, its elegant *mano-à-mano* test of courage pitting man against deadly natural force. Yet the very mechanism of the bullfights has great appeal for the novelist. The worthy onlookers qualify as aficionados because they understand the aesthetics of form and function united in the bullring. The superb torero "becomes one with the bull" in a properly efficient execution of functional procedures.

From the bullfight to camping, this aesthetics of mechanism is a part of Hemingway's deliberately efficient style. In fact, his engineering values show a stylistic alliance with Frank Lloyd Wright. Hemingway's ideas on machine-inspired art appear in his well-known statement on writing in the retrospective (and posthumous) *A Moveable Feast* (1964). There we see Hemingway in full accord with the goal of simplicity which Wright thought inherent to the machine process and exemplary for contemporary artists hemmed in on all sides by affectation. Hemingway's statement begins with his often-cited directive for the writer: "'All you have to do is write one true sentence. Write the truest sentence that you know . . . and then go on from there.'" Critics have found that the phrase on the "one true sentence" succeeding itself lies at the heart of Hemingway's method (EHW 28). In fact, the "one true sentence" is Hemingway's structural component of fiction.

Yet the follow-up passage is more important here, because it underscores Hemingway's allegiance to the values of engineering in efficient prose style. In particular, it allies Hemingway with the principles of Wright's "The Art and Craft of the Machine." "If I started to write elaborately," Hemingway said, "or like someone introducing or presenting something, I found that I could cut that scrollwork or ornament out and throw it away and start with the first true simple declarative sentence I had written" (*EHW* 28).

Hemingway's scorn for ornament and scrollwork is significant. It points up his engineering values of functionalism and efficiency. Back in 1922, as a correspondent for *Toronto Evening Star*, he had expressed his repugnance for nonfunctional ornamentation in a feature article on "The Hotels in Switzerland." The young journalist scorned the "monstrous" Alpine hotels built "on the cuckoo clock style of architecture." They looked, he wrote, "as though they had been cut out . . . with the same scroll saw" by which he meant the thin, ribbonlike saw used for cutting wood into spirals or other ornamental shapes.[13] Much of the so-called gingerbread of Victorian architecture and furnishings was the product of the scroll saw. To reject the Alpine "cuckoo-clock" hotels was to reject bourgeois European tradition and, by extension, to re-

Cecelia Tichi

pudiate its ornate counterpart in American middle-class architecture and home furnishings.

Hemingway's persistent distaste for such nonfunctional ornament, whether in architecture or literature, marks him as a modernist. And his remark on ridding his own work of "scrollwork or ornament" explicitly allies him with Wright's point of view. From the 1920s onward the writer of fiction was really restating the architect's position. As Wright emphasized, all artists must repudiate the inessential and thus discard inauthentic ornament or scrollwork ("jig sawed beams and braces, butted and strutted, to outdo the sentimentality of the already overwrought antique product").[14] Wright, designing houses in Oak Park, the very Chicago suburb in which Hemingway grew up, anticipated Hemingway's theory of writing when he praised the machine for its capacity to accomplish the "wonderful cutting, shaping, smoothing" which produced "clean, strong forms" (65). Hemingway's "true simple declarative sentence" is exactly the verbal "clean, strong form" rid of the "waste," as Wright put it, of nonfunctional scrollwork. Wright's tortured wood is Hemingway's verbiage, but both amount to the same thing—fakery. Hemingway was everywhere sensitive to it, even in the bullring, where inept toreros would enact the wasteful scroll saw motion when the "twisted themselves like corkscrews . . . to give a faked look of danger." The authentic bullfighters, on the contrary, "never made any contortions, always it was the straight and pure and natural in line" (*Sun Also Rises* 167–68).

"Prose is architecture, not interior decoration," Hemingway wrote in a virtual echo of Wright, adding "the Baroque is over," equating its restless curves with the detestable work of the scroll saw (*EHW* 72). The nonfunctional decoration and ornamentation must be thrown out, Hemingway meant, because they are by definition inauthentic. In writing they are padding, mere rhetoric, a charge Hemingway even leveled against Melville, saying his "knowledge is wrapped in the rhetoric like plums in a pudding." Occasionally, he conceded, Melville's knowledge "is there, alone, unwrapped . . . and it is good" (*EHW* 94). But clearly he was too much on guard against nonfunctional ornamentation to undertake the close stylistic analysis that might have vindicated *Moby-Dick*. Stylistic intricacy meant just one thing, lies and evasions. Only essential, demonstrably functional structures were trustworthy.

Hemingway's repugnance for the circular and spiral forms, his appreciation for what he called the "straight" natural line has implications

169

for the shape of the sentence itself. His ethic of efficiency finds expression in the declarative sentence. That sentence becomes geometry's straight line, quite simply the shortest distance between two points. It is the sentence comprised solely of its functional components. It represents discourse as speed in a fast-paced culture. It is thus a different conception of efficacy from that which had governed American writing in the Romantic nineteenth century.

For the American Romantic writer found discourse to be represented adequately in the forms of the circle and spiral. Emerson's essay, "Circles," makes the point. It argues that the expansion of human consciousness takes the form of "a self-evolving circle, which, from a ring imperceptibly small, rushes on all sides outwards to new and larger circles, and that without end" (*Selections* 180). The Romantic conception of history accordingly embraced the figure of the spiral, which described the steady enlargement and progression of human society through time.[15] In an age of machine production and speed, however, Hemingway rejected these forms in favor of the declarative straight line.

He revealed the meaning of that line in his responses to the aesthetics of bullfighting. *The Sun Also Rises* disclosed the depth of Hemingway's commitment to the efficient straight line. The passage on bullfighting is a comment on his own literary style. In his capework the marvelous young bullfighter Romero moves "smoothly and suavely, never wasting the bull." He makes no "contortions," always achieving a line that is "straight and pure and natural," a line of "absolute purity" that he holds even when most exposed to danger. That line, Hemingway believes, is the only form adequate to evoke authentic emotion. It never wastes its materials. The inauthentic writer, like the inept torero, can hide emptiness behind fantastic scrollery. But only the artist who dares to expose himself in the efficient line can achieve the form of truth. Aesthetically, the declarative line surpasses journalism because it transcends the events of the moment. It is unparalleled in power. Stated purely, it endures.

Hemingway shows how it is that writings on a range of subjects can embody the values of machine technology. Stories and novels about hunting or fishing, bullfighting or boxing can exhibit a machine aesthetics, even when machines or structures play no part in the fiction. The pictorial representation of a machine or structure is not necessary and may be irrelevant. The form is what counts, and formally Hemingway's style marks the achievement of machine values in imaginative literature. He proves that the dominant technology does define or re-define the human role in relation to nature. He is full of nostalgia for a preindustrial "natural" environment, but his sentences are irrevocably of another, a gear-and-girder, world.

# Notes

1. Embry Hitchcock, *My Fifty Years in Engineering* (Caldwell, Idaho: Caxton, 1930), p. 112.

2. Carlos Baker, *Ernest Hemingway: A Life Story* (New York: Charles Scribner's Sons, 1969), p. 18.

3. Baker, p. 90.

4. Ernest Hemingway, *Ernest Hemingway on Writing*, ed. Larry W. Phillips (New York: Charles Scribner's Sons, 1984), pp. 120–21. Subsequent references cited as *EHW* and included parenthetically in the text.

5. Hitchcock, pp. 112–13.

6. Baker, p. 34 and Charles A. Fenton, *The Apprenticeship of Ernest Hemingway: The Early Years* (New York: Farrar, Straus, and Young, 1954), p. 33.

7. Fenton, p. 33 and Robert Herrick, *The Common Lot* (New York: Macmillan, 1904), p. 325.

8. Ernest Hemingway, *By-Line: Ernest Hemingway: Selected Articles and Dispatches of Four Decades*, ed. William White (New York: Charles Scribner's Sons, 1967), pp. 30–31.

9. Baker, pp. 90–91.

10. Baker, p. 125.

11. Linda Wagner, *Hemingway and Faulkner: Inventors/Masters* (Metuchen, N. J.: Scarecrow Press, 1975), p. 31. See also *EHW*, p. 34.

12. Baker, p. 17.

13. *By-Line: Ernest Hemingway*, p. 18.

14. Frank Lloyd Wright, *Writings and Buildings*, ed. Edgar Kaufman and Ben Raeburn (New York: Horizon, 1960), p. 65.

15. David Levin, *History as Romantic Art* (Stanford: Stanford University Press, 1959), pp. 1–40.

The Critics

# The Young Hemingway
*Michael S. Reynolds**

. . .Of the several writers living in Oak Park, he knew only enough about them to suspect that they were not the models he wanted. Oliver Marble Gale wrote historical romances that his mother's friends seemed to read. Charles White did architectural pieces for national magazines and there were some local poets. Edgar Rice Burroughs was making a fortune from *Tarzan* novels, one of which had just been made into a movie. Ernest did not know Burroughs, who made a big splash locally while Hemingway was in Italy. Then there were the ladies who wrote children's books—Mrs. Crummer and Helen Smeeth. Ernest had read children's books and magazines. At the lake house in Michigan, his parents kept bound volumes of *St. Nicholas* for summer reading. It was a magazine he devoured as a boy, indeed all through high school.

Now he began to read *St. Nicholas* seriously, looking for the formula, the trick of the story. From Ben Franklin's *Autobiography*, which he read in high school, he knew that imitation was one way to learn. His first real success had been his Ring Lardner imitations, which he continued in Italy. He wrote a "You Know Me, Al" piece for *Ciao*, the irreverent drivers' broadside which Section Four so enjoyed. Because imitation came easy for him, he practiced it throughout his seven-year apprenticeship. Later in Paris, with the apprenticeship done, he wrote a note to himself:

> Imitating everybody, living and dead, relying on the fact that if you imitate someone obscure enough it will be considered original.
>
> Education consists in finding sources obscure enough to imitate so that they will be perfectly safe.[1]

As he had learned by then, the emphasis was on *obscure* if you did not want the reviewers to put you down as someone's protégé.

In the spring of 1919, he had not discovered Stein or Anderson. He had not read Conrad, Lawrence or Turgenev. He had not heard of Ezra

*From *The Young Hemingway* by Michael S. Reynolds (New York: Basil Blackwell, 1986), 48–50. ©1986 by Michael S. Reynolds. Reprinted by permission of Basil Blackwell.

Pound or James Joyce. His reading was rooted in nineteenth-century British fiction. Other than Jack London's stories and *Call of the Wild*, he had read nothing that could be called modern. Few Americans had. The triumvirate—Twain, Howells and Henry James—that dominated the American scene for more than a generation was only lately dead. Twain died in 1910; James in 1916. Howells continued on alone until 1920. At the Scoville Institute, the Big Three could be found with shelves of their own. The 1890s Naturalists—the truly lost generation—left hardly a ripple on the literary consciousness of Oak Park. Dreiser's *Jenny Gerhardt* and *Sister Carrie* came to the library in 1913. Stephen Crane's *Red Badge of Courage* finally appeared in 1914, the single Crane on the shelf. But no one was recommending the Naturalists to Hemingway. Oak Parkers, as genteel as the best of pre-war America, were thoroughly British and Continental in literary taste, and with them was Hemingway.[2]

Growing up inside that protective shell, Hemingway had no way of knowing what lay beyond the edge of good taste. He did not even know the shape of the shell until he went to the war. If he suspected, that spring after the war, that there was more to writing than he had been taught, no evidence remains. There is nothing to suggest that he had any intention of writing great literature. Writing he regarded as an occupation, a job that produced income. Looking for models, he turned to the popular magazines. Had he stuck to those models, he probably would have become financially successful but he would not have become Ernest Hemingway. It was happenstance and blind fortune that changed his direction, a turn that could only take place beyond the Village limits. . . .

## Notes

1. Item 489, Hemingway Collection, Kennedy Library.
2. Acquisition Records, Oak Park Public Library.

# "The Undefeated":
# The Moment of Truth

*Kenneth G. Johnston**

In 1923 Hemingway made his first trip to Pamplona, Spain, to take in
the bullfights. One afternoon he watched the performance of the dark
and spare Manuel García López "Maera," who was having great difficulty making the kill. As the bull charged, Maera leaned hard on his
sword, but the point hit a vertebra. The sword buckled nearly double,
and shot up into the air. Although Maera's wrist was dislocated in this
collision of steel and bone, he refused to leave the ring. But Maera
fared no better in his next four attempts at the kill, striking bone each
time. As Hemingway explains in *Death in the Afternoon*, Maera's honor
demanded that he kill correctly, over the horns: "Now at any time he
could have, without danger or pain, slipped the sword into the neck of
the bull, let it go into the lung or cut the jugular and killed him with
no trouble. But his honor demanded that he kill him high up between
the shoulders, going in as a man should, over the horn, following the
sword with his body. And on the sixth time he went in this way and
the sword went in too."[1] Hemingway would remember this difficult kill
when he sat down to write "The Undefeated" the following year.
There can be little doubt that he named the aging matador of his story
in honor of Manuel García López "Maera" (1896–1924), who on that
memorable afternoon in Pamplona had killed with honor, "as a man
should." "Era muy hombre," declared Hemingway, paying Maera his
highest compliment.[2]

The final sword thrust is what Hemingway calls "the moment of
truth."[3] To appreciate Manuel's performance in "The Undefeated,"
one must clearly understand two essential points: 1) the merit of the
kill is judged by the manner in which the matador goes in on the bull
and by the placement of the sword, not by the quickness of the kill;
2) there are many ways for the matador to trick the killing of a bull
without going straight in on him, without exposing himself to any great
danger.[4] Writes Hemingway in *Death in the Afternoon*: "To kill the bull
with a single sword thrust is of no merit at all unless the sword is placed

*From *The Tip of the Iceberg: Hemingway and the Short Story* by Kenneth G. Johnston
(Greenwood, Fla.: Penkevill Publishing Co., 1987), 85–89. ©1987 by the Penkevill
Publishing Co. Reprinted by permission.

high between the bull's shoulders and unless the man passed over and had his body within reach of the horn at the moment he went in. . . . To kill a bull in his neck or his flank, which he cannot defend, is assassination."[5] Manuel in "The Undefeated" insists on killing the bull properly. *Corto y derecho.* Short and straight, over the horn, thereby exposing himself to very great danger. At any time, if he were without honor, he could have "assassinated" the bull with little or no risk to himself.

"The Undefeated" well illustrates what is meant by the Hemingway code: a personal code of conduct, self-imposed, characterized by courage, stoicism, dignity, and honor. It is a set of inviolable rules by which the code hero imposes order and meaning on a chaotic world, steels himself to the pain and disappointment of life, and retains his dignity and honor. The code permits a character to retrieve victory, usually moral, as he goes down to what the uninitiated would call defeat. The person who abides by the code is motivated, not by a desire to win glory or admiration of others, but by a deep sense of personal honor and integrity. One can be instructed in the code, as is the protagonist in "The Short Happy Life of Francis Macomber," but more often it is instinctively adopted by such "primitives" as Santiago, the old fisherman in *The Old Man and the Sea*; and Manuel Garcia, the illiterate, aging bullfighter in "The Undefeated."

Manuel, it would seem, has every reason to give a perfunctory performance in the bullring this night: he is too old for his profession; he is weak and pale from his recent hospitalization; he is being poorly paid; he is performing for an audience that does not understand and appreciate the finer points of the art; he is a last-minute substitute in a nocturnal in which "kids and bums" perform. It is bad enough to fight at night—the bullfight is a tragedy, traditionally acted out in the sun and shade of the late afternoon—but to follow the comic bullfights, the Charlie Chaplins, is doubly humiliating. Moreover, the crowd laughs during the *tercio* of death, when the bull's splintered horn gets caught in the canvas covering the cowardly picador's dead horse. Their laughter follows immediately upon the heels of Manuel's first abortive attempt to kill his bull, during which he narrowly misses being gored and trampled. Yet Manuel gives a proper performance from beginning to end, even after he is pelted by cushions and bottles, even after he is gored and bloody. Why? The answer is perhaps best summed up in the Spanish word "pundonor." "In Spain honor is a very real thing," Hemingway writes in *Death in the Afternoon*. "Called pundonor, it means honor, probity, courage, self-respect and pride in one word."[6] Manuel is not performing for the President, whose "box he could not see high up in the dark plaza."[7] Nor for the audience that shouts "Olé!" one moment and throws cushions and bottles the next. Manuel, who stands "very much alone in the ring" (257), is performing to satisfy his own high sense of professional dedication and personal honor.

Perhaps only the members of his own *cuadrilla*—Zurito, Fuentes—and Hernandez appreciate the integrity of Manuel's performance. Certainly the crowd does not, nor does the "expert," the substitute bullfight critic of *El Heraldo*. The critic is "slightly bored" (248) and tries to liven up his running account of what he considers to be a dull performance with exaggeration, inflated rhetoric, and slang: The bull "came out at 90 miles an hour" (248), he writes, "showed a tendency to cut into the terrain of the bull-fighters" (249), and "accepted a pair of varas for the death of one rosinante" (250). Hemingway makes a point to undercut the critic's authority and expertise by having him drink warm champagne. Properly served, champagne should be chilled. The critic is neither a connoisseur of wine nor an *aficionado* of the bullfight. Like Manuel, he is a substitute. But his lack of dedication to his craft contrasts sharply with Manuel's deep sense of professional honor. The critic decides it is not worth his while to continue his running account; he will write up the *corrida* back at the office. He makes plans to leave before midnight; "if he missed anything he would get it out of the morning papers" (256). He is no longer taking notes when the fight enters its third act, the *tercio* of death. But apparently he witnesses the difficult kill. For when Manuel is being pelted by cushions, someone from close range (the critic is seated in the front row) throws an empty champagne bottle, striking the matador on the foot.

Manuel, although bloodied and bowed, is truly undefeated. He has fought and killed according to the rules. Despite his bad luck (he has drawn a bull which is all bone), his humiliation by the crowd, and his wound, he kills in the proper manner, on the fifth sword thrust. Manuel's performance is not brilliant; it lacks grace and serenity. But his is a respectable performance, and a remarkable display of personal honor, deserving of our applause and admiration. The picador Zurito, much as he would like to see his aging friend retire, acknowledges the merit of the performance when he refrains from cutting off Manuel's coleta, the traditional badge of the matador's profession.

Kenneth G. Johnston

Hemingway, who did not see his first bullfight until 1923, wrote "The Undefeated" in 1924. But he set his story in 1918.[8] The years 1914–20 are known as "the Golden Age" of bullfighting; these were the years of the great competition between "Joselito" and Juan Belmonte, considered by many the two greatest *toreros* of all time. By selecting a year within the Golden Age, Hemingway places Manuel in the company of the great matadors and, thus, pays the highest tribute to his aging fighter, whose integrity, if not his skill, has earned him this place of honor.

Hemingway, quite likely, saw his own literary situation reflected in "The Undefeated." In 1924 he was, for the most part, performing "without applause,"[9] without editorial understanding or support.

> The rejected manuscripts would come back through the slot in the door of that bare room where I lived over the Montmartre sawmill. They'd fall through the slot onto the wood floor, and clipped to them was that most savage of all reprimands—the printed rejection slip. The rejection slip is very hard to take on an empty stomach and there were times when I'd sit at that old wooden table and read one of those cold slips that had been attached to a story I had loved and worked on very hard and believed in, and I couldn't help crying.[10]

Nevertheless, Hemingway refused to compromise the integrity of his performance. He was determined to write "short and straight," to create honest prose, to maintain the purity of his technique. "With a frequency that makes coincidence impossible," writes John Reardon, "the language which [Hemingway] uses to describe the craft of the bullfighter . . . he also uses to describe the craft of the writer and, beyond that, the ethical attitudes of his heroes. He constructs a metaphorical pattern that at times approaches allegory."[11] Manuel—defiant, uncompromising, bloodied yet undefeated—may well have been Hemingway's romanticized vision of himself. Seen in this light, "The Undefeated" is an oblique tribute to its struggling author at the start of his career. "Writing is a rough trade," he would later write, "et il faut d'abord durer."[12]

# Notes

1. Ernest Hemingway, *Death in the Afternoon* (New York: Scribner's, 1932), pp. 80–81.

2. Ibid., p. 82. Literal translation: "He was much man." Maera actually died from an advanced case of tuberculosis, but Hemingway in his miniature on Maera in *In Our Time* (Chapter XIV) attributes his death to a horn wound.

3. Ibid., p. 174.

4. Ibid., p. 178.

5. Ibid., pp. 245–246.

6. Ibid., p. 91.

7. Ernest Hemingway, "The Undefeated," in *The Short Stories of Ernest Hemingway* (New York: Scribner's, 1953), p. 257. All further references to this story will be cited parenthetically in the text.

8. Manuel tells us that his brother had been killed about nine years ago; the plate under the mounted head of the bull that had killed his brother sets the date of death at April 27, 1909.

The year 1918 figures importantly in Hemingway's life, too, for that was the year in which he had faced his own "moment of truth" on the lower reaches of the Piave River during the war.

9. "You must be prepared to work always without applause," Hemingway wrote ("Old Newsman Writes: A Letter from Cuba," *Esquire*, II [December, 1934], 26).

10. Hemingway, quoted in A. E. Hotchner, *Papa Hemingway: A Personal Memoir* [New York: Random House, 1966], p. 57.

11. John Reardon, "Hemingway's Esthetic and Ethical Sportsmen," *The University Review*, XXXIV [October, 1967], 13.

"Most writers," Hemingway remarked, "slough off the toughest but most important part of their trade—editing their stuff, honing it and honing it until it gets an edge like the bull fighter's *estoque*, the killing sword" (quoted in Hotchner, *Papa Hemingway*, p. 114).

12. EH to Arthur Mizener, 11 January, 1951, *Ernest Hemingway: Selected Letters 1917–1961*, ed. Carlos Baker (New York: Scribner's, 1981), p. 718. Translation: ". . . and first one must endure, last."

# Chronology

1899    Ernest Hemingway born 21 July in Oak Park, Illinois, son of Dr. Clarence E. and Grace Hall Hemingway.

1917    Graduates from Oak Park High School. Works as a reporter on the Kansas City *Star*.

1918    Drives ambulance for the Red Cross in Italy. 8 July, severely wounded by mortar fire at Fossalta di Piave.

1920–1921    Meets and becomes friends with Sherwood Anderson in Chicago.

1920–1924    Feature writer and foreign correspondent for *Toronto Star* and *Toronto Star Weekly*. As correspondent, covers Greco-Turkish War (1922) and interviews Clemenceau and Mussolini.

1921    Marries Hadley Richardson of St. Louis. On Anderson's advice, the newlyweds move to Paris where Hemingway soon becomes friends with Gertrude Stein and Ezra Pound.

1922    Hadley loses the suitcase containing nearly all of Hemingway's work, said to include eleven stories, a novel, and poems.

1923–1925    Publishes *Three Stories and Ten Poems* in Paris (1923); publishes stories and poems in the *Double Dealer, Poetry: A Magazine of Verse, Little Review, Querschnitt, This Quarter*, and the *transatlantic review*, where he assists Ford Madox Ford in editorial duties.

1923    Makes first of many trips to Pamplona, Spain, for the bullfights.

1924    *in our time* published in Paris. "My Old Man" published in Edward O'Brien's anthology *The Best Stories of 1923*.

1925    *In Our Time* published in United States.

1926    *The Torrents of Spring* and *The Sun Also Rises*.

1927 Divorced by Hadley Richardson; marries Pauline Pfeiffer. *Men Without Women.*

1928 Moves to Key West, Florida; until 1938 this home is the base of his various travels. Begins the hobby of sports-fishing on Gulf Stream.

1929 *A Farewell to Arms,* his first major commercial success.

1930 Hurt in automobile accident in Montana.

1932 *Death in the Afternoon.*

1933–1934 *Winner Take Nothing* (1933). Makes first safari in Africa; also visits Paris and Spain.

1933–1939 Sporting pieces and stories (including "The Snows of Kilimanjaro," 1936) published in *Esquire.*

1935 *Green Hills of Africa.*

1936–1938 Covers the Spanish Civil War for the North American Newspaper Alliance. *To Have and Have Not* (1937). Helps prepare film *The Spanish Earth* (1938). *The Fifth Column and the First Forty-nine Stories* (1938).

1939 Buys Finca Vigía at San Francisco de Paula, Cuba, his home until 1958, just before Castro overthrows Batista.

1940 Divorced by Pauline Pfeiffer; marries Martha Gellhorn. *For Whom the Bell Tolls.*

1942–1946 War correspondent in Europe, flies with the Royal Air Force, participates in Normandy invasion, "liberates" Paris and the Ritz Hotel, and attaches himself to the Fourth Infantry Division. Divorces Martha Gellhorn (1945); marries Mary Welsh (1946).

1950 *Across the River and into the Trees.*

1952 Receives the Pulitzer Prize for *The Old Man and the Sea.*

1953–1954 Revisits Africa; suffers two airplane crashes; is reported dead in the world press. Receives the Nobel Prize for Literature in 1954.

1957 The Two Tales of Darkness—"A Man of the World" and "Get a Seeing-Eyed Dog"—appear in *Atlantic Monthly,* becoming Hemingway's last stories published during his lifetime.

1959   Writes "The Art of the Short Story" as a preface for a new student's edition of his collected short stories.

1961   Commits suicide at his home in Ketchum, Idaho, on 2 July.

1964   *A Moveable Feast.*

1970   *Islands in the Stream.*

1972   *The Nick Adams Stories.*

1985   *The Dangerous Summer.*

1986   *The Garden of Eden.*

1987   *The Complete Short Stories of Ernest Hemingway. The Finca Vigía Edition.*

# Bibliography

## Primary Works

### Short Story Collections

*Three Stories and Ten Poems*. Paris and Dijon: Contact Publishing Company, 1923. Includes "Up in Michigan," "Out of Season," "My Old Man," and the poems "Mitragliatrice," "Oklahoma," "Oily Weather," "Roosevelt," "Captives," "Champs d'Honneur," "Riparto d'Assolto," "Montparnasse," "Along with Youth," and "Chapter Heading."

*in our time*. Paris: Three Mountains Press, 1924. Includes the miniatures that later would be used to form the interchapters of the American edition of *In Our Time:* 1. "Everybody was drunk . . ."; 2. "The first matador got the horn . . ."; 3. "Minarets stuck up in the rain . . ."; 4. "We were in a garden at Mons . . ."; 5. "It was a frightfully hot day. . ."; 6. "They shot the six . . ."; 7. "Nick sat against the wall . . ."; 8. "While the bombardment . . ."; 9. "At two o'clock in the morning . . ."; 10. "One hot evening in Milan . . ."; 11. "In 1919 he was traveling . . ."; 12. "They whack whacked the white horse . . ."; 13. "The crowd shouted all the time . . ."; 14. "If it happened right down close . . ."; 15. "I heard the drums coming . . ."; 16. "Maera lay still . . ."; 17. "They hanged Sam Cardinella . . ."; 18. "The king was working. . ."

*In Our Time*. New York: Boni and Liveright, 1925. Includes "Indian Camp," "The Doctor and the Doctor's Wife," "The End of Something," "The Three-Day Blow," "The Battler," "A Very Short Story," "Soldier's Home," "The Revolutionist," "Mr. and Mrs. Elliot," "Cat in the Rain," " Out of Season," "Cross-Country Snow," "My Old Man," "Big Two-Hearted River: Part I," " Big Two-Hearted River: Part II," interchapters 1–15, and "L'Envoi." Two of the *in our time* miniatures are here elevated to the status of short stories (miniature chapter 10 has been titled "A Very Short Story," and miniature chapter 11 has been titled "The Revolutionist"). "On the Quai at Smyrna" was added as the opening story starting with the 1930 edition, published by Charles Scribner's Sons.

*Men Without Women*. New York: Charles Scribner's Sons, 1927. Includes "The Undefeated," "In Another Country," "Hills Like White Elephants," "The Killers," "Che Ti Dice La Patria?," "Fifty Grand," "A Simple Enquiry," "Ten Indians," "A Canary for One," "An Alpine Idyll," "A Pursuit Race," "Today Is Friday," "Banal Story," and "Now I Lay Me."

*Winner Take Nothing.* New York: Charles Scribner's Sons, 1933. Includes "After the Storm," "A Clean, Well-Lighted Place," "The Light of the World," "God Rest You Merry, Gentlemen," "The Sea Change," "A Way You'll Never Be," "The Mother of a Queen," "One Reader Writes," "Homage to Switzerland," "A Day's Wait," "A Natural History of the Dead," "Wine of Wyoming," "The Gambler, the Nun, and the Radio," and "Fathers and Sons."

*The Fifth Column and the First Forty-nine Stories.* New York: Charles Scribner's Sons, 1938. (Reprinted without the play as *The Short Stories of Ernest Hemingway.* New York: Charles Scribner's Sons, 1954.) Includes all stories found in *In Our Time, Men Without Women,* and *Winner Take Nothing,* plus "The Capital of the World," "Old Man at the Bridge," "Up in Michigan," "The Short Happy Life of Francis Macomber," "The Snows of Kilimanjaro," and the play *The Fifth Column.*

*The Fifth Column and Four Stories of the Spanish Civil War.* New York: Charles Scribner's Sons, 1969. Includes *The Fifth Column,* "The Denunciation," "The Butterfly and the Tank," "Night Before Battle," and "Under the Ridge."

*Ernest Hemingway's Apprenticeship: Oak Park, 1916–1917.* Edited by Matthew J. Bruccoli. Washington: Microcard Editions, National Cash Register Company, 1971. Includes thirty-nine articles written by Hemingway for the Oak Park High School newspaper the *Trapeze.* Also includes three stories ("Judgment of Manitou," "A Matter of Color," and "Sepi Jingan"), several poems ("How Ballad Writing Affects Our Seniors," "The Worker," "Athletic Verse," and "The Inexpressible") and a piece called "Class Prophecy" published in the Oak Park High School literary magazine *Tabula.*

*The Nick Adams Stories.* Edited by Philip Young. New York: Charles Scribner's Sons, 1972. Includes "Three Shots," "Ten Indians," "The Indians Moved Away," "The Last Good Country," "Crossing the Mississippi," "Night Before Landing," "Summer People," "Wedding Day," and "On Writing," as well as the previously collected "Indian Camp," "The Doctor and the Doctor's Wife," "The Light of the World," "The Battler," "The Killers," interchapter 6 from *In Our Time* ("Nick sat against the wall . . ."), "Now I Lay Me," "A Way You'll Never Be," "In Another Country," "Big Two-Hearted River," "The End of Something," "The Three-Day Blow," "An Alpine Idyll," "Cross-Country Snow," and "Fathers and Sons."

*Along With Youth: Hemingway, the Early Years.* Edited by Peter Griffin. New York: Oxford University Press, 1985. Includes five otherwise uncollected apprentice stories: "The Mercenaries," "Crossroads—An Anthology," "Portrait of the Idealist in Love," "The Ash Heel's Tendon," and "The Current."

*The Complete Short Stories of Ernest Hemingway. The Finca Vigía Edition.* New

Bibliography

York: Charles Scribner's Sons, 1987. Includes all stories found in *The First Forty-nine Stories*, the stories in *The Fifth Column*, plus: "One Trip Across," "The Tradesman's Return," "Nobody Ever Dies," "The Good Lion," "The Faithful Bull," "Get a Seeing-Eyed Dog," "A Man of the World," "Summer People," "The Last Good Country," "An African Story," "A Train Trip," "The Porter," "Black Ass at the Cross Roads," "Landscape with Figures," "I Guess Everything Reminds You of Something," "Great News from the Mainland," and "The Strange Country."

## Novels

*The Torrents of Spring*. New York: Charles Scribner's Sons, 1926.
*The Sun Also Rises*. New York: Charles Scribner's Sons, 1926.
*A Farewell to Arms*. New York: Charles Scribner's Sons, 1929.
*To Have and Have Not*. New York: Charles Scribner's Sons, 1937.
*For Whom the Bell Tolls*. New York: Charles Scribner's Sons, 1940.
*Across the River and Into the Trees*. New York: Charles Scribner's Sons, 1950.
*The Old Man and the Sea*. New York: Charles Scribner's Sons, 1952.
*Islands in the Stream*. New York: Charles Scribner's Sons, 1970.
*The Garden of Eden*. New York: Charles Scribner's Sons, 1986.

## Nonfiction

*Death in the Afternoon*. New York: Charles Scribner's Sons, 1932.
*Green Hills of Africa*. New York: Charles Scribner's Sons, 1935.
*The Spanish Earth*. Cleveland: J. B. Savage Co., 1938.
*Men at War*. Edited with an introduction by Ernest Hemingway. New York: Crown Publishers, 1942.
*The Wild Years*. Edited by Gene Z. Hanrahan. New York: Dell, 1962. Seventy-three articles from the *Toronto Star Weekly* and the *Toronto Daily Star*.
*A Moveable Feast*. New York: Charles Scribner's Sons, 1964.
*By-Line: Ernest Hemingway, Selected Articles and Dispatches of Four Decades*. Edited by William White. New York: Charles Scribner's Sons, 1967.
*Ernest Hemingway, Cub Reporter: "Kansas City Star" Stories*. Edited by Matthew J. Bruccoli. Pittsburgh: University of Pittsburgh Press, 1970. Twelve articles from December 1917 through April 1918.
*Dateline: Toronto. The Complete "Toronto Star" Dispatches, 1920–1924*. Edited by William White. New York, Charles Scribner's Sons, 1985.
*The Dangerous Summer*. Introduction by James A. Michener. New York: Charles Scribner's Sons, 1985.

## Poetry, Letters, Interviews

*88 Poems.* Edited by Nicholas Gerogiannis. New York: Harcourt Brace Jovan-
ovich/Bruccoli Clark, 1979. Paperback reprint. *Complete Poems.* University
of Nebraska Press, 1983.
*Ernest Hemingway: Selected Letters, 1917–1961.* Edited by Carlos Baker. New
York: Charles Scribner's Sons, 1981.
*Hemingway on Writing.* Edited by Larry W. Phillips. New York: Charles Scribner's Sons, 1984.
*Conversations with Ernest Hemingway.* Edited by Matthew J. Bruccoli. Jackson
and London: University Press of Mississippi, 1986.

# *Secondary Works*

## Books and Parts of Books

Baker, Carlos, ed. *Hemingway and His Critics: An International Anthology.* New
York: Hill & Wang, 1961.
———. *Ernest Hemingway: A Life Story.* New York: Charles Scribner's Sons,
1969.
———. *Hemingway: The Writer as Artist.* 4th ed. Princeton: Princeton Univer-
sity Press, 1972.
Baker, Sheridan. *Ernest Hemingway: An Introduction and Interpretation.* New
York: Holt, Rinehart & Winston, 1967.
Barrett, William. "Winner Take Nothing." In *Time of Need: Forms of Imagination
in the Twentieth Century,* 64–95. New York: Harper & Row, 1972.
Benson, Jackson J. *Hemingway . . . The Writer's Art of Self-Defense.* Minneapolis:
University of Minnesota Press, 1969.
———, ed. *The Short Stories of Ernest Hemingway: Critical Essays.* Durham,
N.C.: Duke University Press, 1975.
Brenner, Gerry. *Concealments in Hemingway's Works.* Columbus: Ohio State Uni-
versity Press, 1983.
Brooks, Cleanth. "Ernest Hemingway: Man on His Moral Uppers." In *The
Hidden God. Studies in Hemingway, Faulkner, Yeats, Eliot, and Warren,* 8–
16. New Haven: Yale University Press, 1963.
Burgess, Anthony. *Ernest Hemingway and His World.* New York: Charles Scrib-
ner's Sons, 1978.
Cooper, Stephen. *The Politics of Ernest Hemingway.* Ann Arbor, Mich.: UMI
Research Press, 1987.
De Falco, Joseph. *The Hero in Hemingway's Short Stories.* Pittsburgh: University
of Pittsburgh Press, 1963.

Bibliography

Donaldson, Scott. *By Force of Will: The Life and Art of Ernest Hemingway.* New York: Viking, 1977.

Fenton, Charles A. *The Apprenticeship of Ernest Hemingway: The Early Years.* New York: Farrar, Straus & Cudahy, 1954.

Flora, Joseph M. *Hemingway's Nick Adams.* Baton Rouge: Louisiana State University Press, 1982.

Grebstein, Sheldon Norman. *Hemingway's Craft.* Carbondale: Southern Illinois University Press, 1973.

Griffin, Peter. *Along with Youth: Hemingway, The Early Years.* New York: Oxford University Press, 1985.

Grimes, Larry E. *The Religious Design of Hemingway's Early Fiction.* Ann Arbor, Mich.: UMI Research Press, 1985.

Gurko, Leo. *Ernest Hemingway and the Pursuit of Heroism.* New York: Thomas Y. Crowell Co., 1968.

Hemingway, Gregory H., M.D. *Papa: A Personal Memoir.* Boston: Houghton Mifflin Co., 1976.

Hemingway, Leicester. *My Brother, Ernest Hemingway.* Cleveland: World Publishing Co., 1961.

Hemingway, Mary Welsh. *How It Was.* New York: Alfred A. Knopf, 1976.

Hotchner, A. E. *Papa Hemingway: A Personal Memoir.* New York: Random House, 1966. Reprinted with postscript and new subtitle, "The Ecstasy and Sorrow." New York: William Morrow & Co., 1983.

Hovey, Richard B. *Hemingway: The Inward Terrain.* Seattle: University of Washington Press, 1968.

Howell, John M., ed. *Hemingway's African Stories: The Stories, Their Sources, Their Critics.* New York: Charles Scribner's Sons, 1969.

Jain, S. P. *Hemingway: A Study of His Short Stories.* New Delhi: Arnold-Heinemann Publishers, 1985.

Johnston, Kenneth G. *The Tip of the Iceberg: Hemingway and the Short Story.* Greenwood, Fla.: Penkevill Publishing Co., 1987.

Kazin, Alfred. "Hemingway the Painter." In *An American Procession*, 357–73. New York: Alfred A. Knopf, 1984.

Kert, Bernice. *The Hemingway Women.* New York: Norton & Co., 1983.

Killinger, John. *Hemingway and the Dead Gods: A Study in Existentialism.* Lexington: University of Kentucky Press, 1960.

Lewis, Robert W., Jr. *Hemingway on Love.* Austin: University of Texas Press, 1965.

Lynn, Kenneth. *Hemingway.* New York: Simon and Schuster, 1987.

McCaffery, John K. M., ed. *Ernest Hemingway: The Man and His Work.* Cleveland: World Publishing, 1950. Reprint. New York: Cooper Square Publishers, 1969.

Meyers, Jeffrey, ed. *Hemingway: The Critical Heritage.* Boston and London: Routledge & Kegan Paul, 1982.

———. *Hemingway: A Biography.* New York: Harper & Row, 1985.

Nahal, Chaman. *The Narrative Pattern in Ernest Hemingway's Fiction*. Rutherford, N.J.: Fairleigh Dickinson University Press, 1971.

Nelson, Raymond S. *Hemingway: Expressionist Artist*. Ames: Iowa State University Press, 1979.

O'Connor, Frank. "A Clean, Well-Lighted Place." In *The Lonely Voice: A Study of the Short Story*, 156–69. Cleveland: World Publishing Co., 1963.

O'Connor, Richard. *Ernest Hemingway*. New York: McGraw-Hill Co., 1971.

Peterson, Richard K. *Hemingway: Direct and Oblique*. The Hague and Paris: Mouton, 1969.

Raeburn, John. *Fame Became of Him: Hemingway as Public Writer*. Bloomington: Indiana University Press, 1984.

Reynolds, Michael S. *Hemingway's First War: The Making of "A Farewell to Arms."* Princeton: Princeton University Press, 1976.

————. *The Young Hemingway*. New York: Basil Blackwell, 1986.

————, ed. *Critical Essays on Hemingway's "In Our Time."* Boston: G. K. Hall & Co., 1983.

Ross, Lillian. *Portrait of Hemingway*. New York: Simon & Schuster, 1961.

Rovit, Earl, and Gerry Brenner. *Ernest Hemingway*. Boston: Twayne, 1962. Revised edition, 1986.

Sanford, Marcelline Hemingway. *At the Hemingways: A Family Portrait*. Boston: Atlantic–Little, Brown, 1962.

Smith, Paul. *The Short Stories of Ernest Hemingway: A Reference Guide*. Boston: G. K. Hall, 1989.

Stephens, Robert O., ed. *Ernest Hemingway: The Critical Reception*. New York: Burt Franklin & Co., 1977.

Tanner, Tony. "Ernest Hemingway's Unhurried Sensations." In *The Reign of Wonder: Naivety and Reality in American Literature*, 228–57. Cambridge: Cambridge University Press, 1965.

Tichi, Cecelia. "Opportunity: Imagination Ex Machina II." In *Shifting Gears: Technology, Literature, Culture in Modernist America*, 216–29. Chapel Hill: University of North Carolina Press, 1987.

Wagner, Linda Welshimer, ed. *Ernest Hemingway: Six Decades of Criticism*. East Lansing: Michigan State University Press, 1987.

Waldhorn, Arthur, Ed. *Ernest Hemingway: A Collection of Criticism*. New York: McGraw-Hill, 1973.

————. *A Reader's Guide to Ernest Hemingway*. New York: Farrar, Straus & Giroux, 1972.

Watts, Emily Stipes. *Ernest Hemingway and the Arts*. Urbana: University of Illinois Press, 1971.

Weeks, Robert P., ed. *Hemingway: A Collection of Critical Essays*. Englewood Cliffs, N.J.: Prentice-Hall, 1962.

Williams, Wirt. *The Tragic Art of Ernest Hemingway*. Baton Rouge: Louisiana State University Press, 1981.

Bibliography

Workman, Brooke. *In Search of Ernest Hemingway: A Model for Teaching a Literature Seminar.* Urbana, Ill.: National Council of Teachers of English, 1979.

Wylder, Delbert. *Hemingway's Heroes.* Albuquerque: University of New Mexico Press, 1969.

Young, Philip. *Ernest Hemingway.* New York: Rinehart, 1952. Enlarged and reissued as *Ernest Hemingway: A Reconsideration.* University Park: Pennsylvania State University Press, 1966.

## Recorded Lectures

Kazin, Alfred. *Fiction in the Twenties: The Lost Generation—Ernest Hemingway.* Mount Vernon, N.Y.: Gould Media. Audiotape cassette: twenty-eight-minute lecture.

Wylder, Delbert. *Ernest Hemingway: "Early Short Stories," "Middle Short Stories," and "Late Short Stories."* Mount Vernon, N.Y.: Gould Media. Audiotape cassettes: thirty-five-minute lecture, forty-two-minute lecture, forty-minute lecture.

# Index

Abortion, 31–32, 34–35. *See also* Pregnancy; Relationships, male-female

Absurdism, 64

Adams, Henry: *The Education of Henry Adams*, 27

Adams, Nick. *See* Nick Adams stories

Adams, Samuel (novelist): *Success*, 163–64

Adultery, 76, 80. *See also* Marriage; Relationships, male-female: end of

Aesthetics of Hemingway prose, 166–67

Africa, safari in, 74, 110

African stories, 74–88, 100, 105; and Spanish Civil War stories, 99. *See also* Hemingway, Ernest: and Africa

Albee, Edward, 64

Alcohol. *See* Drinking

Alienation, 19–20. *See also* Individual; Isolation

Allegory, 20, 177; of death, 82–86

American West. *See* West, Old

Anderson, Sherwood, 100, 112, 140–41, 160, 172; *Dark Laughter*, 140; "I'm a Fool," 141; *Triumph of the Egg*, 141; *Winesburg, Ohio*, 26, 141

Andreson, Andre, 139

Anonymous: *Art of Dying Well* (woodcut in), 82

Anthology technique: in early Hemingway fiction, xiv. *See also* Sequence

Apprentice work. *See* Hemingway, Ernest: apprentice work

Architecture: and writing, 5–6, 168–69. *See also* Functionalism

Art, discipline of, 104. *See also* Painting

Atomic bomb, 143n10

Authority figure, 98, 101

Autobiographical fallacy. *See* Hemingway, Ernest: autobiographical fallacy

Baker, Carlos, 7, 32, 61, 98, 112

Barnes, Jake. *See* Hemingway, Ernest: WORKS (*The Sun Also Rises*)

Bartender figure, 19–25, 92–95, 101, 113

Bellow, Saul, 45–46

Belmonte, Juan (bullfighter), 177. *See also* Bullfighting: bullfighter figure

Benson, Jackson J., xii–xiii

Berry, Walter, 159

Betts, Doris, 8–9

Bible, 55–56, 67; King James Version's influence on Hemingway's work, 20, 40, 110; and women, 72

Bierce, Ambrose: "An Occurrence at Owl Creek Bridge," 86

Bishop, John Peale, 3–4, 6

"Black ass," 104, 108–109, 113, 116–17. *See also* Despair; Hemingway, Ernest: depression of

Blair, Robert: "The Grave," 75

Blake, William: "The Death of the Good Old Man" and "The Death of the Strong Wicked Man," 75, 82

# Index

Bliss, P. P., 67

Blixen, Bror von, 76

Blyth, Mr. and Mrs. Audley James, 76

Bonding, Male. *See* Sexual roles: male bonding

Boredom, 85, 88

Boulton, Nick: as model for Nick Adams, 27

Bourne, Catherine: understanding of her husband's writing, 10–11, 14, 15

Bourne, David (protagonist of *The Garden of Eden*), 56; and theory of writing, 10–16. See also Hemingway, Ernest: WORKS (*The Garden of Eden*)

Boxing, 131–33; boxer figure, 56–57, 67, 131–32; as symbol, xiv

Brenner, Gerry, and Earl Rovit, 11, 86, 100, 153–56

British literature, influence on Hemingway of, 173

Britton, Jack (boxer), 131

Bullfighting, 7, 129, 150, 167–68; aesthetics of, 170; bullfighter figure, 54, 122n63, 174–77, 177, 178n2; compared with writing, 178n11; critics of, undercut, 176; in fable, 111–12; "Golden Age" of, 177; "Maera" (Manuel García López), 54; mechanics of, 165

Bunyan, John: *Pilgrim's Progress*, 55

Burroughs, Edgar Rice, 172

Byron, George Gordon, Lord, 6

"Cablese," 5

Camping, ritual of, 51–52, 166–67

Carroll, Lewis: *Alice in Wonderland*, 68

Castro, Fidel, 141

Catholicism, Roman. *See* Roman Catholicism

Censorship, 103, 118n10; self-, 142nn1, 3, 4, 7

Cézanne, Paul, 5

Characterization, 20, 132; God as character, 124n89; names and

namelessness, 37, 38–39, 41, 91, 115; voices and, 33, 68–69, 106

Chaucer, Geoffrey: "The Wife of Bath's Tale," 57

Chauvinism, 30. *See also* Hemingway, Ernest: and women; Women

Chicote's bar. *See* Drinking: Chicote's bar

Children, 47–48, 85; as infringement on personal freedom, 31–32; stories for, 109–14; *See also* Hemingway, Ernest: childhood

Christianity, 24–25, 67, 104; and marriage, 43. *See also* Hemingway, Ernest: and Christianity; ———: and Roman Catholicism; ———: WORKS ("Today Is Friday"); Jesus Christ

Class consciousness, 87

Clemens, Samuel Langhorne, 148. *See also* Twain, Mark

Code: of authors, 76; of behavior, in early fiction, xv; of bullfighting, 174–77; of fishing, 51, 175; Hemingway's, 175; professional, 154–55, 174–77; of silence, 142n8

Commitment. *See* Relationship, male-female: and commitment

Companion stories, 87, 107, 110, 112–15

Concealment, Art of, 2, 13, 49, 91, 130–31, 139–40, 147–49; and narrator, 37; in fable, 109–10

Conrad, Joseph, 14–15, 25, 172

*Constater,* concept of, 133–34

Context, stories in their, xvi, 36, 59–60, 61–62

Conventionality: in face of despair, 155; intensity of the mundane in, 150; of marriage, 65; of middle-class values rejected, 168–69; and Switzerland, 44, 64. *See also* Family; Hemingway, Ernest: conventionality of; Responsibility

Cooper, Stephen, 99

Courage, 80–81, 155–56, 175–76; and cowardice, 18–19, 78–79, 80;

<br>

of Hemingway protagonist, 11. *See also* Stoicism
Cowley, Malcolm, 29, 108
Crane, Stephen: *The Red Badge of Courage*, 173
"Craziness" as redeeming feature, 72
Criminals in early Hemingway works, xv
Crummer, Mrs., 172

Dante Alighieri, 41, 144n16
Darkness and light, 20, 67, 116, 117, 120n38
Death, 75, 76, 82, 121n55; as allegorical figure, 82–86; and contest of good and evil, 82, 83–84; and dying well, 82–84, 85–88; fear of, 54–55; and grace, 87–88; Hemingway's encounter with, 178n8; irony in, 93; in life, 77–78; as release, 116; as transfiguration, 110; in war, 95–96, 154; violent, 81
"Depersonalization," T. S. Eliot's concept of, 17–19. *See also* Eliot, T. S.
Depression. *See* "Black ass"; Despair
Despair, 22–23, 35, 120n38, 120n41, 155. *See also* "Black ass"
Detail, wealth of, 147–53
Di Robillant, Carlo, 109
Dialogue, 21–24, 34, 120n41; editorial emendation of, in "A Clean, Well-Lighted Place," 21–24
Didion, Joan, 15
Dignity, 155–56, 175
Dinesen, Isak, 76
Divorce, 38, 64. *See also* Relationships, male-female: end of
Doctorow, E. L., 78
Domesticity. *See* Family
Donne, John, 41, 82
Dos-Passos, 5, 112, 157
Dos Passos, Katy Smith, 108
Doubles. *See* Companion stories
Dreiser, Theodore: *Jenny Gerhardt* and *Sister Carrie*, 173

Drinking, xv, 77, 85, 137; Chicote's bar, 92–95, 101, 113; Hemingway's, 138; and husband-wife relationship, 115; as ritual, 114; sociability of, 92–93; and war, 94–95

Eakins, Thomas, 5; *The Pair-Oared Shell*, 165
Early works. *See* Hemingway, Ernest: apprentice work
Editing of Hemingway's works, xiii, 132–33
Efficiency Movement, 157, 161
Efficient style. *See* Style: economy of. *See also* Writing
Eliot, T. S., 43, 118n20, 119n21; "Tradition and the Individual Talent," 16–17; *The Waste Land*, 35, 41; "Whispers of Immortality," 82
Emerson, Ralph Waldo, 149, 170
Emotion, 58, 149–50, 152; basis in action, 163; presentation of, 46; of war, 97; writing as expression of, 19
Epigraph, 82, 84
Epiphany (James Joyce's concept of), 150
Epistolary mode, xiv–xv, 61–64. *See also* Hemingway, Ernest: WORKS ("One Reader Writes")
Europe, values of, 65–66
Experience and fiction, 14–15, 27, 39, 131, 134–35, 139–40, 141. *See also* Hemingway, Ernest: autobiographical elements in the works of; ———: autobiographical fallacy; Objective Correlative

Fable, 109–14, 124n89
Family, 109, 113–14, 117; fear of domesticity in, 58–59; and individual, 33; relationships, 104; tensions in, 56
Fascists: in Italy, 109; in Spanish Civil War, 91, 92, 98

Father figure: as archetype, 47; positive view of, 42. *See also* Father-son relationships; Hemingway, Ernest: and his father; ———: and his sons

Father-son relationships, 18–19, 28, 34, 44–45, 46–51, 54, 104–107, 107–108, 123–24n88, 144n16; and affection, show of, 53; and hunting, 48–49; and instruction in sexuality, 48–49; normalcy in, 46; in *The Old Man and the Sea*, 109; "Prodigal son" motif in, 110–11; ritual and memory of father in, 51–53; and suicide of father, 52; and values, 52. *See also* Hemingway, Ernest: and his father; ———: and his sons; ———: WORKS ("My Old Man")

Faulkner, William, 60; "The Bear," 137; Hemingway on, 137; *The Sound and the Fury*, 65

Female figure, 110; absence of, 57, 62, 63–64. *See also* Relationships, male-female; Wife figure; Women

Finca Vigía edition of Hemingway's stories: and emendation of "A Clean, Well-Lighted Place," 22. *See also* Hemingway, Ernest: WORKS (*The Complete Short Stories of Ernest Hemingway: The Finca Vigía Edition*)

Fishing, 51, 54, 175; mechanics of, 165–66

Fitzgerald, F. Scott, 9, 30, 60, 76–77, 85, 131–33, 161; "Babylon Revisited," 87, 92; *The Great Gatsby*, 94–95

Flaubert, Gustave, 3

Food, ritual preparation of, 52–53

Ford, Ford Madox, 164

Forgiveness, 55–56, 60

Franklin, Benjamin: *Autobiography*, 172

Frontier, American: values of, 45–46, 66. *See also* Stoicism; West, Old

Frost, Robert, 45; "Mending Wall," 23

Functionalism, 5–6; aesthetic of, 157–71 *passim*, 167–68

Gale, Marble, 172

Gambler figure, 69–70, 73–74, 94–95; writer as, 136

García López, Manuel ("Maera"), 174, 178n2

Gardner, Ava, 143n12; in movie version of "The Killers," 139

Gilbert, Billy, xiv

Gilbert, Prudence, xiv

Griffin, Peter, xii, xiii, xixn4, 100

Hagopian, John, 21–22

Happiness, 59. *See also* Pleasure

Harling, Robert, xvii

Hawthorne, Nathaniel: "Rappaccini's Daughter," 10; "Roger Malvin's Burial," 11

Heinz, W. C.: "The Professional," 133

Hemingway, Clarence (father), 108–109, 120n42. *See also* Hemingway, Ernest: and his father

Hemingway, Ernest: and adultery, 76; and the aesthetics of the short story, 9–10; and Africa, 136; and America, 59; anthologies of stories by, 127; and anti-Semitism, 119n21; apprentice work by, xiii–xv, xvi–xvii, 4–5, 112, 162–63, 172; and his audience, 139; autobiographical elements in the works of, xiii–xv, xvii, 6–7, 12–13, 17–18, 26, 26–27, 26–60 *passim*, 31–32, 39–40, 41–42, 44, 47, 57, 76–77, 88, 90, 98, 99–100, 110, 113, 114, 120n42, 121n48, 134–35, 141, 177 (*See also* listings for other Hemingway family members); autobiographical fallacy regarding life of, 102, 121–22n57, 136, 141; biographies of, xi–xii; childhood of, xi–xii; and Christianity, 40–41;

conventionality of, 40–41; as critic, 18, 41, 129–42, 130, 137, 140–41, 143n10; crying by, 177; and cult of personality, 6–7, 16; and his debt to previous writers, 119n27; depression of, 104–105, 108–109, 113; drinking by, 138; encounter with death of, 178n8; his erysipelas, 113; and his father, 18, 28, 108–109; and feelings of mortality, 8; and genre, xv, 8–10, 62–63, 74, 89–90, 102, 117, 117, 123n86; and homosexuality, 119n21; and the human condition, 19–20, 155, 156; in Italy, xiv, 26–27, 30, 141; journalistic work of, 4–5, 162–63, 168; and market for writing, 14, 101; and marriage, 10, 18, 41; and misspellings of his name, 118–19n20; and his models for writing, 172–73; as a modernist, 169; as mythic figure, 7; narrative theory of, xvii; Nobel Prize acceptance speech of, 17; in Paris, 4, 87, 127, 131, 141, 160–61, 162, 172; places of residence of, 127; politics of, 119n22; publication of stories by, xiii; as reader, 17; and the "registered particular," 147–53; religious background of, 16, 160; and Roman Catholicism, 16; sexual identity of, xi–xii; and his sons, 105–107, 108–109, 123–24n88, 144n16; and Spain, 7, 34, 35, 127, 167; stories for children by, 109; and the straight line, 166–67, 169–70; and his "surrogate children," 109; and Switzerland, 36, 41–42, 43–44, 168–69; themes in the fiction of, 12; theory of the short story, 3–25; and therapeutic value of writing, 11–15, 19; views on architecture, 168–69; views on his audience, 142n2; views on civil war, 90; views on compulsion to write, 130; views on editors and editing, 132–33; views on the epic, 9; views on himself as writer, 138, 177; views on the human condition, 155; views on humility, 131–32; views on imitation of obscure sources, 172; views on interviews, 137–38; views on movies based on his work, 139; views on the "one true sentence," 168; views on pride vs. arrogance, 131; views on reading from his own works, 143n10; views on the rejection slip, 177; views on relationship between reader and writer, 14, 22–24, 135; views on requisites of a writer, 134–35; views on self-righteousness, 140–41; views on the short story, 129–42; views on symbolism, 132, 133; views on unpublished stories, 141; views on his own work, 15–16, 78–79, 89, 129–42; views on writing, 46, 168, 177; and his wives, 110, 114; and women, 7–8, 119n21, 133–35; and women readers, 62; works by—*see separate listing under WORKS at end of this entry;* in World War I, 160, 178n8; and writer as critic, 15–16; writes three stories in one day, 138; and writing method, 89–90, 123n81, 127–28, 177 (*See also* Writing); youth of, xiii, 172–73

WORKS (Primary references in italics)

BOOKS
*Across the River and Into the Trees,* 8, 109
*By-line: Ernest Hemingway,* 162
*Complete Short Stories of Ernest Hemingway: The Finca Vigía Edition, The,* xiii, 22, 100, 102, 103, 105
*Dangerous Summer, The,* xiii, 129

# Index

*Death in the Afternoon*, 5–6, 9, 13, 16, 46, 111, 147, 174–76
*Ernest Hemingway on Writing*, 163
*Farewell to Arms, A*, 3, 31, 39, 42, 61, 89, 91, 103, 120n43, 150
*Fifth Column, The*, 97, 124n92, 127
*Fifth Column and Four Stories of the Spanish Civil War, The*, xiii, xvi, xvii, xix–xxn8, 8, 74, 77, 89, 90, 127–28
*For Whom the Bell Tolls*, 8, 9, 10, 89–90, 90, 94, 95, 99, 100, 152
*Garden of Eden, The*, xi, xiii, *10–16*, 56, 78, 118n12, 123n86
*Green Hills of Africa*, 6, 45, 74, 75, 90, 151
*in our time*, 62, 149
*In Our Time*, xvi, xviii, 26, 28, 32, 41, 54, 55, 56, 57, 59, 61, 62, 90, 95, 100, 102, 103, 108, 164
*Islands in the Stream*, 8, 75, 104–105, 123n86
*Men Without Women*, xvi, 33, 34, 36, 55, 59, 61, 62, 100, 108
*Moveable Feast, A*, 4, 9, 39–40, 112, 113, 114, 116–17, 168
*Nick Adams Stories, The*, xvi, 123n86
*Old Man and the Sea, The*, 8, 9–10, 15–16, 40, 89, 109, 175
*Sun Also Rises, The*, xviii, 3, 16, 34, 40, 78, 127, 151–52, 167, 169, 170
*Three Stories and Ten Poems*, xv–xvi, 26, 164
*To Have and Have Not*, 62, 63, 74, 127
*Torrents of Spring, The*, 140
*Winner Take Nothing*, xv, xvi, 8, 19, 44, 46, 55, 59, 61, 62, 63, 66, 74, 100

SHORT STORIES AND ESSAYS
"African Betrayal, An." *See* "African Story, An"
"African Story, An," 105
"After the Storm, " 46, 62

"Art of the Short Story, The" (essay), xvii–xviii, 19, 102, 120n36, *129–42*, 142, 143n14
"Ash Heel's Tendon—A Story, The," xv
"Battler, The," 46, *56–57*, 68, 113
"Big Two-Hearted River," 18, *51–60*, 60, 61, 72, 82, 112, 130–31, 166–67
"Black Ass at the Cross Roads," *102–104*, 112, 141
"Butterfly and the Tank, The," 89, 91, *93*, 93–94, 96, 97, 100, 123n85
"Canary for One, A," *36–39*, 64, 149–50
"Cat in the Rain," 31
"Clean, Well-Lighted Place, A," *19–25*, 31, 42, 60, 72, 89, 94, 113, 120nn38–42, 127, 140
"Cross Roads, The." *See* "Black Ass at the Cross Roads"
"Cross-Country Snow," 31, *41–43*, 44, 45, 57, 58
"Crossroads—An Anthology," xiv
"Current, The," xiii–xiv
"Day's Wait, A," *44–46*, 48, 65, 105, 107, 109
"Denunciation, The," 89, 91, *92–93*, 93, 95, 101
"Divine Gesture, A," 124n89
"Doctor and the Doctor's Wife, The," *18–19*, 28, 49, 52, 77, 110, 119n33
"End of Something, The," *28–30*, 33, 37, 58, 107, 165–66
"Faithful Bull, The," 109–10, *111–12*
"False Spring, A," 114, 116, 116–17
"Fathers and Sons," 34, *46–51*, 60, 61, 62, 82
"Fifty Grand," 109, *131–33*
"Gambler, the Nun, and the Radio, The," 60, *69–74*, 76, 82
"Get a Seeing-Eyed Dog," 102, 112, *113–17*, 124n92

194

"Good Lion, The," 109–10, *110–11*

"Great News from the Mainland," *107–108*

"Hills Like White Elephants," *33–35*, 37, 38, 38–39, 43, 66, 123n81, 127

"Homage to Switzerland," *43–44*, 64, 65, 108

"I Guess Everything Reminds You of Something," *105–107*

"In Another Country," 34, 54, 127, *153–56*

"Indian Camp," 18, 28, 52, 54, 149

"Indian Country and the White Army," 123n87

Interchapter 3 of *In Our Time*, 103

Interchapter 14 of *In Our Time*, 54, 54–55

Interchapter 15 of *In Our Time*, 54–55, 59

"Killers, The," xv, 34, 46, 60, 121n53, 127, 138, 139–40

"L'Envoi," 59

"Landscape with Figures," 89, 90, *96–98*, 100, 109

"Last Good Country, The," xvi, 26, 33, 51, 123n86

"Light of the World, The," *66–69*, 73, 89, 127, 133–34

"Man of the World, A," *112–13*

"Mercenaries—A Story, The," xv, 100–101, 113

"Mr. and Mrs. Elliott," 16

"Monument, The," 123n87

"Mr. Johnson Talks About It at Vevey," 64

"My Old Man," xvi, 54, 141

Nobel Prize acceptance speech, 17

"Night Before Battle," 89, 91, *93–95*, 97, 98

"Nobody Ever Dies," 89, 90, 95, *98–99*, 100, 141

"Now I Lay Me," 36, 47, 54, *55–56*, 60

"Old Man at the Bridge," *90–92*, 99, 127

"One Reader Writes," xv, *61–64*, 64, 65

"Out of Season," xvi, *30–33*, 36, 116

"Porter, The," 123n86. *See also* "Train Trip, A"

"Portrait of Mr. Wheeler in Montreux," 64

"Portrait of the Idealist in Love—A Story," xiv–xv

"Revolutionist, The," 99

"Room on the Garden Side, A," 123n87

"Sea Change, The," 18, 66, 123n81, 131

"Short Happy Life of Francis Macomber, The," *74–81*, 84, 85, 87, 89, 107, 110, 123n77, 127, 134–35, 175

"Simple Enquiry, A," 36

"Snows of Kilimanjaro, The," 74–75, 77, *81–88*, 89, 100, 107, 110, 112, 114–16, 122n71, 127, 136–37, 148

"Soldier's Home," 33, 84, 87

"Son of a Fellow Member at Territet, The," 64

"Strange Country, The," 123n86

"Summer People," 108

"Ten Indians," 36, 39, 52, 53, 58, 121n53, 127, 138

"Three-Day Blow, The," 28, 30, 41, 42–43, 52, 56, 107, 114, 152

"Today Is Friday," *24–25*, 104, 121n53, 127, 138

"Train Trip, A," 123n86. *See also* "Porter, The"

"Two Tales of Darkness," 112, 116. *See also* "Get a Seeing-Eyed Dog" and "Man of the World, A"

"Undefeated, The," 140, *174–77*

"Under the Ridge," 89, *95–96*, 100

# Index

Unnamed and/or unpublished
  stories, 123n87, 141
"Up in Michigan," xvi, 26, 56, 63,
  127
"Very Short Story, A," *30*, 38, 61,
  63
"Way You'll Never Be, A," 54, 57,
  *58*, 62, 72, 89, 127, 139
"Wedding Day," 35
"Wine of Wyoming," 50, 53, *65–
  66*

Hemingway, Grace Hall (mother),
  xi–xii, xixn6, 67, 108–109, 122n67
Hemingway, Gregory Hancock (son),
  xii, 102, 105–106, 108–109, 123–
  24n88, 144n16
Hemingway, Hadley Richardson
  (first wife), xiv, 18, 26, 31–32, 39–
  40, 41, 116–17. *See also*
  Hemingway, Ernest: WORKS (*A
  Moveable Feast*)
Hemingway, John Nicanor
  ("Bumby") (son), 44, 47, 102, 109
Hemingway, Marcelline (later Mrs.
  Marcelline Hemingway Sanford)
  (sister), xi–xii, 26
Hemingway, Martha Gellhorn (third
  wife), 97, 102, 110; on
  Hemingway's style, 6
Hemingway, Mary Welsh (fourth
  wife), 114, 129
Hemingway, Patrick (son), 102
Hemingway, Pauline Pfeiffer (second
  wife), 47
Hemingway Society, 7. *See also*
  Hemingway, Ernest: and cult of
  personality
Henry, Edwin (narrator of Spanish
  Civil Stories), 90–101
Hero: and antihero, in modern
  literature, 155–56; stoicism of, 11.
  *See also* Stoicism
Herrick, Robert, 161
Honor, 174–77; Spanish view of,
  175–76
*Horizon*, interview with Hemingway
  in, 138

Hotchner, A. E., 16, 109
Howells, William Dean, 173
Humor, 65, 69–70, 98, 162; in
  fables, 111; and joking as relief in
  war, 96–97
Hunt, Holman, 67
Hunting, 45, 47, 48–49, 76
Huston, John: as scriptwriter for
  movie version of "The Killers,"
  139
Hutton, Virgil, 78

Idealism, 53; of youth, 62
Identity, sexual. *See* Sexual roles
Imagism, 4, 13, 90, 148, 165. *See
  also* Pound, Ezra
Indian (native American), figure of,
  18, 27, 28, 36, 47–49, 68, 131. *See
  also* Hemingway, Ernest: WORKS
  ("Ten Indians")
Individual: and community, 33, 175–
  76; and crowd, 54, 122n63; and
  larger world, 53–54. *See also*
  Isolation
Innocence, 103; Edenic, 57; of
  youth, 66–67
Interchapters of *In Our Time*, 28, 46,
  54, 62, 91, 95, 103. *See also*
  listings for specific interchapters
  under Hemingway, Ernest:
  WORKS (Interchapter —)
Ionesco, Eugene, 64
Isolation and the senses, 151. *See
  also* Alienation; Individual
Ivancich, Adriana, 109

James, Henry, 36, 173; prefaces by,
  158
James, Henry, Sr., 121n48
Jesus Christ, 24–25, 73, 155
Johnston, Kenneth G., 32; on "The
  Undefeated," 174–77
Jones, James, 7
"Joselito" (bullfighter), 177. *See also*
  Bullfighting: bullfighter figure
Journalism: Hemingway's
  background in, 160, 161–65;
  journalist figure, 90–101; journalist

figure as female, 97–98; and perception, 152; writing style of, 161–63, 170. *See also* Hemingway, Ernest: journalistic work
Journey motif, 47; as sexual symbol, 49
Joyce, James, 150, 173

*Kansas City Star,* Hemingway's work on, 5, 160–61
Kurowsky, Agnes von, xiv, 30

Lancaster, Burt: in movie version of "The Killers," 139
Language, nuances of, 115
Lardner, Ring, 172
Lawrence, D. H., 80, 172
Leaf, Munro: *Ferdinand the Bull,* 111
Lee, Basil (Fitzgerald character): contrasted with Nick Adams, 60
Leonard (boxer), 131
Lesbian relationships, 66. *See also* Relationships, male-female
Listening: reader as listener, 22–24; importance of, 38
London, Jack: *The Call of the Wild,* 173
Long, Ray, 132
Love, 30–32; as risk, 38; sacred and profane, 41; in wartime, 99. *See also* Marriage; Relationships, male-female; Sexual roles; Sexuality
Loyalists (in Spanish Civil War), 92, 94, 95–96, 98, 100
Lynn, Kenneth, xi–xii, xixn4, 17–18, 18, 61

Machine: images of, in early Hemingway works, 161; as metaphor, 157–71; values of, 170–71
Machismo. *See* Masculinity
Macomber, Francis (protagonist of "The Short Happy Life of Francis Macomber"): inspirations for name of, 76–77

"Maera" (bullfighter). *See* García López, Manuel ("Maera"); *See also* Bullfighting: bullfighter figure
Marriage, 24, 35, 41, 56–57, 63–66, 79, 80, 85, 87–88, 114–17; blessings of, 43–44; death of spouse in, 154; discord in, 31–32; end of, 36–40; in *Ethan Frome,* 160; normalcy of, 44; skepticism regarding, 36. *See also* Divorce; Hemingway, Ernest: and marriage; ———: and his wives; Relationships, male-female; Wife figure
Mary, Virgin, 71–74
Masculinity, 16, 75, 76, 77, 80; and bull fable, 112; fear of emasculation, 58–59, 76–78, 83, 113; machismo of bullfighter, 174, 178n2
Mason, Jane: as inspiration for Margot Macomber, 76
Masters, Edgar Lee: *Spoon River Anthology,* xiv
Maturity, 92. *See also* Responsibility
Maugham, Somerset, 130
Maupassant, Guy de: "La Maison Tellier," 67
McGrady, John: *Swing Low, Sweet Chariot,* 82
Melville, Herman, 7, 169
Memory, 47–48, 52, 82, 84, 114–15, 148; as both hunger and pleasure, 116–17; of childhood, 55; function of, in writing, 12–13, 13 14; and women, 57–58
*Métier,* concept of, 3–4, 6, 9, 11, 25, 69, 111, 177. *See also* Profession; Writing
Meyers, Jeffrey, xii, 26, 31, 41, 42, 76, 78, 122n71
Minimalism. *See* Style: economy of
Mitchell, Trudy (character in "Fathers and Sons"), 47–49
Monroe, Harriet: *Poetry* (journal), 161
Morality of Hemingway's works, 34–35

Mother figure, 37; absence of, 49, 64; and children, 85; domination by, 55–56, 122n67; stepmother, 50
Movies of Hemingway's works, 74, 139, 143n12
Music, 73
Myth, 153. *See also* Hemingway, Ernest: as mythic figure

*Nada*, Hemingway's concept of, 19–20, 25, 72, 155
Names and namelessness. *See* Characterization: names and namelessness
Narrator, 32, 66, 81, 93, 101; as adolescent, 66–67; and art of concealment, 21, 37 (*See also* Concealment, Art of); as engineer (in *Ethan Frome*), 158–59; and female perspective/voice, 62–63, 66, 78, 80; first-person, 45, 56, 60, 67, 68, 90–91, 95–96, 99–100, 101; hidden, 37; implied, 67, 68, 121n56; irony of, 99; male voice of, 62; maturity of, 92; and Nick Adams, 33–34, 121n56; shift in, 37, 99; of Spanish stories, 90–101 *passim*; third-person, in Spanish Civil War stories, 98–99; as tutor, 97–98; as tyro, 154; unnamed, xv; variation of, 67, 78; and war, 104
Native American. *See* Indian (native American), figure of
Naturalist school of American literature, 173
Nature. *See* Camping; Fishing; Food; Hunting; Indian; Outdoors
Neroni, Nick: as model for Nick Adams, 26–27
Newspaper apprenticeship. *See* Hemingway, Ernest: journalistic work
Nick Adams stories, xvi, 18–19, 26–30, 33–34, 36, 39, 41–60, 55, 62, 64, 67–68, 72, 81–82, 87, 107, 107–108, 109, 119n33, 121n56, 165–67; Nick Adams contrasted with Fitzgerald's Basil Lee, 60;

Nick Adam's persona, 91–92; origin of Nick's name, 26–27
Nihilism. See *Nada*, Hemingway concept of
Normalcy. *See* Conventionality; Hemingway, Ernest: conventionality of
Nothingness. See *Nada*, Hemingway concept of
Novelty: values by Hemingway, 62

O'Neill, Eugene: *Hughie*, 94
Oak Park, Illinois, 172–73. *See also* Hemingway, Ernest: childhood; ———: youth
Objective Correlative, 15, 46, 152–53, 163
Old age. *See* Youth: and old age
*Omertà* (code of silence), 137, 142n8
Omission. *See* Concealment, Art of
Order, longing for, 51–52. *See also* Conventionality; Sequence
Ornamentation, 167–69. *See also* Style
Outdoors, 45. *See also* Ritual

Painting, 5, 40, 67, 75, 82, 96, 118n4, 122n69, 165; and engineering values, 158
Parent-child relationships, 51, 109. *See also* Father figure; Father-son relationships; Hemingway, Ernest: and his father; ———: and his sons; Mother figure
Parenthood, 58–59
*Paris Review:* and "The Art of the Short Story," 142, 143n11; interview with Hemingway in, 41, 138
Past, 58; indebtedness of writer to, 16–17, 119n27
Patterson, John Henry, 76
Paul, Saint, 52
Perception, 147–53
Percival, Philip, 76
Periodicals, Hemingway published in: *Atlantic Monthly*, 112;

*Cosmopolitan*, 74–75, 89, 132; *Esquire*, 74, 89; *Family Circle*, 105; *Holiday*, 109; *Horizon*, 138; *Paris Review*, 41, 138, 142, 143n11; *Poetry*, 161; *Redbook*, 100–101; *Saturday Evening Post*, 101; *Scribner's Magazine*, 19; *Sports Illustrated*, 105; *Tabula* (Hemingway's high school's literary magazine), xiii
Perkins, Maxwell, 61, 62, 66, 89, 90, 95, 132, 142n3
Play form in stories, 34, 64
Pleasure, 42. *See also* Happiness
Plimpton, George, 41; his interview with Hemingway, 138, 143n11
Poe, Edgar Allan, 87; "The Fall of the House of Usher," xii
*Poetry* (journal), Hemingway poem submitted to, 161
Point-of-view. *See* Narrator
Politics, 98–99; Hemingway's neutrality in, 119n22
Pope, Alexander, 52
Porter, Katherine Anne, 60
Pound, Ezra, 3, 4, 27, 100, 157, 161, 166, 172–73; and efficient style, 157, 165; and imagism, 13
Predecessors, Literary. *See* Past: indebtedness of writer to
Pregnancy, 41–42, 58–59. *See also* Abortion
Profession: codes of, 154–55, 174–77; importance of, 25; as self-discipline, 70. See also *Métier*
Prostitute figure, 67–69, 133
Protagonist. *See* Hero
*Pundonor*, Spanish concept of, 175–76
Puritanism, 48. *See also* Sexuality

*Reader's Digest:* Hemingway's distaste for, 133
Realism, 43
Reality, Hemingway's perception of, 147–53
Reardon, John, 177
Reid, Marjorie, 164

Relationships, male-female, 29, 57–58, 77, 92, 120n43; beginnings of, 35, 121n55; and commitment, 29–30, 108; end of, 30, 34–35, 36, 36–40, 41, 58, 117, 166; and infidelity, 39–40, 58; in late Hemingway work, 113–14. *See also* Abortion; Love; Hemingway, Ernest (*passim*); Marriage; Sexual roles; Sexuality
Responsibility, 42, 87, 88; and conscience, 48; in father-son relationship, 105; of pregnancy, 42–43; in sexual relationships, 48. *See also* Marriage
Retreat: and healing, 59
Reynolds, Michael S., xii, 40; on Hemingway's early years, 172–73
Ritual: of bullfighting, 167–68; of camping, 51–52, 166–67; of drinking, 114; of fishing, 51–52, 165–66; of food preparation, 52–53; and memory of father, 51–53; and technique, 165–67
Roles, sexual. *See* Sexual roles
Roman Catholicism, 120n43; and abortion, 35; in America, 65; as Hemingway's own religion, 16; and nun figure, 70–74; and sainthood, 73; and Virgin Mary, 71–74. *See also* Christianity; Hemingway, Ernest: religious background of; Jesus Christ
Romance. *See* Relationships, male-female
Rovit, Earl, and Gerry Brenner, 11, 86, 100; on "In Another Country," 153–56

Safari, African. *See* Africa, safari in
*St. Nicholas* (magazine) and Hemingway's youth, 172
Saga form, 60
Santiago (protagonist of *The Old Man and the Sea*), 175
Satire, 37; of genre, xiv–xv
Scribner, Charles, Jr., 129, 142, 143n11, 143n14, 143–44n15, 162

# Index

Scribner's (publisher), 132
Sedgwick, Ellery, 133
Senses, perception and relation of details by, 147–53
Sequences of stories, 36, 62, 63, 77, 99–100
Sexual roles, xi, 8, 12, 31–32, 35; male bonding, 30. *See also* Marriage; Relationships, male-female; Sexuality
Sexuality, 26, 58, 64; awakening of, 47–50; as commodity, 63; conflict of values regarding, 49–50; and creativity, 116–17, 117; and lesbian relationships, 66; and sex as opiate in war, 97; and terse writing style, 165
Shakespeare, William: *Henry IV, Part I*, 76, 81
Sheeler, Charles, 158
Sherwood, Bob, 141
"Significant emotion," concept of, 19. *See also* Emotion
Silence, 37; code of, 137, 142n8
Smeeth, Helen, 172
Soldier figure, 24, 24–25, 30, 33, 62, 84, 94, 95, 103, 103–104, 153–56. *See also* War
Spain, view of honor in, 175–76. *See also* Hemingway, Ernest: and Spain
Spanish Civil War stories, 89–101; compared with Hemingway's African stories, 99
Spenser, Edmund: "Prothalamion," 43–44
Sports, 71–72
Stegner, Wallace, 27, 45–46
Stein, Gertrude, 4, 28, 40, 100, 161, 172; quoted by Hemingway, 129
Steinbeck, John, xii–xiii, 123n85
Stoicism, 11, 23, 67, 69, 75, 113, 122nn62–63, 175; in the elderly, 24; in face of death, 55; in face of ruined relationships, 39; hard won, 45–46; and pain, 74; in soldiers, 154–56. *See also* Courage

Structure of *In Our Time*, 32
Style: economy of, xv–xvi, 4–5, 13, 20, 31, 35, 40, 44, 46, 62, 82, 88, 108, 130, 139–40, 152–53, 157, 157–71; economy of, in *Ethan Frome*, 159–60; economy of, notable by its absence, 46; journalistic, 162–65; ornate, 158; simplicity of, 158, 168–69; and the telegraph, 162–64; verbose, 164. *See also* Concealment, Art of; Imagism; Ornamentation; Writing
Suicide, 22–24, 32, 47, 116, 120n42; of father, 52
Switzerland: and conventional values, 44, 64; and function of form, 168–69
Symbolism, 27, 33, 36, 58, 107, 137; arcaneness of, 32; and the Bible, 40; of bull, in fables, 111–12; of death, 54–55, 82–84, 85–86, 116; of food, 53; Hemingway on, 132, 133; lack of, in setting, 47; and the natural object, 4, 27–28, 35, 42, 56, 116; overdone, 150; of parenthood, 59; of ruined relationships, 30, 31; of setting, 28–29, 34, 38; sexual, 49
Syntax of "engineering style," 158

*Tabula* (high school literary magazine), Hemingway stories in, xiii
Talent, stewardship of, 76–77, 88
Talking, 37, 70, 73; in interviews, 137–38; as opiate for war, 103; pleasures of, 116–17; therapeutic value of, 94; and writer's private thoughts, 114; and writing, 137–38
Tanner, Tony: on sensory detail in Hemingway, 147–53
Teacher figure. *See* Tutor figure
Technics, 165–67
Thinking, 62, 74; necessity of, 55; "thinking inside" an animal, 135; unavoidability of, 81–82

200

Thoreau, Henry David, 153; *Walden*, 59, 83
Tichi, Cecelia, 5–6; on engineering values in Hemingway's prose, 157–71
Tolstoy, Leo: *The Death of Ivan Ilyich*, 75, 77
*Torero.* See Bullfighting: bullfighter figure
*Toronto Star,* Hemingway's work on, 5, 160, 162, 168
Tradition, 51–59; desire for, 49–51; in shaping child's views, 49–50. *See also* Past
Tunney, Gene, 139
Turgenev, Ivan Sergeevich, 105, 172; *Fathers and Sons*, 50
Tutor figure, 97–98, 129, 153–55
Twain, Mark, 48, 162,173. *See also* Clemens, Samuel Langhorne

Violence, 33, 62
Void, See *Nada*, Hemingway's concept of
Vorticism, 165

War, 36, 54, 62, 89–101 *passim*, 102, 130–31; and Hemingway apprentice stories, 101; civil war, 90, 92–93; as theme in Hemingway's fiction, 91, 99, 104; unpublished stories about, 123n87; and writing, 90; World War II, 102
Webster, John, 82
Weeks, Edward, 133
West, Old: ideal of, 112–13
Wharton, Edith: *A Backward Glance*, 158, 159; *Ethan Frome*, 157–61; *Madame de Treymes*, 158–59
White, Charles, 172
Whitman, Walt, 148
Wife figure, 65–66, 78–79, 84; as ideal figure, 84–85. *See also* Marriage; Women

Wives, of Ernest Hemingway. *See* Hemingway, Ernest: and marriage; ————: and his wives; Hemingway, Hadley Richardson (first wife); Hemingway, Martha Gellhorn (third wife); Hemingway, Mary Welsh (fourth wife); Hemingway, Pauline Pfeiffer (second wife)
Wolfe, Thomas, 12–13, 15, 33, 60
Women, xiv, 66, 68–69, 72–73, 77–78, 85, 86–87, 115; as heroic figures, 99; ideal of, 87; minimal surface treatment of, 61; sympathetic view of, 78–80, 99; viewpoint of, 63–64; in war stories, 97
Woolf, Virginia, 62
Wright, Frank Lloyd, 5, 168–69
Writer: figure of, 70, 163–64; figure of, as father, 106; Hemingway's view of himself as, 177; as observer/reporter, 95–96; as protagonist, 10–16, 88, 91, 92–93, 94, 100, 107, 114, 116–17; as truth-teller, 93, 99, 100. *See also* Hemingway, Ernest: WORKS (*For Whom the Bell Tolls* [Robert Jordan, protagonist] and *The Garden of Eden* [David Bourne, protagonist]; Henry, Edwin; Narrator
Writing, 111–12; aesthetics of, 163–64; compared with bullfighting, 178n11; as confession, 56; as discovery, 15; fulfillment in, 116–17; Hemingway to his son on, 105; market for, 14, 173; need for, 55, 56; "rules" of, 132; sentence as basic unit of, 168; theory of, in *The Garden of Eden*, xi, 10–16. *See also* Hemingway, Ernest: *passim*
Writing style. *See* Style

Young, Philip, xvi, 44
Youth, 66–67; and old age, 21–24

# The Author

Joseph M. Flora is professor of English and chairman of the department at the University of North Carolina at Chapel Hill. He is the author of *Hemingway's Nick Adams* (1982), *Vardis Fisher* (1962), *William Ernest Henley* (1970), *Frederick Manfred* (1974), and articles on Hemingway and others. He is editor of *The English Short Story* (1985) and co-editor of *Southern Writers: A Biographical Dictionary* (1979), *Fifty Southern Writers Before 1900* (1987), and *Fifty Southern Writers After 1900* (1987).

# The Editor

General editor Gordon Weaver earned his B.A. in English at the University of Wisconsin-Milwaukee in 1961; his M.A. in English at the University of Illinois, where he studied as a Woodrow Wilson Fellow, in 1962; and his Ph.D. in English and creative writing at the University of Denver in 1970. He is the author of several novels, including *Count a Lonely Cadence, Give Him a Stone, Circling Byzantium,* and *The Eight Corners of the World.* Many of his numerous short stories are collected in *The Entombed Man of Thule, Such Waltzing Was Not Easy, Getting Serious, Morality Play,* and *A World Quite Round.* Recognition of his fiction includes the St. Lawrence Award for Fiction (1973), two National Endowment for the Arts fellowships (1974, 1989), and the O. Henry First Prize (1979). He edited *The American Short Story, 1945–1980: A Critical History.* He is a professor of English at Oklahoma State University and serves as an adjunct member of the faculty of the Vermont College Master of Fine Arts in Writing Program. Married, and the father of three daughters, he lives in Stillwater, Oklahoma.

| DATE DUE | | | |
|---|---|---|---|
| FEB 2 7 1991 | | | |
| APR 2 6 1991 | | | |
| | | | |
| DEC 1 7 1968 | | | |
| 10-13-94 | | | |
| FEB 1 7 1996 | | | |
| SEP 1 1 1996 | | | |
| NOV 19 2001 | | | |
| | | | |
| | | | |
| | | | |